DreamHOMESource

350 SMALL HOME PLANS

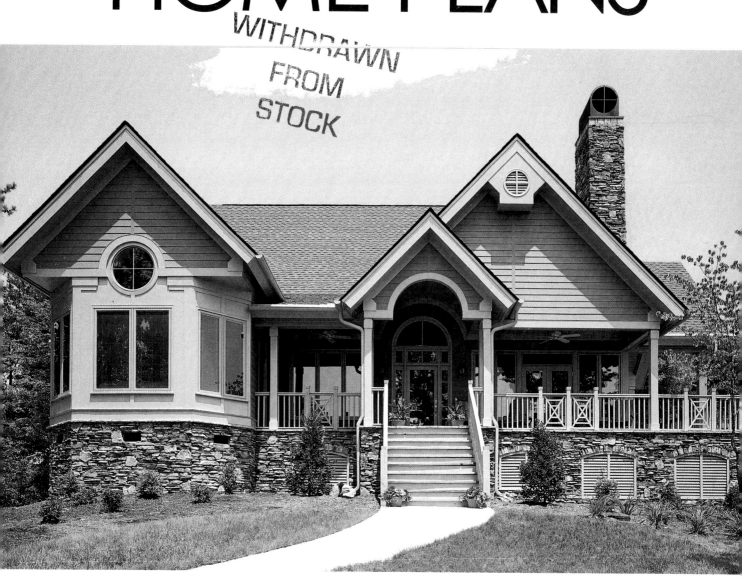

UP TO 2,500 SQUARE FEET

DreamHOMESource
350 SMALL
HOME PLANS

hanley▲wood

Published by Hanley Wood
One Thomas Circle, NW, Suite 600
Washington, DC 20005

Distribution Center
29333 Lorie Lane
Wixom, Michigan 48393

Group Publisher, Andrew Schultz
Associate Publisher, Editorial Development, Jennifer Pearce
Managing Editor, Hannah McCann
Senior Editor, Nate Ewell
Associate Editor, Simon Hyoun
Senior Plan Merchandiser, Morenci C. Clark
Plan Merchandiser, Nicole Phipps
Proofreader/Copywriter, Dyana Weis
Graphic Artist, Joong Min
Plan Data Team Leader, Susan Jasmin
Production Manager, Brenda McClary

Vice President, Retail Sales, Scott Hill
National Sales Manager, Bruce Holmes
Director, Plan Products, Matt Higgins

Most Hanley Wood titles are available at quantity discounts with bulk purchases for educational, business, or sales promotional use. For information, please contact Bruce Holmes at bholmes@hanleywood.com.

VC Graphics, Inc.
Creative Director, Veronica Vannoy
Graphic Designer, Jennifer Gerstein
Graphic Designer, Denise Reiffenstein

Photo Credits
Front Cover, Main: Design HPK1200032, for details see page 91.
Photo © 1998 Donald A. Gardner, Inc., Photography courtesy of Donald A. Gardner Architects, Inc.
Front Cover, Lower Right: Design HPK120001, for details see page 6 and 24. Photo by Dummond Designs.
Back Cover, Left and Top: Photo by Marc Samu.

10 9 8 7 6 5 4 3 2 1

Library of Congress Control Number: 2005927711

ISBN-13: 978-1-93113-142-1
ISBN-10: 1-931131-42-2

DreamHOMESource
350 SMALL HOME PLANS

CONTENTS

ONLINE EXTRA!

PASSAGEWAY

For access to bonus home plans, articles, online ordering, and more go to: **www.hanley woodbooks.com/350smallhomeplans**

Features of this site include:

- A dynamic link that lets you search and view bonus home plans
- Online related feature articles
- Built-in tools to save and view your favorite home plans
- A dynamic web link that allows you to order your home plan online
- Contact details for the Hanley Wood Home Plan Hotline
- Free subscriptions to Hanley Wood Home Plan e-news

hanley▲wood

Rethink Small

Small homes are ideal for those looking to build a smart, flexible, cost-efficient, and energy-saving residence that is no larger than what the family needs or what the plot allows. In general, smaller structures cost less at initial construction because they require fewer raw materials and have uncomplicated floor plans. Similarly, small designs need less power to heat and illuminate, which means cost and energy savings over time. In fact, by investing what will be saved at initial construction toward environmentally friendly methods and materials, a small home can reinforce its fundamental design efficiencies to become a truly "green" home.

K. Yamashita / NGSImages.com

NOT TOO TIGHT

Prospective homeowners should rightly stay away from smaller homes that feel cramped and inadequate. A well-fitting small home for your family should demonstrate the designer's skill at balancing aesthetics, necessity, and utility. For example, look for a floor plan that offers comfortable compromise between shared spaces and private zones. Look also for a design that can forgo strict assignments to rooms, which can cut up a floor plan into uncomfortable squares. Smartly built smaller homes call for spaces that flow easily between household hotspots and perform "on demand."

A good principle to remember is that a well-designed small space can create a sense of order through travel paths and visual paths as well as with physical structures such as walls. This will allow areas of the home to retain definition without being closed off. Just as a few pillars can establish a separation between, say, the dining room and kitchen, a diminished foyer can remain meaningful if it serves to contrast a two-story great room.

LIVING LARGER

Small homes can also live beyond their square footage in outdoor areas that are extensions of interior rooms. In climates that invite outdoor enjoyment for most of the year, homeowners can nearly double living and entertaining spaces by building porches and decks that adjoin interior rooms and circulate traffic throughout the home. Read on to our feature homes for a closer look at how flexible designs maximize utility and generate easy indoor/outdoor sequences. For examples of plans with great outdoor living spaces, turn to our collection beginning on page 240.

MODIFY A PLAN

In terms of aesthetics, let the home's elevations satisfy your style preference, bearing in mind the prevailing trend of the architecture within your new neighborhood. Discuss with your builder what exterior materials will suit the home's style and environment. Also, remember that almost all predrawn home plans can be modified at time of purchase. If you feel, for instance, that a front-loading garage

compromises the home's curbside presence, inquire with our service representatives (or with any qualified architect) about the possibility of customizing the garage to load from the side or rear of the plan. Modifying a design may also augment interior views. For example, opting to eliminate an unneeded bedroom on the second floor can create two-story volume and give scale to a first-floor living room. More information of home plan customization can be found on pages 378-379.

HOW TO USE THIS BOOK

Following this introduction, our featured homes section will take you on a tour of two designs that exemplify the above-outlined advantages of small living. Take time to visualize the flow of interior spaces and imagine how this home—and others like it—would feel to you. The rest of the book is divided into five sections. Section one is our selection of sensible, easy-living plans for first-time builders. Section two features homes friendly to empty nesters and owners with special needs.

SMALL HOMES REQUIRE US TO ASK WHAT WE NEED and want in a home. They help reveal the scale of our own lives and encourage a more intimate experience with our surroundings.

Continue to section three's cottages and vacation homes—perfect for waterfront lots and hillsides with a view. Or enjoy everyday vacations in our homes with great outdoor spaces, collected in section four. Lastly, put the finishing touches on your new home with one of the perfectly matching landscape plans (and other projects) found in section five.

Every plan discussed in this book is available to own. Turn to page 376 to learn how to order a plan and what you will receive with your purchase. Materials lists, customization, home automation, and other options are also explained in this part of the book, followed by the list of prices on page 382. Please note that the plans are organized by plan number. Any time you have a question or simply would like a second opinion about a home, please feel free to contact our representatives.

Just Right at Home

A spirited design shows good sense and a taste for personal comforts

This revisited Craftsman home offers effortless good-looks on the outside and candid living spaces inside. The moderately pitched front-gable roof, off-center chimney, tall windows, and a simply elegant entryway resound with a spirit of clean design. All the built-in advantages of a smaller home have been given full expression in a plan that's sure to satisfy prospective homeowners who value a smart, unfussy way of living.

The interior prefers sleek, high-end materials that emphasize the home's attention to understated details—a good rule of thumb for finishing a small home. Beyond the entryway, the foyer is a brief but meaningful space that introduces the dramatic verticality of the central living room. The height of the ceiling is given balance by tall windows topped with radials, a slim-line stairway, and a fireplace anchoring the living room at the bottom of the plan. The flow of the living room into the dining and kitchen area also serves to establish this bright and open space in the heart of the home.

❷ **A STRIKING FIRST IMPRESSION** comes courtesy of a brief foyer that gives scale to the living room's surprising height.

Photo by Drummond Designs, Inc.

① CRISP ROOFLINES PUNCTUATED BY A ROBUST CHIMNEY are attractive complements to a minimal but expressive exterior. Nested gables, an off-center entryway, and windows of varying sizes establish a pleasingly balanced asymmetry. Lastly, a bold color option casts a final flourish to this little attention-getter.

3 **A FIREPLACE DEFINES THIS COZY CONVERSATION AREA** in the living room. Nonetheless, low profile furnishings allow the eye to move the entire length of the first floor, encouraging circulation between spaces. The second-floor bedrooms have been given Shoji-style sliding doors with brushed glass that let in light and preserve privacy.

FIRST FLOOR

SECOND FLOOR

This home, as shown in photographs, may differ from the actual blueprints. For more detailed information, please check the floor plans carefully.

The contemporary kitchen is designed to handle demanding orders with aplomb. Booth-style seating nearby accommodates casual dining, as does the center island. When company calls, turn to the formal dining room, which flows over into the covered porch.

THE OWNERS HAVE OPTED TO MODIFY THE ORIGINAL PLAN to include ④ a dining room (previously the kitchen, as seen right), with overflow into an adjacent sun room. The resulting layout feels more formal, but quite appropriate for families that enjoy entertaining. ⑤ The kitchen has been moved to the top right of the plan (previously a bedroom), where it now has room enough for a center island and booth seating for casual meals. The attending closet serves well as a pantry. To see more of the original plan, turn to page 24.

The porch can also bring year-round enjoyment to the home as a reading room, bar, or artists' space.

Two bedrooms on the upper level share a full bath. A compartmented toilet makes sharing more comfortable. The bedroom at the bottom of the plan is slightly larger, with room enough for a reading area beside the window. A full-length closet located between the rooms serves additionally to insulate the rooms from noise.

ORIGINAL

Easy Street

Make a clean getaway to this postcard-perfect vacation home

Building a second home is an opportunity to loosen your tie and get creative, as the owners of this home have done. By modifying the base plan, the owners have brought out the more casual, warm-weather side of this Country design. The two-tiered porch originally planned for the rear elevation now faces the street, offering a classic Southern demeanor and attractive fenestration to passersby. Similarly, the two-car garage at the front of the initial floor plan is now a recreation room at the back of the home and offers a cozy vantage from which to watch a tropical sunset turn to moonlit sky.

Photo by Doug Thompson. This home, as shown in photographs, may differ from the actual blueprints. For more detailed information, please check the floor plans carefully.

1 **FORMERLY THE BACK OF THE HOME,** a two-tiered porch and paired gables distinguish the front of the plan.

2 **THE BRIGHT LIVING ROOM FEATURES** a 10-foot ceiling and French doors that serve as a main entry. Built-in niches for a television and artwork keep the room tidy and attractive.

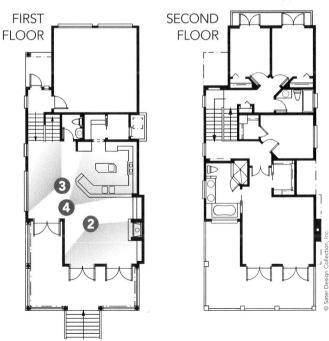

FIRST FLOOR

SECOND FLOOR

© Sater Design Collection, Inc.

The balanced floor plan works well within a narrow footprint. The layout borrows from the strategy of the Caribbean "shotgun" houses, so named for their one-room-wide layout that could be sighted front-to-back without interruption. This modern take of the shotgun house contains more polished details, but still maintains open lines of sight and low-key spatial sequences. The pair of off-center gables is a contemporary element.

The friendly island kitchen is ready for company, with a prep sink, plenty of counter space, and serving bar. The attending pantry and laundry area are hard-working details tucked quietly out of sight. A half-bath rounds out this home's shared spaces.

Upstairs, double French doors open the master suite to a sundeck, also enjoyed from the master bath's soaking tub. Circle-head windows and a vaulted ceiling bring a degree of refinement for the owners, as do the art niches on both upper-level landings. The mid-level holds to two additional bedrooms that share a bath. Each of the bedrooms enjoys private access to a shared balcony at the rear of the home.

THE TWO-CAR GARAGE would have faced the street. Instead, the owners opted for a recreation room and a separate garage (not pictured). A garage at the rear of the lot was another option. To see more of the original design, turn to page 68.

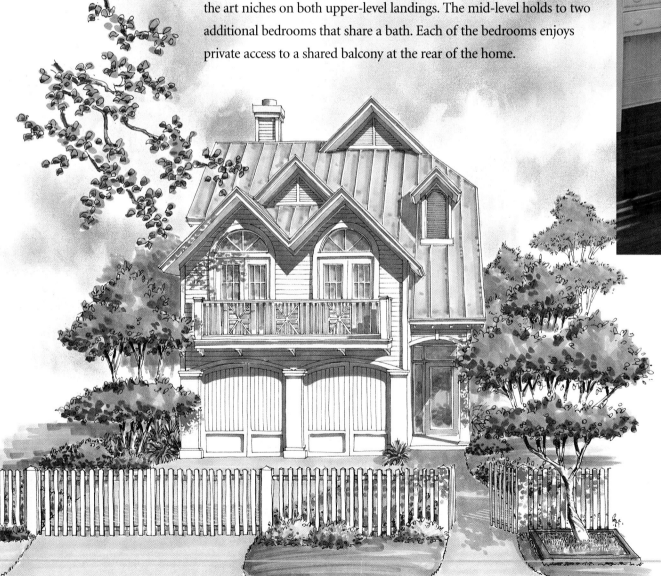

3 DINING IN THE BREAKFAST NOOK IS SUNNY and appropriately casual. Small families may choose to forgo the dining area and take their meals in the **4** eat-in kitchen. Bar-style seating around the peninsula serves four comfortably.

Brilliant Beginnings—Beautiful Homes for First-Time Builders

Few experiences measure up to the joy of building a new home, especially if it is for the first time. Starter homes mark the beginning of a new time in the life of a small family or individual, and our designers mean to celebrate the occasion with homes that will feel just right for a long time.

First-time builders generally appreciate amenities such as a clustered bedroom plan—with a nearby nursery or study—and a casual kitchen with breakfast nook. A larger family or gathering room opens up the heart of the plan and lets cozy private spaces exist at the corners.

The economy of these plans will appeal to everyone. But perhaps the most tempting feature is their flexibility. A small home plan is a great opportunity to incorporate customized spaces that provide for growth. A study can become a nursery or a third bedroom; a den becomes a media room or home office. Or consult our modification designers to add or change rooms in the original plan. If you haven't done so already, read the

CASEMENT WINDOWS and matching treatment are perfect for this small coastal home. In the attending bath, quality materials and artful touches continue to make every space special.

ELEVATE CORNERS, nooks, and other inconspicuous areas that could be overlooked in a larger home.

features "Just Right at Home" and "Easy Street" to find out more about what modification can do for you, or turn to page 378.

Selecting a design for the first time requires a lot of imagination and a bit of instinct. This section offers 79 plans, ordered by square footage, for you to start from—and thousands more are available at www.eplans.com. Each design promises a winning blend of style and function—a home you'll love for years to come.

FIRST FLOOR

SECOND FLOOR

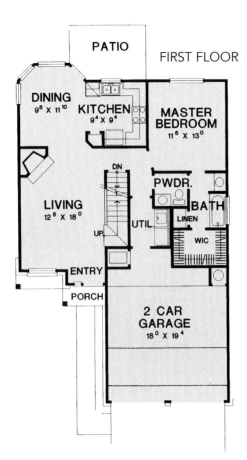

PATIO

DINING
9⁸ X 11¹⁰

KITCHEN
9⁴ X 9⁴

MASTER BEDROOM
11⁸ X 13⁰

DN

LIVING
12⁸ X 18⁰

PWDR.

BATH

UP

UTIL

LINEN

WIC

ENTRY

PORCH

2 CAR GARAGE
18⁰ X 19⁴

BEDRM. 2
10⁸ X 10⁶

BATH 2

BEDRM. 3
10⁰ X 10⁶

DN

OPEN TO LIVING BELOW

A STEEPLY PITCHED ROOFLINE, muntin windows, sidelights, and a paneled door topped by a fanlight provide a welcoming entrance to this home. The two-story living room includes a corner fireplace; a powder room for guests is across the hall. A U-shaped kitchen adjoins a dining bay with access to a rear patio. The master suite offers a full bath and a walk-in closet; the laundry room is nearby. Two second-level bedrooms overlook the living room and share a bath.

HPK1200064

HOME PLAN

Style: Traditional

First Floor: 889 sq. ft.

Second Floor: 373 sq. ft.

Total: 1,262 sq. ft.

Bedrooms: 3

Bathrooms: 2 ½

Width: 32' - 7"

Depth: 51' - 2"

Foundation: Crawlspace, Slab, Unfinished Basement

eplans.com

© 1992 Donald A. Gardner Architects, Inc.

B. NATHAN

THIS ECONOMICAL PLAN makes an impressive visual statement with its comfortable and well-proportioned appearance. The entrance foyer leads to all areas of the house. The great room, dining area, and kitchen are all open to one another, allowing visual interaction. The great room and dining area share a dramatic cathedral ceiling and feature a grand fireplace flanked by bookshelves and cabinets. The master suite has a cathedral ceiling, walk-in closet, and bath with double-bowl vanity, whirlpool tub, and shower. Two family bedrooms and a full hall bath complete this cozy home.

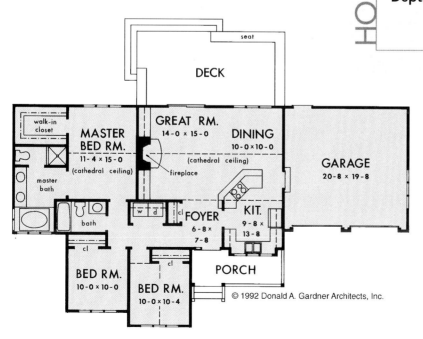

seat

DECK

MASTER BED RM.
11-4 x 15-0
(cathedral ceiling)

walk-in closet

master bath

bath

GREAT RM.
14-0 x 15-0

(cathedral ceiling)

fireplace

DINING
10-0 x 10-0

GARAGE
20-8 x 19-8

w d

cl

FOYER
6-8 x 7-8

KIT.
9-8 x 13-8

cl

BED RM.
10-0 x 10-0

cl

BED RM.
10-0 x 10-4

PORCH

© 1992 Donald A. Gardner Architects, Inc.

MAIN LEVEL

LOWER LEVEL

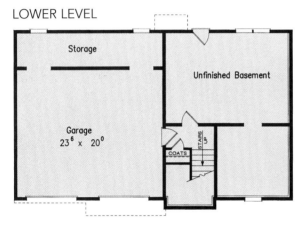

WITH A DOUBLE GARAGE and unfinished basement space on the lower level, this design lives like a one-story home, but has the space of two levels. A vaulted great room features a fireplace flanked by windows. The U-shaped kitchen features a large dining area and a corner window sink. Bedrooms are split for privacy, with the master suite to the right of the great room and family bedrooms to the left. Note the many pampering amenities in the master suite.

HOME PLAN

HPK1200062

Style: Country Cottage

Main Level: 1,249 sq. ft.

Lower Level: 46 sq. ft.

Total: 1,295 sq. ft.

Bedrooms: 3

Bathrooms: 2

Width: 45' - 0"

Depth: 31' - 4"

Foundation: Unfinished Walkout Basement

eplans.com

THIS **COUNTRY-STYLE HOUSE** seems bigger than it is, because the open layout draws the dining and great rooms together with the kitchen. This spaciousness continues as the great room opens through a French door to a wide deck facing the backyard. The deck can also be entered through the master suite, which enjoys a private bath. Two other bedrooms, located on the right side, share a bath. One could be used as a library. The courtyard between the garage doors and the foyer, along with the rustic brick-and-siding facade, will draw appreciative looks from passersby.

 # HPK1200035

Style: Country Cottage

Square Footage: 1,315

Bedrooms: 3

Bathrooms: 2

Width: 50' - 0"

Depth: 54' - 8"

Foundation: Unfinished Walkout Basement

eplans.com

Deck

Master Bedroom
12'-4" x 13'-0"

Great Room
18'-8" x 17'-4"

Bedroom
11'-4" x 10'-8"

Bath

Bath

Dining

Kitchen
13'-4" x 9'-11"

Foyer

Bedroom
12'-4" x 10'-10"

Laun.

Porch

Garage
20'-0" x 26'-2"

OPTIONAL LAYOUT

Bath

Optional Library

FIRST FLOOR

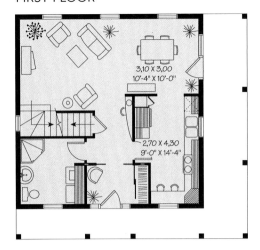

3,10 X 3,00
10'-4" X 10'-0"

2,70 X 4,30
9'-0" X 14'-4"

SECOND FLOOR

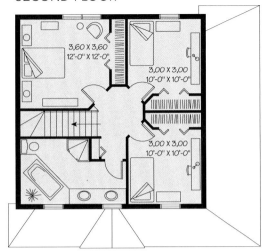

3,60 X 3,60
12'-0" X 12'-0"

3,00 X 3,00
10'-0" X 10'-0"

3,00 X 3,00
10'-0" X 10'-0"

A VISION OF EARLY AMERICAN ARCHITECTURE, this Colonial design is the picture of New England family perfection. A relaxing covered front porch encloses an alluring plan. The entry holds a coat closet. A shower bath is located to the left, and the kitchen sits to the right. The formal living and dining rooms are placed to the rear. Upstairs, three family bedrooms share a full hall bath that includes a separate shower and a corner tub.

HOME PLAN # HPK1200023

Style: Colonial
First Floor: 676 sq. ft.
Second Floor: 676 sq. ft.
Total: 1,352 sq. ft.
Bedrooms: 3
Bathrooms: 2
Width: 26' - 0"
Depth: 26' - 0"
Foundation: Unfinished Basement

eplans.com

HOME PLAN

HPK1200006

Style: Country Cottage

Square Footage: 1,352

Bedrooms: 3

Bathrooms: 2

Width: 71' - 6"

Depth: 36' - 0"

Foundation: Slab, Crawlspace, Unfinished Walkout Basement

eplans.com

THE FRONT COVERED PORCH that wraps around two sides of the house and the rear sundeck expand the living space of this modest one-story home. A lavish master suite with all the amenities you've dreamed about and two bedrooms that share a bath will make your family relaxed and comfortable. The kitchen, with a sweeping curved counter, is open to the dining areas and the living room. This not only enhances the feeling of open space, but makes serving both formal and informal meals a joy. A delightful breakfast bay that looks out over the sundeck will make the first morning cup of coffee something to remember. The well-equipped laundry is nestled between the kitchen and garage.

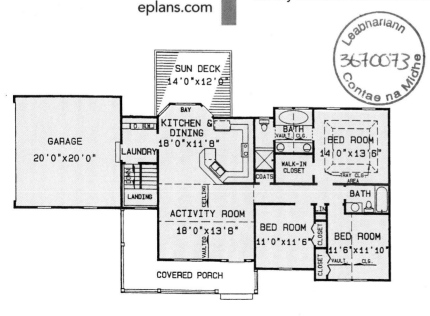

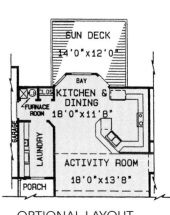

OPTIONAL LAYOUT

A STEEP GABLE ROOFLINE punctuated with dormer windows and a columned front porch give a traditional welcome to this family home. A vaulted ceiling tops the family and dining rooms, which are nicely accented with a fireplace and bright windows. An amenity-filled kitchen opens to the breakfast room. The master suite has a refined tray ceiling and a vaulted bath. Two family bedrooms, a laundry center, and a full bath—with private access from Bedroom 3—complete this stylish plan.

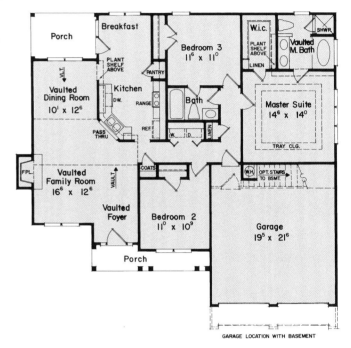

GARAGE LOCATION WITH BASEMENT

HPK1200004

HOME PLAN

Style: Country Cottage

Square Footage: 1,373

Bedrooms: 3

Bathrooms: 2

Width: 50' - 4"

Depth: 45' - 0"

Foundation: Unfinished Walkout Basement, Crawlspace

eplans.com

HOME PLAN

HPK1200067

Style: Craftsman
First Floor: 436 sq. ft.
Second Floor: 792 sq. ft.
Third Floor: 202 sq. ft.
Total: 1,430 sq. ft.
Bedrooms: 2
Bathrooms: 2
Width: 16' - 0"
Depth: 54' - 0"
Foundation: Crawlspace

FIRST FLOOR   SECOND FLOOR

THIRD FLOOR

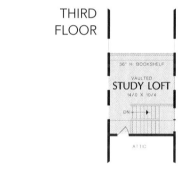

FIRST FLOOR   SECOND FLOOR

HOME PLAN

HPK1200029

Style: Colonial
First Floor: 728 sq. ft.
Second Floor: 728 sq. ft.
Total: 1,456 sq. ft.
Bedrooms: 3
Bathrooms: 2
Width: 26' - 0"
Depth: 28' - 0"
Foundation: Unfinished Basement

FIRST FLOOR

HOME PLAN

HPK1200001

Style: Cape Cod

First Floor: 958 sq. ft.

Second Floor: 510 sq. ft.

Total: 1,468 sq. ft.

Bedrooms: 3

Bathrooms: 2

Width: 35' - 0"

Depth: 29' - 8"

Foundation: Unfinished Basement

eplans.com

SECOND FLOOR

THIS FINE BRICK HOME features a bay-windowed sunroom, perfect for admiring the view. Inside this open floor plan, a family room features a fireplace and a spacious eat-in kitchen with access to the sunroom. A bedroom, full bath, and laundry facilities complete this floor. Upstairs, two more bedrooms share a compartmented bath, as well as an overlook to the family room below.

Photo by Drummond Designs, Inc. This home, as shown in photographs, may differ from the actual blueprints. For more detailed information, please check the floor plans carefully.

HOME PLAN

 # HPK1200025

Style: European Cottage

Square Footage: 1,475

Bedrooms: 2

Bathrooms: 2 ½

Width: 38' - 0"

Depth: 79' - 2"

Foundation: Slab

eplans.com

THIS QUAINT COTTAGE-STYLE home is enhanced by country European accents and an amenity-filled interior. Double doors open into a petite welcoming foyer. Double doors from the family room and dining room access the back porch. The kitchen features an efficient storage pantry. A powder room and laundry room are placed just outside of the two-car garage. The master bedroom enjoys a private bath and walk-in closet, and Bedroom 2 is located near the hall bath.

FIRST FLOOR

SECOND FLOOR

A TRADITIONAL NEIGHBORHOOD LOOK is accented by stone and decorative arches on this stylish new design. Simplicity is the hallmark of this plan, giving the interior great flow and openness. The foyer, with a coat closet, leads directly into the two-story great room with abundant natural light and a warming fireplace. The island kitchen and dining area are to the left and enjoy rear-porch access. Upstairs, a vaulted master suite with a private bath joins two additional bedrooms to complete the plan.

HOME PLAN

HPK1200063

Style: Traditional

First Floor: 716 sq. ft.

Second Floor: 784 sq. ft.

Total: 1,500 sq. ft.

Bedrooms: 3

Bathrooms: 2 ½

Width: 36' - 0"

Depth: 44' - 0"

Foundation: Crawlspace

eplans.com

THE FOYER OPENS TO A SPACIOUS great room with a fireplace and a cathedral ceiling in this lovely traditional home. Sliding doors open to a rear deck from the great room, posing a warm welcome to enjoy the outdoors. The U-shaped kitchen features an angled peninsula counter with a cooktop. A private hall leads to the family sleeping quarters, which includes two bedrooms and a full bath with a double-bowl lavatory. Sizable bonus space above the garage provides a skylight.

HOME PLAN

HPK1200074

Style: Traditional

Square Footage: 1,517

Bonus Space: 287 sq. ft.

Bedrooms: 3

Bathrooms: 2

Width: 61' - 4"

Depth: 48' - 6"

eplans.com

DECK

(cathedral ceiling)

master bath

fireplace

DINING
12-0 x 12-0

walk-in closet

BED RM.
11-0 x 11-0

bath

GREAT RM.
15-0 x 17-10

MASTER
BED RM.
13-0 x 15-0

walk-in closet

FOYER
6-2 x
6-0

KIT.
12-0 x
12-2

UTIL.
6-4 x
6-0

BED RM.
11-0 x 11-0

storage

up

PORCH

GARAGE
20-0 x 20-4

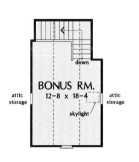

down

BONUS RM.
12-8 x 18-4

attic storage

attic storage

skylight

FIRST FLOOR

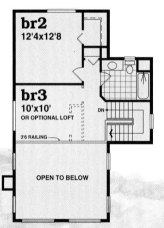

PORCH

mbr
12'4x12'8

W | D

CABINETS

din
12'x10'

k
8'4x10'

DN

UP

BREAKFAST BAR

great rm
17'x13'6

PORCH

SECOND FLOOR

br2
12'4x12'8

br3
10'x10'
OR OPTIONAL LOFT

DN

3'6 RAILING

OPEN TO BELOW

HPK1200047

Style: Country Cottage

First Floor: 1,012 sq. ft.

Second Floor: 556 sq. ft.

Total: 1,568 sq. ft.

Bedrooms: 3

Bathrooms: 2 ½

Width: 34' - 0"

Depth: 48' - 0"

Foundation: Unfinished Basement, Crawlspace

eplans.com

COUNTRY COMES HOME to this plan with details such as a metal roof, horizontal siding, multipane double-hung windows, and front and rear porches. The recessed front entry leads to the great room, flanked by a breakfast bar and formal dining room with access to both the front and rear porches. The great room is warmed by a fireplace and features a two-story ceiling. The master suite on the first level includes a private bath and walk-in closet.

BUILT-IN VIEWS!
GET A CUT ABOVE THE REST

in this multilevel home. A flight of stairs leads to the foyer, where another short flight reveals a wonderful floor plan. An intricate ceiling and arched windows in the activity room create a sense of drama as a fireplace gently soothes. The kitchen and bayed dining area are bright and open, accessing the rear sun-deck. The master suite is elegant and luxurious, and includes a vaulted resort-style bath. Two additional bedrooms share a full bath and hall linen closet.

HPK1200060

Style: Traditional

Main Level: 1,504 sq. ft.

Lower Level: 68 sq. ft.

Total: 1,572 sq. ft.

Bedrooms: 3

Bathrooms: 2 ½

Width: 51' - 2"

Depth: 32' - 4"

Foundation: Unfinished Walkout Basement

eplans.com

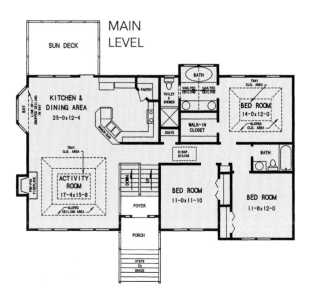

MAIN LEVEL

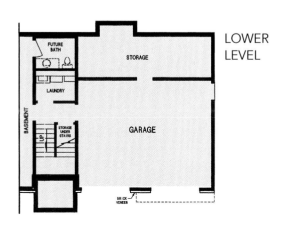

LOWER LEVEL

MULTIPLE GABLES, a transom over the entry door, and a brick-and-stone exterior combine to create an exciting front on this beautiful one-story home. The open foyer offers a view through the great room to the rear yard. A dramatic fireplace and sloped ceiling decorate the fashionable great room. The spacious kitchen and breakfast room feature a favorable indoor/outdoor relationship. The first-floor master bedroom with a tray ceiling, private bath, and extra-large walk-in closet pampers homeowners with its size and luxury. Two additional bedrooms complete this spectacular home.

HOME PLAN

HPK1200066

Style: Transitional

Square Footage: 1,593

Bedrooms: 3

Bathrooms: 2

Width: 60' - 0"

Depth: 48' - 10"

Foundation: Unfinished Basement

eplans.com

HOME PLAN

HPK1200008

THIS LOVELY VICTORIAN HOME has a perfect balance of ornamental features making it irresistible, yet affordable. The beveled-glass front door invites you into a roomy foyer. The open kitchen and breakfast room and abundant counter space make cooking a pleasure. A large family room with a warming fireplace is convenient for either informal family gatherings or formal entertaining. The upper level includes a master suite with a multifaceted vaulted ceiling, a separate shower, and a six-foot garden tub. Two additional bedrooms share a conveniently located bath. A special feature is the large, closed-in storage space at the back of the two-car garage.

Style: Country Cottage
First Floor: 812 sq. ft.
Second Floor: 786 sq. ft.
Total: 1,598 sq. ft.
Bedrooms: 3
Bathrooms: 2 ½
Width: 52' - 0"
Depth: 28' - 0"
Foundation: Slab, Crawlspace

eplans.com

FIRST FLOOR

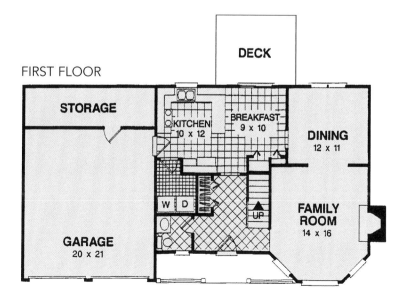

DECK

STORAGE

KITCHEN 10 x 12

BREAKFAST 9 x 10

DINING 12 x 11

W D

UP

FAMILY ROOM 14 x 16

GARAGE 20 x 21

SECOND FLOOR

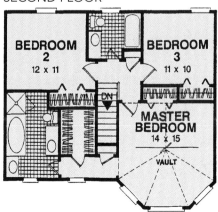

BEDROOM 2 12 x 11

BEDROOM 3 11 x 10

DN

MASTER BEDROOM 14 x 15

VAULT

FIRST FLOOR

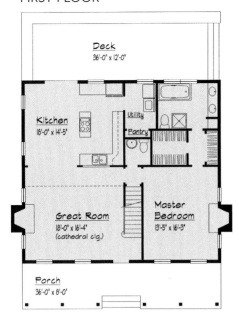

SECOND FLOOR

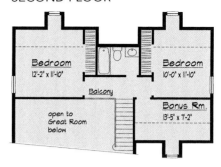

THREE DORMERS, TWO CHIMNEYS, and a covered front porch combine to make this home attractive in any neighborhood. Inside, a great room greets both family and friends with a cathedral ceiling and a warming fireplace. An L-shaped kitchen features a cooktop island. The nearby dining area offers rear-porch access. Upstairs, two secondary bedrooms share a hall bath and access a bonus room—perfect for a study or computer room.

HOME PLAN

HPK1200009

Style: Farmhouse

First Floor: 1,152 sq. ft.

Second Floor: 452 sq. ft.

Total: 1,604 sq. ft.

Bonus Space: 115 sq. ft.

Bedrooms: 3

Bathrooms: 2 ½

Width: 36' - 0"

Depth: 40' - 0"

Foundation: Crawlspace, Unfinished Basement

eplans.com

HPK1200016

Style: Country

First Floor: 808 sq. ft.

Second Floor: 808 sq. ft.

Total: 1,616 sq. ft.

Bedrooms: 3

Bathrooms: 1 ½

Width: 45' - 0"

Depth: 32' - 0"

Foundation: Unfinished Basement

HOME PLAN

FIRST FLOOR

SECOND FLOOR

HERE'S AN ATTRACTIVE HOME that provides all that a small family needs and sits lightly on the land. The lower level establishes comfortable gathering and eating areas, such as the efficient kitchen and adjoining nook. A formal dining room awaits larger parties. Upstairs, three bedrooms share a large bath. A corner space can act as an office; or, convert one of the bedrooms into a full-sized study. A single-car garage is a discrete presence at the right of the plan.

HOMES FOR FIRST-TIME BUILDERS

FIRST FLOOR

4,40 X 4,30
14'-8" x 14'-4"

3,60 x 4,10
12'-0" x 13'-8"

3,60 x 5,70
12'-0" x 19'-0"

SECOND FLOOR

3,40 X 3,00
11'-4" X 10'-0"

3,40 X 3,30
11'-4" X 11'-0"

3,40 X 4,50
11'-4" X 15'-0"

HOME PLAN

HPK1200041

Style: Country

First Floor: 831 sq. ft.

Second Floor: 791 sq. ft.

Total: 1,622 sq. ft.

Bedrooms: 3

Bathrooms: 2 ½

Width: 28' - 8"

Depth: 32' - 8"

Foundation: Unfinished Basement

eplans.com

A CLASSIC CROSS-GABLED DESIGN and full-length porch bring country charm to this small home. The lower level provides homeowners open spaces for dining and entertainment, as well as a compartmented laundry and pantry. A rear entry near the kitchen enables backyard access for chores and cookouts. Upstairs, two smaller bedrooms share a bath. The master suite achieves a comfortable compromise of space-saving and self-pampering amenities.

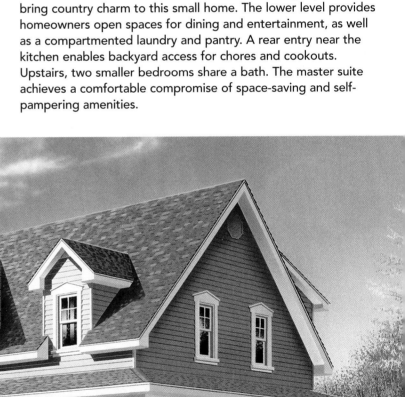

© 1998 Donald A. Gardner, Inc.

A COLUMNED, ARCHED ENTRANCE and windows add classic style to the exterior of this plan. The foyer leads to the great room warmed by an extended-hearth fireplace. Adjacent to the U-shaped kitchen, a bay-windowed dining room provides views to the rear property and rear deck, which includes a built-in seat. One of two family bedrooms is highlighted by a vaulted ceiling. The master bedroom boasts cathedral dimensions, a roomy walk-in closet, and a private bath with a dual-sink vantity, tub, and separate shower. An upstairs bonus room offers space for future expansion.

HOME PLAN

HPK1200057

Style: Country Cottage
Square Footage: 1,629
Bonus Space: 316 sq. ft.
Bedrooms: 3
Bathrooms: 2
Width: 58' - 6"
Depth: 49' - 8"

eplans.com

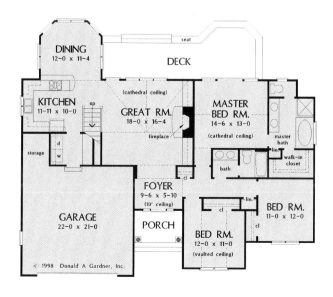

DINING
12-0 x 11-4

DECK
seat

(cathedral ceiling)

KITCHEN
11-11 x 10-0

GREAT RM.
18-0 x 16-4

MASTER
BED RM.
14-6 x 13-0

(cathedral ceiling)

fireplace

master
bath

storage

walk-in
closet

bath

FOYER
9-6 x 5-10
(10' ceiling)

BED RM.
11-0 x 12-0

GARAGE
22-0 x 21-0

PORCH

BED RM.
12-0 x 11-0
(vaulted ceiling)

© 1998 Donald A Gardner, Inc.

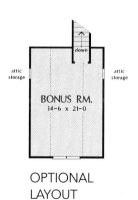

attic
storage

BONUS RM.
14-6 x 21-0

down

attic
storage

OPTIONAL
LAYOUT

A **BUNGALOW-STYLE PLAN**, this home is enhanced with unique pillars, horizontal siding, square clerestory windows, and muntin windows. Covered porches grace both the front and rear of this inviting home. Two doors access the spacious living room, where a fireplace heats up the space. The dining room and kitchen run into one smooth area and the kitchen accesses the rear covered porch. The right side of the plan is devoted to sleeping quarters: a master suite, with a private full bath, and two additional bedrooms complete with walk-in closets.

HOME PLAN

HPK1200065

Style: Bungalow

Square Footage: 1,657

Bedrooms: 3

Bathrooms: 2

Width: 64' - 0"

Depth: 58' - 0"

Foundation: Unfinished Basement, Crawlspace, Slab

eplans.com

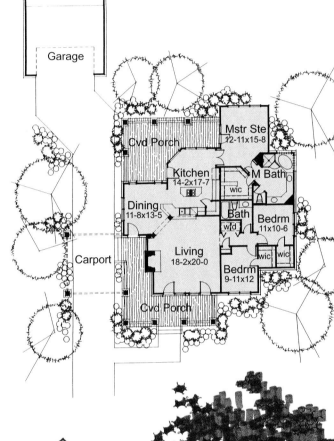

THE WRAPAROUND FRONT PORCH WELCOMES you home to this classic country farmhouse design. Two floors of family-friendly space await inside. The first level is devoted to living spaces. An island kitchen with plenty of space for helping hands has direct access to both a formal dining room and an informal niche backed by a wall of windows with views to the rear yard. Assemble the kids and some friends in the great room for a movie or a board game. Three bedrooms are situated upstairs, including the master bedroom with a large walk-in closet. The bathroom is shared by all rooms and has a dual-sink vanity, separate tub and shower, and plenty of space.

HOME PLAN

(#) HPK1200031

Style: Farmhouse

First Floor: 860 sq. ft.

Second Floor: 840 sq. ft.

Total: 1,700 sq. ft.

Bedrooms: 3

Bathrooms: 1 ½

Width: 30' - 0"

Depth: 29' - 0"

Foundation: Unfinished Basement

eplans.com

HOMES FOR FIRST-TIME BUILDERS

FIRST FLOOR

SECOND FLOOR

COUNTRY STYLE SHAPES the exterior of this lovely family home. A covered front porch welcomes you inside to a foyer that opens to the gathering areas. A fireplace warms the dining room and family room. The kitchen provides a pantry and island workstation and opens to the casual breakfast nook. The rear deck is perfect for outdoor cooking and entertainment. The master suite features a luxury bath and His and Hers walk-in closets. Two additional family bedrooms are situated to the right side of the plan and share a hall bath. Extra storage space is available in the two-car garage.

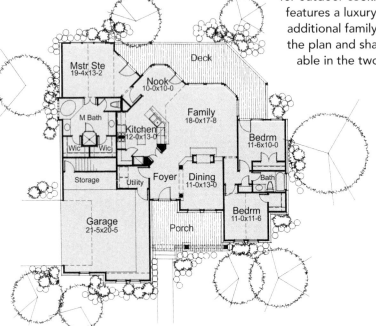

HOME PLAN

**HPK1200056**

Style: Farmhouse

Square Footage: 1,715

Bedrooms: 3

Bathrooms: 2

Width: 58' - 0"

Depth: 59' - 6"

Foundation: Crawlspace, Slab, Unfinished Basement

eplans.com

FIRST FLOOR

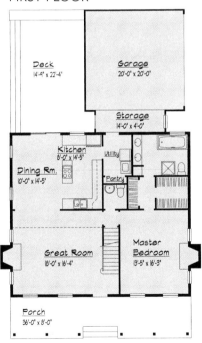

SECOND FLOOR

SIMPLICITY IS OFTEN THE BEST APPROACH to design. Twin chimneys serve as anchors to the home, while a deep front porch welcomes visitors. Inside, the cathedral ceiling and natural light from the dormers above enliven the great room. The well-appointed master suite also enjoys a private fireplace. Two additional bedrooms are located on the second floor along with the bonus room, which will add 115 square feet if finished.

 # HPK1200061

HOME PLAN

Style: Country Cottage

First Floor: 1,152 sq. ft.

Second Floor: 567 sq. ft.

Total: 1,719 sq. ft.

Bonus Space: 115 sq. ft.

Bedrooms: 3

Bathrooms: 2 ½

Width: 36' - 0"

Depth: 64' - 0"

Foundation: Crawlspace, Unfinished Basement

eplans.com

HOMES FOR FIRST-TIME BUILDERS

FIRST FLOOR

SECOND FLOOR

A **STONE-AND-SIDING EXTERIOR** brings dimension and color to the exterior of this charming home. A two-story foyer greets you upon arrival, and the great room, with views to the rear and side yards, offers a 12-foot ceiling. The breakfast bay and entry to a covered porch create a bright and cheery place to start the day. Counter space that wraps around from the kitchen provides additional storage and a convenient writing desk. A furniture alcove adds space to the formal dining room and a rear entry hall offers storage closets and a large laundry room. A second-floor master bedroom, with a ceiling that slopes to nine feet, keeps the parents close at hand to younger family members. This home has a full basement that can be developed for additional square footage.

HOME PLAN

HPK1200037

Style: Craftsman

First Floor: 941 sq. ft.

Second Floor: 786 sq. ft.

Total: 1,727 sq. ft.

Bedrooms: 3

Bathrooms: 2 ½

Width: 57' - 10"

Depth: 42' - 4"

Foundation: Unfinished Basement

eplans.com

COME HOME TO A COUNTRY GEM with a unique portico entry and dazzling windows. Inside, the foyer directs family and guests to the two-story great room where a fireplace warms any gathering. Just ahead, the angled island kitchen serves casual snacks in the breakfast nook, and elegant meals in the dining room. The master suite is tucked to the rear for privacy, and enjoys a lavish spa bath. Upstairs, two bedrooms share a full bath and access to an expansive bonus room. Walk-in storage (not included in the square footage) is a wonderful amenity.

HOME PLAN

HPK1200021

Style: Cape Cod

First Floor: 1,251 sq. ft.

Second Floor: 505 sq. ft.

Total: 1,756 sq. ft.

Bonus Space: 447 sq. ft.

Bedrooms: 3

Bathrooms: 2 ½

Width: 50' - 0"

Depth: 39' - 0"

Foundation: Unfinished Walkout Basement, Crawlspace, Slab

eplans.com

FIRST FLOOR

SECOND FLOOR

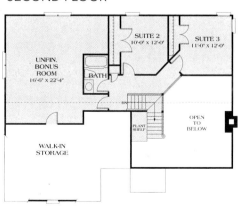

FIRST FLOOR

THIS COUNTRY VICTORIAN design comes loaded with charm and amenities. The entry leads to open living space, defined by a two-sided fireplace and a large bay window. An island counter with a snack bar highlights the L-shaped kitchen. A quiet sitting area opens to the outdoors. Upstairs, the master suite allows plenty of sunlight from the turret's bay window and boasts a step-up tub, dual-sink vanity, and separate shower. Bonus space above the garage offers room for future expansion.

HOME PLAN

HPK1200030

Style: Victorian

First Floor: 880 sq. ft.

Second Floor: 880 sq. ft.

Total: 1,760 sq. ft.

Bonus Space: 256 sq. ft.

Bedrooms: 3

Bathrooms: 2 ½

Width: 42' - 0"

Depth: 40' - 0"

Foundation: Unfinished Basement

SECOND FLOOR

eplans.com

**THIS COZY
1,770-SQUARE-FOOT
COTTAGE** is reminiscent of a simpler time. It is a flexible and full-featured design with particular appeal for an established neighborhood, a narrow lot, or a vacation retreat. The covered front porch and the screened porch make this home perfect for those who enjoy the outdoors. Upon entering, your first glance will be of the formal dining room, adorned with decorative columns. Just beyond is the carefully planned kitchen boasting a double oven and recipe desk. Decorative columns surround the breakfast room, providing openness to the family room. A fireplace, lot's of glass, and a tray ceiling make this family room most dramatic. The master suite also has a tray ceiling and offers direct access to the screened porch. While modest in size, rooms are spacious and the living areas are quite open. And, with the optional bonus room, there's an additional 14' x 53'-9" for future expansion. Ceiling heights are nine feet except for vaulted areas.

HOME PLAN

HPK1200068

Style: Traditional

Square Footage: 1,770

Bonus Space: 762 sq. ft.

Bedrooms: 3

Bathrooms: 2

Width: 52' - 4"

Depth: 66' - 0"

Foundation: Crawlspace, Unfinished Basement

eplans.com

OPTIONAL LAYOUT

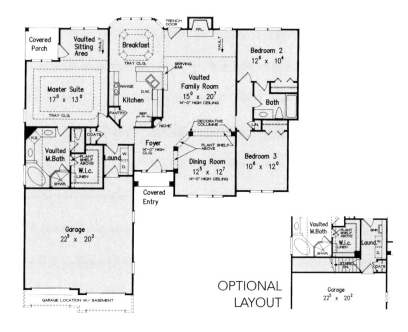

OPTIONAL
LAYOUT

HOME PLAN

HPK1200046

Style: European Cottage

Square Footage: 1,779

Bedrooms: 3

Bathrooms: 2

Width: 57' - 0"

Depth: 56' - 4"

Foundation: Unfinished Walkout Basement, Crawlspace

eplans.com

EUROPEAN STYLE SHINES from this home's facade in the form of its stucco detailing, hipped rooflines, fancy windows, and elegant entryway. Inside, decorative columns and a plant shelf define the formal dining room, which works well with the vaulted family room. The efficient kitchen offers a serving bar to both the family room and the deluxe breakfast room. Located apart from the family bedrooms for privacy, the master suite is sure to please with its many amenities, including a vaulted sitting area and a private covered porch. The two secondary bedrooms share a full hall bath.

HOME PLAN

HPK1200051

Style: Traditional

Square Footage: 1,787

Bonus Space: 263 sq. ft.

Bedrooms: 3

Bathrooms: 2

Width: 55' - 8"

Depth: 56' - 6"

Foundation: Unfinished Walkout Basement, Slab, Crawlspace

eplans.com

THIS STRIKING AND DISTINCTIVE RANCH home includes all the frills. From the inviting front porch to the screened porch and deck, this home provides dramatic spaces, luxurious appointments, and spacious living areas. It's carefully designed to provide the feel and features of a much larger home. The bonus room and basement provide plenty of space for expansion, so this home is one that won't soon be outgrown. Soaring ceilings enhance the entryway. To the left is the dining room—open to the entry and family room. The kitchen is open and provides both a breakfast and serving bar. The dramatic master suite is loaded with amenities such as a double step tray ceiling, direct access to the screened porch, a sitting room, deluxe bath, and His and Hers walk-in closets. The secondary bedrooms share a second bath.

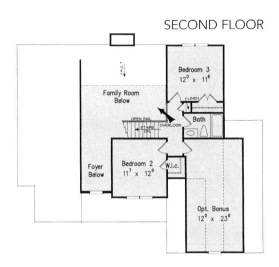

VARIETY IN THE FACADE is just a prelude to the charm to be found inside this attractive three-bedroom home. The two-story foyer opens on the right to a formal dining room, then leads back to a vaulted family room—complete with a warming fireplace. The efficient kitchen offers a breakfast bar and easy access to the breakfast area. The master suite is lavish with its amenities. Included here is a huge walk-in closet, a separate tub and shower, and a tray ceiling. Upstairs, two family bedrooms share a full hall bath. An optional bonus room is available for future development.

HPK1200026

HOME PLAN

Style: Country Cottage

First Floor: 1,382 sq. ft.

Second Floor: 436 sq. ft.

Total: 1,818 sq. ft.

Bonus Space: 298 sq. ft.

Bedrooms: 3

Bathrooms: 2 ½

Width: 52' - 4"

Depth: 45' - 10"

Foundation: Crawlspace, Unfinished Walkout Basement, Slab

eplans.com

HOME PLAN

HPK1200069

Style: Country Cottage

First Floor: 1,242 sq. ft.

Second Floor: 577 sq. ft.

Total: 1,819 sq. ft.

Bedrooms: 3

Bathrooms: 2 ½

Width: 43' - 0"

Depth: 47' - 0"

Foundation: Slab, Crawlspace

eplans.com

THIS PETITE AND EFFICIENT home offers a charming floor plan with a stunning front porch. The first floor provides a formal living room with a fireplace and an opening to the dining area. The kitchen opens to the breakfast room, which overlooks the rear deck. Secluded on the first floor for privacy, the master bedroom includes a spacious walk-in closet and a bathroom with a whirlpool tub. Upstairs, two secondary bedrooms with walk-in closets share a bathroom.

FIRST FLOOR

SECOND FLOOR

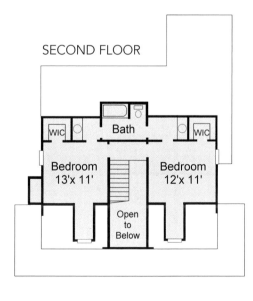

STONE BAYS AND WOOD SIDING make up the exterior facade on this one-story home. The interior revolves around the living room with an attached dining room and the galley kitchen with a breakfast room. The master suite has a fine bath and a walk-in closet. One of three family bedrooms on the left side of the plan could be used as a home office.

HOME PLAN

HPK1200034

Style: Farmhouse

Square Footage: 1,822

Bedrooms: 3

Bathrooms: 2

Width: 58' - 0"

Depth: 67' - 2"

Foundation: Unfinished Basement, Finished Basement

eplans.com

HOME PLAN

HPK1200027

Style: Farmhouse

Square Footage: 1,830

Bedrooms: 3

Bathrooms: 2

Width: 75' - 0"

Depth: 43' - 5"

Foundation: Unfinished Basement

eplans.com

THIS CHARMING ONE-STORY traditional home greets visitors with a covered porch. A uniquely shaped galley-style kitchen shares a snack bar with the spacious gathering room where a fireplace is the focal point. The dining room furnishes sliding glass doors to the rear terrace, as does the master bedroom. This bedroom area also includes a luxury bath with a whirlpool tub and separate dressing room. Two additional bedrooms, one that could double as a study, are located at the front of the home. The two-car garage features a large storage area and can be reached through the service entrance or from the rear terrace.

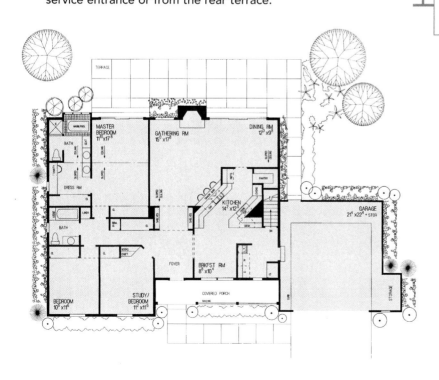

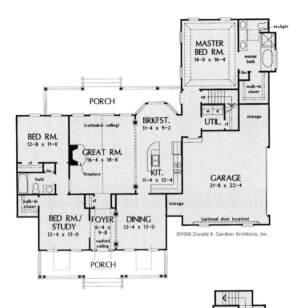

MASTER BED RM.
14-0 x 16-4

skylight

master bath

walk-in closet

PORCH

up

storage

BRKFST.
11-4 x 9-2

UTIL.

w d

cl

BED RM.
12-8 x 11-0

(cathedral ceiling)

GREAT RM.
16-4 x 18-8

fireplace

cl

lin.

bath

KIT.
11-4 x 12-4

GARAGE
21-8 x 22-4

walk-in closet

storage

BED RM./
STUDY
12-4 x 13-0

cl

FOYER
6-4 x 9-8

vaulted ceiling

DINING
12-4 x 13-0

(optional door location)

©1995 Donald A. Gardner Architects, Inc.

PORCH

attic storage

storage

down

skylights

BONUS RM.
12-8 x 22-4

THIS CHARMING COUNTRY plan boasts a cathedral ceiling in the great room. Dormer windows shed light on the foyer, which opens to a front bedroom/study and to the formal dining room. The kitchen is completely open to the great room and features a stylish snack-bar island and a bay window in the breakfast nook. The master suite offers a tray ceiling and a skylit bath. Two secondary bedrooms share a full bath on the opposite side of the house. Bonus space over the garage may be developed in the future.

HPK1200054

HOME PLAN

Style: **Farmhouse**
Square Footage: **1,832**
Bonus Space: **425 sq. ft.**
Bedrooms: **3**
Bathrooms: **2**
Width: **65' - 4"**
Depth: **62' - 0"**

eplans.com

© 1995 Donald A. Gardner Architects, Inc.

B. LATON

PILLARS, BEAUTIFUL

TRANSOMS, and sidelights set off the entry door and draw attention to this comfortable home. The foyer leads to a formal dining room and a great room with a ribbon of windows pouring in light. To the left of the kitchen is a roomy laundry area, with lots of storage space for those extra household supplies. Privacy is assured with a master suite—a large walk-in closet and full bath with separate shower and large tub add to the pleasure of this wing. Two family bedrooms occupy the right side of the design and share a full bath.

HOME PLAN

HPK1200077

Style: Traditional

Square Footage: 1,836

Bedrooms: 3

Bathrooms: 2

Width: 65' - 8"

Depth: 55' - 0"

Foundation: Crawlspace, Slab, Unfinished Basement

eplans.com

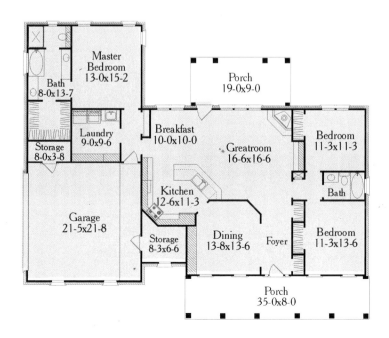

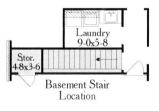

Basement Stair Location

FIRST FLOOR

SECOND FLOOR

HOME PLAN

HPK1200010

Style: Traditional

First Floor: 919 sq. ft.

Second Floor: 927 sq. ft.

Total: 1,846 sq. ft.

Bedrooms: 4

Bathrooms: 2 ½

Width: 44' - 0"

Depth: 40' - 0"

eplans.com

THIS WONDERFUL DESIGN begins with the wraparound porch. Explore further and find a two-story entry with a coat closet and plant shelf above and a strategically placed staircase alongside. The island kitchen with a boxed window over the sink is adjacent to a large bay-windowed dinette. The great room includes many windows and a fireplace. A powder room and laundry room are both conveniently placed on the first floor. Upstairs, the large master suite contains His and Hers walk-in closets, corner windows, and a bath area featuring a double vanity and whirlpool tub. Two pleasant secondary bedrooms have interesting angles, and a third bedroom in the front features a volume ceiling and an arched window.

©1998 Donald A. Gardner, Inc.

GABLE TREATMENTS along with stone and horizontal siding give a definite country flavor to this two-story home. Inside, the foyer opens to a great room, which boasts a fireplace, built-ins, and a magnificent view of the backyard beyond an inviting rear porch. The kitchen is designed for high style with a column-defined cooktop island and serving-bar access to the dining area. The master suite finishes this level and includes two walk-in closets and a private bath. Two bedrooms share a full bath and bonus space on the second floor.

HOME PLAN

HPK1200005

Style: Country Cottage

First Floor: 1,336 sq. ft.

Second Floor: 523 sq. ft.

Total: 1,859 sq. ft.

Bonus Space: 225 sq. ft.

Bedrooms: 3

Bathrooms: 2 ½

Width: 45' - 0"

Depth: 53' - 0"

eplans.com

FIRST FLOOR

SECOND FLOOR

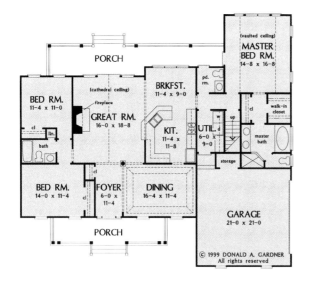

PORCH

BED RM.
11-4 x 11-0

(cathedral ceiling)

fireplace

GREAT RM.
16-0 x 18-8

BRKFST.
11-4 x 9-0

pd. rm.

MASTER
BED RM.
14-8 x 16-8

(vaulted ceiling)

KIT.
11-4 x 11-8

UTIL.
6-0 x 9-0

walk-in closet

master bath

storage

cl

BED RM.
14-0 x 11-4

FOYER
6-0 x 11-4

DINING
16-4 x 11-4

GARAGE
21-0 x 21-0

PORCH

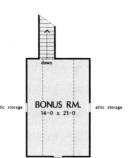

BONUS RM.
14-0 x 21-0

attic storage   attic storage

down

AN ARCHED WINDOW in a center front-facing gable lends style and beauty to the facade of this three-bedroom home. An open common area features a great room with a cathedral ceiling, a formal dining room with a tray ceiling, a functional kitchen, and an informal breakfast area that separates the master suite from the secondary bedrooms for privacy. The master suite provides a dramatic vaulted ceiling, access to the back porch, and abundant closet space. Access to a versatile bonus room is near the master bedroom.

HPK1200076

HOME PLAN

Style: Country

Square Footage: 1,882

Bonus Space: 363 sq. ft.

Bedrooms: 3

Bathrooms: 2 ½

Width: 61' - 4"

Depth: 55' - 0"

eplans.com

HOME PLAN

HPK1200045

Style: Santa Fe

Square Footage: 1,895

Bedrooms: 3

Bathrooms: 2

Width: 65' - 10"

Depth: 59' - 9"

eplans.com

GIDDYUP! SANTA FE STYLE at its best brings you back to the days of open skies and covered wagons. Rich with history on the outside, this plan's interior has all the up-to-date amenities that today's families require. The arched loggia entry opens to a soaring foyer, flanked on the right by a formal dining room. To the left is a bedroom that could easily become a study. Straight ahead, the hearth-warmed great room enjoys sliding-glass-door access to the rear loggia. Another bedroom is tucked in the back left corner, convenient to a full hall bath. On the other side of the great room, a roomy kitchen opens to a breakfast nook with a curved wall of windows. Secluded to the back is the luxurious master suite, featuring a 10-foot ceiling and spectacular private bath. The two-car garage opens to a utility room with a handy linen closet.

THE WELCOMING CHARM of this country farmhouse is expressed by its many windows and its covered wrap-around porch. A two-story foyer is enhanced by a Palladian window in a clerestory dormer above to let in natural lighting. The first-floor master suite allows privacy and accessibility. The master bath includes a whirlpool tub, separate shower, double-bowl vanity, and walk-in closet. The first floor features nine-foot ceilings throughout with the exception of the kitchen area, which sports an eight-foot ceiling. The second floor contains two additional bedrooms, a full bath, and plenty of storage space. The bonus room provides room to grow.

HOME PLAN

HPK1200024

Style: Farmhouse

First Floor: 1,356 sq. ft.

Second Floor: 542 sq. ft.

Total: 1,898 sq. ft.

Bonus Space: 393 sq. ft.

Bedrooms: 3

Bathrooms: 2 ½

Width: 59' - 0"

Depth: 64' - 0"

eplans.com

FIRST FLOOR

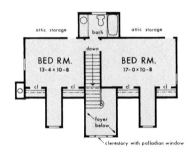

©1991 Donald A. Gardner Architects, Inc.

SECOND FLOOR

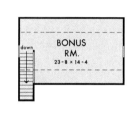

© 1991 Donald A. Gardner, Architects, Inc.

B. NATHAN

HPK1200042

Style: European Cottage

First Floor: 880 sq. ft.

Second Floor: 1,029 sq. ft.

Total: 1,909 sq. ft.

Bedrooms: 4

Bathrooms: 2 ½

Width: 32' - 8"

Depth: 38' - 0"

Foundation: Unfinished Basement

eplans.com

SHARPLY DEFINED ROOFLINES, arch-top windows, and a wraparound porch mark this European cottage as a home that begs to make you comfortable. All the sleeping quarters and two baths are located on the second level. A wraparound dual-sink vanity, an oversize tub, and a shower in the master suite promise to pamper. Two downstairs sitting rooms, one with a fireplace and space for elegant dining at one end, provide ample room for formal get-togethers and family relaxation. A peninsular snack bar helps define the other sitting room from the kitchen. A half-bath, laundry room, and one-car garage complete the plan.

HOMES FOR FIRST-TIME BUILDERS

FIRST FLOOR

SECOND FLOOR

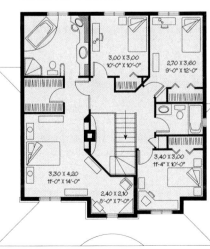

FIRST FLOOR

SECOND FLOOR

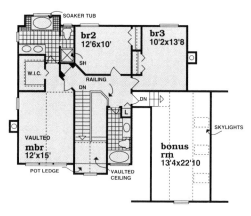

THIS CHARMING COUNTRY EXTERIOR conceals an elegant interior, starting with formal living and dining rooms, each with a bay window. Decorative columns help define an elegant dining room. The gourmet kitchen features a work island and a breakfast area with its own bay window. A fireplace warms the family room, which opens to the rear porch through French doors. Upstairs, two family bedrooms share a full bath and a gallery hall with a balcony overlook to the foyer. Also on this floor, a master suite boasts a vaulted ceiling, a walk-in closet, and a tiled bath.

HOME PLAN

HPK1200053

Style: Country Cottage

First Floor: 1,007 sq. ft.

Second Floor: 917 sq. ft.

Total: 1,924 sq. ft.

Bonus Space: 325 sq. ft.

Bedrooms: 3

Bathrooms: 2 ½

Width: 53' - 0"

Depth: 44' - 0"

Foundation: Crawlspace, Unfinished Basement

eplans.com

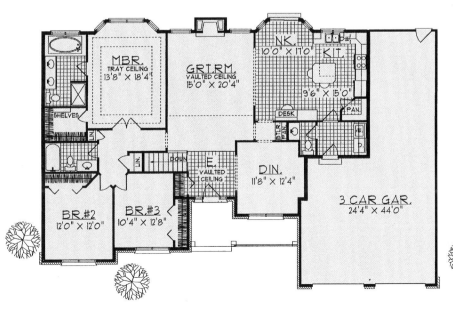

HPK1200050

THIS HIPPED ROOF HOME has an exterior that tastefully mixes brick and siding. The recessed entrance with sidelights creates the formal entry. The foyer opens to a formal dining room with butler's pantry to the right, and to the vaulted great room featuring a fireplace. There is a large, open kitchen with ample cupboard space, and a spacious breakfast area that leads to the backyard. The spacious main-floor master bedroom has a large walk in closet, private bath, and bay windows overlooking the backyard. The private master bath amenities start with a whirlpool tub, double vanity, and a large shower. Two additional bedrooms share a full bath and each has a large closets. The large triple tandem garage provides plenty of storage or workshop space. The laundry room is on the main level between the garage and the kitchen, and adjoins the guest bath.

Style: Ranch

Square Footage: 1,926

Bedrooms: 3

Bathrooms: 2 ½

Width: 69' - 8"

Depth: 46' - 0"

Foundation: Unfinished Basement

eplans.com

HOME PLAN

HOMES FOR FIRST-TIME BUILDERS

SECOND FLOOR

FIRST FLOOR

TRADITIONAL FEATURES get a boost with an appealing front turret. Inside, flexible room design rules. The formal dining area is to the left of the foyer and discreetly accesses the kitchen. The great room sits to the rear of the plan and features a fireplace and rear-porch access. Unobstructed views of the fireplace can be enjoyed during casual meals or cooking in the breakfast room and kitchen. A first-floor master suite, located in the front turret, includes a corner garden tub in the private bath. The second floor is composed of two family bedrooms and a bonus room—all sharing a full hall bath with dual-sink vanity.

HPK1200049

HOME PLAN

Style: Transitional

First Floor: 1,420 sq. ft.

Second Floor: 549 sq. ft.

Total: 1,969 sq. ft.

Bonus Space: 268 sq. ft.

Bedrooms: 3

Bathrooms: 2 ½

Width: 58' - 0"

Depth: 44' - 4"

Foundation: Unfinished Basement

eplans.com

 # HPK1200072

HOME PLAN

Style: Craftsman

First Floor: 1,060 sq. ft.

Second Floor: 914 sq. ft.

Total: 1,974 sq. ft.

Bedrooms: 3

Bathrooms: 3

Width: 32' - 0"

Depth: 35' - 0"

Foundation: Crawlspace

eplans.com

FIRST FLOOR

GARAGE
20'-0" x 22'-0"

SECOND FLOOR

LIN.

MASTER BATH

DN

SUITE 2
12'-2" x 13'-4"

W.I.C.

LAUN.

BATH

ATTIC STOR.

MASTER SUITE
14'-0" x 15'-8"

W.I.C.

ATTIC STOR.

HOME OFFICE / GUEST SUITE
13'-2" x 13'-10"

W.I.C.

COVERED PORCH

PANT.

KITCHEN
12'-0" x 15'-8"

BATH

OPT. BUILT-IN BREAKFAST BOOTH

OPT. 2ND SINK

UP

OPT. CABINETS

GATHERING ROOM
18'-6" x 14'-4"

DINING ROOM
12'-0" x 14'-4"

COVERED PORCH

THIS CHARMING CRAFTSMAN DESIGN
offers a second-story master bedroom with four windows under the gabled dormer. The covered front porch displays column and pier supports. The hearth-warmed gathering room opens to the dining room on the right, where the adjoining kitchen offers enough space for an optional breakfast booth. A home office/guest suite is found in the rear. The second floor holds the lavish master suite and a second bedroom suite with its own private bath.

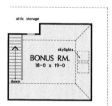

A TWO-STORY FOYER with a Palladian window above sets the tone for this sunlit home. Columns mark the passage from the foyer to the great room, where a central fireplace and built-in cabinets are found. A screened porch with four skylights above and a wet bar provides a pleasant place to start the day or wind down after work. The kitchen is flanked by the formal dining room and the breakfast room. Hidden quietly at the rear, the master suite includes a bath with dual vanities and skylights. Two family bedrooms (one an optional study) share a bath that has twin sinks.

HPK1200012

Style: Traditional

Square Footage: 1,977

Bonus Space: 430 sq. ft.

Bedrooms: 3

Bathrooms: 2

Width: 69' - 8"

Depth: 59' - 6"

HOME PLAN

eplans.com

© 1994 Donald A. Gardner Architects, Inc.

HOME PLAN

(#) HPK1200020

Style: Craftsman

First Floor: 1,106 sq. ft.

Second Floor: 872 sq. ft.

Total: 1,978 sq. ft.

Bedrooms: 3

Bathrooms: 2 ½

Width: 38' - 0"

Depth: 35' - 0"

Foundation: Slab, Unfinished Basement

eplans.com

THOUGH THIS HOME GIVES THE IMPRESSION OF THE NORTHWEST, it will be the winner of any neighborhood. From the foyer, the two-story living room is just a couple of steps up and features a through-fireplace. The U-shaped kitchen has a cooktop work island, an adjacent nook, and easy access to the formal dining room. A spacious family room shares the fireplace with the living room, is enhanced by built-ins, and also offers a quiet deck for stargazing. The upstairs consists of two family bedrooms sharing a full bath and a vaulted master suite complete with a walk-in closet and sumptuous bath. A two-car, drive-under garage has plenty of room for storage.

FIRST FLOOR

SECOND FLOOR

BASEMENT

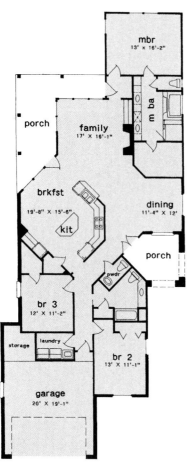

HPK1200036

Style: European Cottage

Square Footage: 2,007

Bedrooms: 3

Bathrooms: 2 ½

Width: 40' - 0"

Depth: 94' - 10"

Foundation: Slab

eplans.com

AN ORNATE STUCCO FACADE with brick highlights refines this charming French cottage. The double-door entrance sits to the side—perfect for a courtyard welcome. A dining and family room utilize an open layout for easy traffic flow. The circular kitchen space features an island and complementary breakfast bay. Bedrooms 2 and 3 share a hall bath. The master suite, apart from the main living areas, enjoys privacy and a full bath with a spacious walk-in closet. The rear porch encourages outdoor relaxation.

HOME PLAN

HPK1200033

Style: Traditional

First Floor: 1,411 sq. ft.

Second Floor: 618 sq. ft.

Total: 2,029 sq. ft.

Bonus Space: 214 sq. ft.

Bedrooms: 4

Bathrooms: 2 ½

Width: 63' - 8"

Depth: 48' - 4"

eplans.com

SHUTTERS, MULTIPANE GLASS WINDOWS, and a cross-hatched railing on the front porch make this a beautiful country cottage. To the left of the foyer is a roomy great room and a warming fireplace, framed by windows. To the right of the foyer, two family bedrooms feature walk-in closets and share a fully appointed bath. The efficient kitchen centers around a long island workstation and opens to the large dining/sitting room. The rear porch adds living space to view the outdoors. French doors, a fireplace, and columns complete this four-bedroom design.

FIRST FLOOR

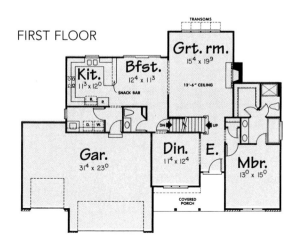

SECOND FLOOR

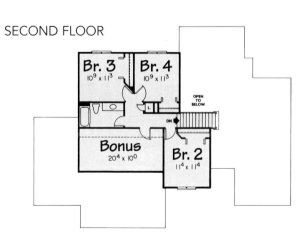

FIRST FLOOR

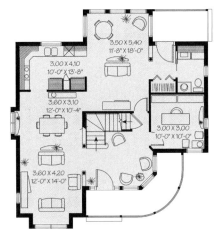

SECOND FLOOR

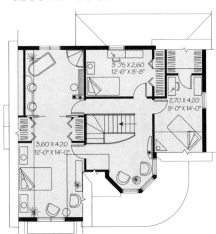

VICTORIAN STYLING can come in an affordable size, as this home shows. A sitting area inside the front hall connects with the family room for handling large parties. An enclosed room off the sitting area can be used as a study or extra bedroom. A combination half-bath and laundry is just inside the rear entrance for quick cleanup; the covered rear porch is accessed from a door just beyond the laundry area. For easy upkeep, the three bedrooms on the second floor share a full bath that includes a corner tub. One of the bedrooms offers access to a private balcony.

HOME PLAN

HPK1200040

Style: Victorian

First Floor: 1,070 sq. ft.

Second Floor: 970 sq. ft.

Total: 2,040 sq. ft.

Bedrooms: 3

Bathrooms: 1 ½

Width: 36' - 0"

Depth: 40' - 8"

Foundation: Unfinished Basement

eplans.com

HOME PLAN
HPK1200073

Style: Farmhouse
Square Footage: 2,076
Bedrooms: 3
Bathrooms: 2
Width: 64' - 8"
Depth: 54' - 7"
Foundation: Unfinished Basement

HOME PLAN
HPK1200022

Style: European Cottage
First Floor: 1,172 sq. ft.
Second Floor: 912 sq. ft.
Total: 2,084 sq. ft.
Bedrooms: 3
Bathrooms: 2 ½
Width: 50' - 0"
Depth: 42' - 6"
Foundation: Unfinished Basement

FIRST FLOOR

SECOND FLOOR

FIRST FLOOR

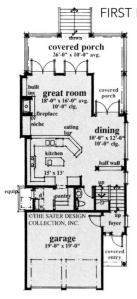

covered porch
26'-0" x 10'-0" avg.

built ins

great room
18'-0" x 16'-0" avg.
10'-0" clg.

covered porch

fireplace

tv niche

eating bar

dining
10'-0" x 12'-0"
10'-0" clg.

kitchen
15' x 13'

half wall

equip

pantry

up

up
foyer

©THE SATER DESIGN COLLECTION, INC.

garage
19'-0" x 19'-0"

covered entry

SECOND FLOOR

sundeck
26'-0" x 10'-0" avg.

master
16'-6" x 15'-0"
vault. clg.

sundeck

w.i.c.

art

study/br.
12'-0" x 10'-0"
9'-0" clg.

w.i.c.

dn.

landing

up

art

br. 2
9'-8" x 11'-0"
9'-0" clg.

br. 3
9'-8" x 11'-0"
9'-0" clg.

KEY WEST CONCH style blends Old World charm with New World comfort in this picturesque design. A glass-paneled entry lends a warm welcome and complements a captivating front balcony. Two sets of French doors open the great room to wide views and extend the living areas to the back covered porch. A gourmet kitchen is prepared for any occasion with a prep sink, plenty of counter space, an ample pantry, and an eating bar. The midlevel landing leads to two additional bedrooms, a full bath, and a windowed art niche. Double French doors open the upper-level master suite to a sundeck.

HPK1200002

HOME PLAN

Style: Contemporary

First Floor: 876 sq. ft.

Second Floor: 1,245 sq. ft.

Total: 2,121 sq. ft.

Bedrooms: 4

Bathrooms: 2 ½

Width: 27' - 6"

Depth: 64' - 0"

Foundation: Crawlspace, Pier

eplans.com

THE HIPPED ROOF with its eyebrow dormers settles beautifully above the columns and shuttered windows of this three-bedroom home. A courtyard separates the house from the street. Inside, three bedrooms line the left of the plan, and a living area sits to the right. The master suite features a large bath with two walk-in closets. A hearth-warmed living room accesses the rear porch. The island kitchen shares natural light from the bayed breakfast nook and easily serves the formal dining room.

HPK1200028

HOME PLAN

Style: Country Cottage
Square Footage: 2,155
Bedrooms: 3
Bathrooms: 2
Width: 50' - 4"
Depth: 101' - 9"
Foundation: Slab

eplans.com

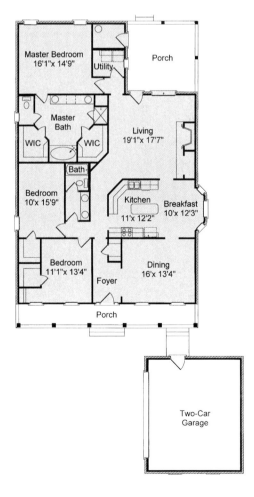

FIRST FLOOR

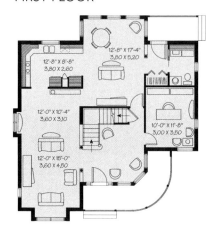

SECOND FLOOR

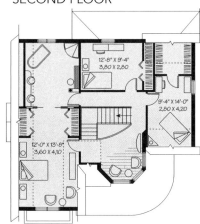

HOME PLAN

HPK1200015

Style: Victorian

First Floor: 1,130 sq. ft.

Second Floor: 1,030 sq. ft.

Total: 2,160 sq. ft.

Bedrooms: 3

Bathrooms: 1 ½

Width: 36' - 8"

Depth: 40' - 8"

Foundation: Unfinished Basement

eplans.com

A CROSS-GABLED DESIGN, central tower, semi-circular porch with bracketed posts, and other Victorian details make this home an easy fit for established neighborhoods. Inside, enjoy modern conveniences like a home office and an island kitchen, as well as an expansive master suite. The generous amount of full-height windows in a small plan means plenty of natural light for all the home's spaces. The adorable sitting area within the tower is one such example.

HOME PLAN

HPK1200007

Style: European Cottage

Square Footage: 2,163

Bedrooms: 3

Bathrooms: 2

Width: 44' - 0"

Depth: 83' - 0"

Foundation: Slab

eplans.com

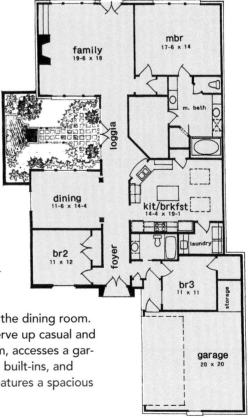

THIS COZY STUCCO design fits a shady lane in town or takes advantage of the views in the country. French doors open from an arched entryway with a transom window to the foyer. Two family bedrooms flank the foyer, and a hallway opens to the dining room. Across the hall, the kitchen and breakfast room serve up casual and formal meals. A loggia, just before the family room, accesses a garden courtyard. The family room sports a fireplace, built-ins, and French doors to the rear yard. The master suite features a spacious walk-in closet and an amenity-filled bath.

FIRST FLOOR

SECOND FLOOR

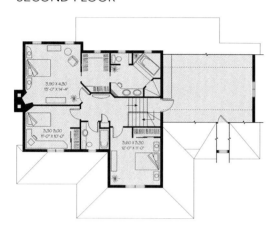

THIS BEAUTIFUL THREE-BEDROOM HOME boasts many attractive features. Two covered porches will entice you outside; inside, a special sunroom on the first floor brings the outdoors in. The foyer opens on the right to a comfortable family room that may be used as a home office. On the left, the living area is warmed by the sunroom and a cozy corner fireplace. A formal dining area lies adjacent to an efficient kitchen with a central island and breakfast nook overlooking the back porch. The second level offers two family bedrooms served by a full bath. A spacious master suite with a walk-in closet and luxurious bath completes the second floor.

HOME PLAN

HPK1200055

Style: Victorian

First Floor: 1,232 sq. ft.

Second Floor: 951 sq. ft.

Total: 2,183 sq. ft.

Bonus Space: 365 sq. ft.

Bedrooms: 3

Bathrooms: 2 ½

Width: 56' - 0"

Depth: 38' - 0"

Foundation: Unfinished Basement

eplans.com

HOME PLAN

HPK1200013

Style: Farmhouse

First Floor: 1,085 sq. ft.

Second Floor: 1,110 sq. ft.

Total: 2,195 sq. ft.

Bedrooms: 4

Bathrooms: 2 ½

Width: 49' - 0"

Depth: 47' - 0"

Foundation: Crawlspace

eplans.com

FARMHOUSE DESIGN IS POPULAR throughout the country—this plan is an outstanding example. The corner entry leads to a formal parlor on the left and dining room on the right—each sports a bay window. To the rear of the first floor you will find the casual living area, which encompasses a family room with a vaulted ceiling and cheerful fireplace, and an L-shaped island kitchen with a sunny nook and built-in planning desk. A nearby powder room and laundry facilities complete this floor. Upstairs are four bedrooms (or three and a den). The master bedroom beckons with a vaulted ceiling and a lovely private bath.

FIRST FLOOR

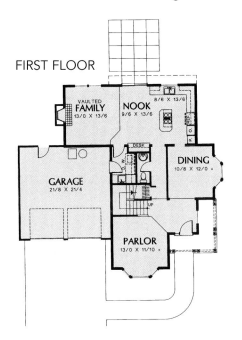

SECOND FLOOR

FIRST FLOOR

SECOND FLOOR

THE BRICK ACCENTS OF THIS home give it a European flavor. The vaulted foyer introduces the formal dining room plus a built-in shelf to the right and the den or Bedroom 4 to the left. The massive great room enjoys a vaulted ceiling and includes a cozy fireplace. The vaulted master bedroom features a walk-in closet and private access to the utility room. The private bath is entered through French doors and boasts dual vanities and an oversized soaking tub. Upstairs, two additional bedrooms share a hall with a large bonus room and a full bath with dual vanities—Bedroom 2 features a walk-in closet.

HPK1200018

HOME PLAN

Style: Country Cottage
First Floor: 1,658 sq. ft.
Second Floor: 538 sq. ft.
Total: 2,196 sq. ft.
Bonus Space: 496 sq. ft.
Bedrooms: 4
Bathrooms: 2 ½
Width: 50' - 0"
Depth: 56' - 0"
Foundation: Crawlspace

eplans.com

THIS VACATION HOME is certain to be a family favorite. The two-story great room boasts a built-in media center, access to a front deck, and a two-sided fireplace, shared by the adjacent den. The spacious island kitchen is ideal for entertaining. The second floor houses the master suite, two additional family bedrooms, and a full bath. A workshop and extra storage space in the garage are added bonuses.

FIRST FLOOR

HPK1200058

Style: Craftsman
First Floor: 1,302 sq. ft.
Second Floor: 960 sq. ft.
Total: 2,262 sq. ft.
Bedrooms: 3
Bathrooms: 2 ½
Width: 40' - 0"
Depth: 40' - 0"
Foundation: Crawlspace

eplans.com

SECOND FLOOR

BASEMENT

LAP SIDING, SPECIAL WINDOWS, and a covered porch enhance the elevation of this popular-style home. The spacious two-story entry surveys the formal dining room, which includes hutch space. An entertainment center, a through-fireplace, and bayed windows add appeal to the great room. Families will love the spacious kitchen with its breakfast and hearth rooms. Comfortable secondary bedrooms and a sumptuous master bedroom feature privacy by design. Bedroom 3 is highlighted by a half-round window, volume ceiling, and double closets, while Bedroom 4 contains a built-in desk. The master suite possesses a vaulted ceiling, large walk-in closet, His and Hers vanities, and an oval whirlpool tub.

HPK1200017

HOME PLAN

Style: **Farmhouse**

First Floor: **1,150 sq. ft.**

Second Floor: **1,120 sq. ft.**

Total: **2,270 sq. ft.**

Bedrooms: **4**

Bathrooms: **2 ½**

Width: **46' - 0"**

Depth: **48' - 0"**

eplans.com

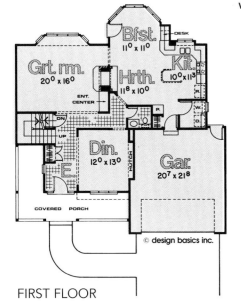

FIRST FLOOR

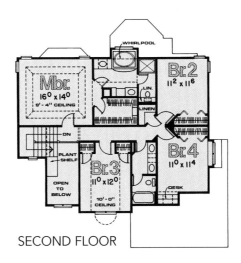

SECOND FLOOR

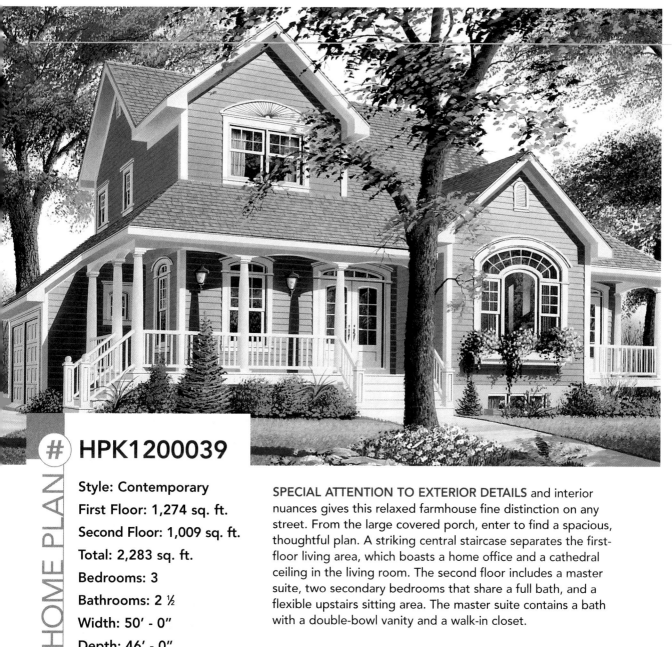

HOME PLAN # HPK1200039

Style: Contemporary

First Floor: 1,274 sq. ft.

Second Floor: 1,009 sq. ft.

Total: 2,283 sq. ft.

Bedrooms: 3

Bathrooms: 2 ½

Width: 50' - 0"

Depth: 46' - 0"

Foundation: Unfinished Basement

eplans.com

SPECIAL ATTENTION TO EXTERIOR DETAILS and interior nuances gives this relaxed farmhouse fine distinction on any street. From the large covered porch, enter to find a spacious, thoughtful plan. A striking central staircase separates the first-floor living area, which boasts a home office and a cathedral ceiling in the living room. The second floor includes a master suite, two secondary bedrooms that share a full bath, and a flexible upstairs sitting area. The master suite contains a bath with a double-bowl vanity and a walk-in closet.

SECOND FLOOR

FIRST FLOOR

FIRST FLOOR

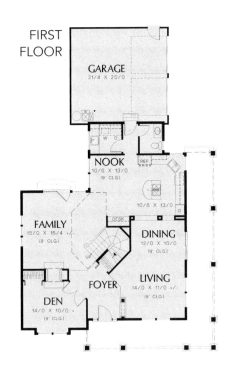

GARAGE
21/4 X 20/0

NOOK
10/6 X 13/0
(9' CLG.)

REF.

FAMILY
15/0 X 16/4
(9' CLG.)

DESK

DINING
12/0 X 10/0
(9' CLG.)

10/6 X 13/0

UP

FOYER

LIVING
14/0 X 11/0 +/-
(9' CLG.)

DEN
14/0 X 10/0
(9' CLG.)

SECOND FLOOR

BR. 3
10/6 X 13/0

PLANT SHELF

FAMILY BELOW

DN

BR. 2
12/4 X 11/0

VAULTED
MASTER
12/0 X 15/0

HOME PLAN

HPK1200038

Style: Craftsman

First Floor: 1,371 sq. ft.

Second Floor: 916 sq. ft.

Total: 2,287 sq. ft.

Bedrooms: 3

Bathrooms: 2 ½

Width: 43' - 0"

Depth: 69' - 0"

Foundation: Crawlspace

eplans.com

THE DECORATIVE PILLARS and the wraparound porch are just the beginning of this comfortable home. Inside, an angled U-shaped stairway leads to the second-floor sleeping zone. On the first floor, French doors lead to a bay-windowed den that shares a see-through fireplace with the two-story family room. The large island kitchen includes a writing desk, a corner sink, a breakfast nook, and access to the laundry room, the powder room, and the two-car garage. Upstairs, the master suite is a real treat with its French-door access, vaulted ceiling, and luxurious bath. Two other bedrooms and a full bath complete the second floor.

HPK1200003

Style: Country Cottage

First Floor: 1,266 sq. ft.

Second Floor: 1,026 sq. ft.

Total: 2,292 sq. ft.

Bedrooms: 3

Bathrooms: 2 ½

Width: 58' - 0"

Depth: 40' - 0"

Foundation: Unfinished Basement

eplans.com

STONE ACCENTS ENHANCE THE EXTERIOR of this two-story farmhouse. A country kitchen opens to the wraparound front porch and is conveniently located near the dining room. A breakfast bar divides the kitchen from the living room, which features a fireplace. A few steps down, on the garage level, the family room can be used as a home office. Upstairs, the master suite features a private luxurious bathroom, walk-in closet, fireplace, and sitting area. Two additional bedrooms upstairs complete the sleeping zone.

FIRST FLOOR

SECOND FLOOR

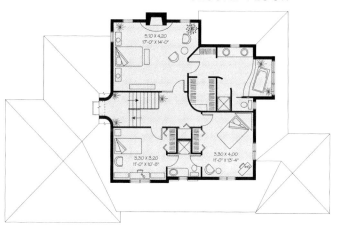

MULTIPLE ROOFLINES, SHUTTERS, and a charming vaulted entry lend interest and depth to the exterior of this well-designed three-bedroom home. Inside, double doors to the left open to a cozy den. The dining room, open to the family room and foyer, features a stunning ceiling design. A fireplace and patio access and view adorn the family room. Two family bedrooms share a double-sink bathroom to the right, and the master bedroom resides to the left. Note the private patio access, two walk-in closets, and luxurious bath that ensure a restful retreat for the homeowner.

HOME PLAN

HPK1200351

Style: International

Square Footage: 2,293

Bonus Space: 509 sq. ft.

Bedrooms: 3

Bathrooms: 2

Width: 51' - 0"

Depth: 79' - 4"

Foundation: Slab

eplans.com

HPK1200059

Style: Greek Revival

First Floor: 1,688 sq. ft.

Second Floor: 630 sq. ft.

Total: 2,318 sq. ft.

Bonus Space: 506 sq. ft.

Bedrooms: 3

Bathrooms: 3 ½

Width: 44' - 4"

Depth: 62' - 4"

Foundation: Crawlspace, Unfinished Walkout Basement

eplans.com

FIRST FLOOR

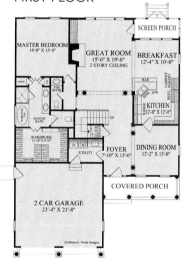

SECOND FLOOR

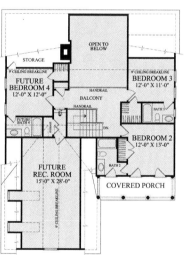

THIS SOUTHERN COLONIAL BEAUTY features three porches: one welcomes visitors to the first floor, the second offers a pleasant retreat from a bedroom upstairs, and the third, a screened porch, sits at the rear of the house, accessed from the great room. A centrally located fireplace in the great room warms the entire area, including the kitchen and the breakfast room. The spacious kitchen is a family favorite with a snack bar and a scenic view of the backyard. The left side of the plan is dominated by the master suite. The master bath boasts a dual sink vanity, a whirlpool tub, a separate shower, a compartmented toilet, and His and Hers walk-in closets. Upstairs, there are two additional family bedrooms, each with a full bath. Future space on the second floor invites the possibility of a fourth bedroom and a recreation room. A two-car garage completes the plan.

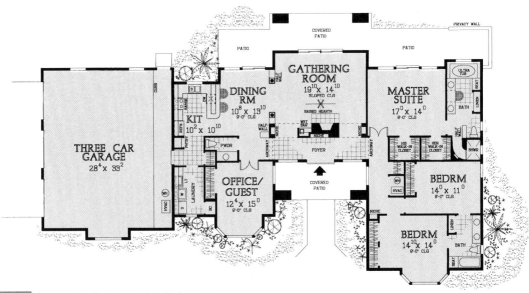

HOME PLAN

HPK1200011

Style: Mission

Square Footage: 2,319

Bedrooms: 3

Bathrooms: 2 ½

Width: 97' - 2"

Depth: 57' - 4"

Foundation: Slab

eplans.com

THE TILED FOYER of this Sun Country design invites guests into a gathering room with a fireplace and views of the rear grounds. Half-walls define the formal dining area, which offers rear-patio access. The kitchen is equipped to serve formal and informal occasions, and includes a snack counter for meals on the go. An office or guest room has a sunny bay window and an adjacent powder room. The outstanding master suite contains twin walk-in closets, a whirlpool tub, a sit-down vanity, and a stylish doorless shower. Two secondary bedrooms share a bath.

HOME PLAN

HPK1200044

Style: Country Cottage

First Floor: 1,633 sq. ft.

Second Floor: 705 sq. ft.

Total: 2,338 sq. ft.

Bonus Space: 203 sq. ft.

Bedrooms: 3

Bathrooms: 2 ½

Width: 58' - 6"

Depth: 49' - 0"

Foundation: Unfinished Basement

eplans.com

FIRST FLOOR

Patio

Great Room
15'2" x 18'2"

Breakfast
11'10" x 9'10"

Laun.

Dressing

Kitchen
11'10" x 11'11"

pantry

Bath

Master
Bedroom
13' x 17'

Foyer

Dining Room
11' x 13'

Porch

Two Car
Garage
20' x 21'

SECOND FLOOR

Great Room
Below

walk-in closet

Loft
10'4" x 13'8"

Bedroom
13'1" x 10'8"

Down

Bedroom
11' x 15'4"

walk-in closet

Bath

Sloped
Ceiling

Bonus
11'1" x 17'3"

THIS FINE COTTAGE DESIGN offers two levels of livability. The front porch invites you inside to a foyer introducing a graceful staircase to the second floor. The island kitchen easily serves the breakfast and dining rooms. The two-story great room is warmed by a fireplace. The master bedroom offers a whirlpool bath with a walk-in closet. A laundry room and two-car garage complete the plan. Upstairs, two additional family bedrooms share a loft and hall bath with the bonus room—great for attic space, a home office, or another bedroom.

HOMES FOR FIRST-TIME BUILDERS

FIRST FLOOR

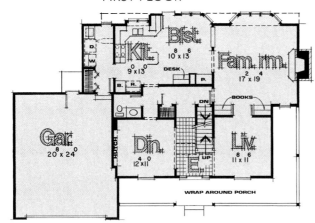

SECOND FLOOR

HOME PLAN #

HPK1200048

Style: Farmhouse

First Floor: 1,188 sq. ft.

Second Floor: 1,172 sq. ft.

Total: 2,360 sq. ft.

Bedrooms: 4

Bathrooms: 2 ½

Width: 58' - 0"

Depth: 40' - 0"

eplans.com

BEGINNING WITH THE INTEREST OF A WRAP-AROUND PORCH, there's a feeling of country charm in this two-story plan. Formal dining and living rooms, visible from the entry, offer ample space for gracious entertaining. The large family room is truly a place of warmth and welcome with its gorgeous bay window, fireplace, and French doors to the living room. The kitchen, with an island counter, pantry, and desk, makes cooking a delight. Upstairs, the secondary bedrooms share an efficient compartmented bath. The expansive master bedroom has its own luxury bath with a double vanity, whirlpool tub, walk-in closet, and dressing area.

J.N. HANSEN P.T.L.

HOME PLAN #

HPK1200075

Style: Contemporary

Square Footage: 2,362

Bedrooms: 4

Bathrooms: 3

Width: 65' - 8"

Depth: 73' - 4"

Foundation: Slab

eplans.com

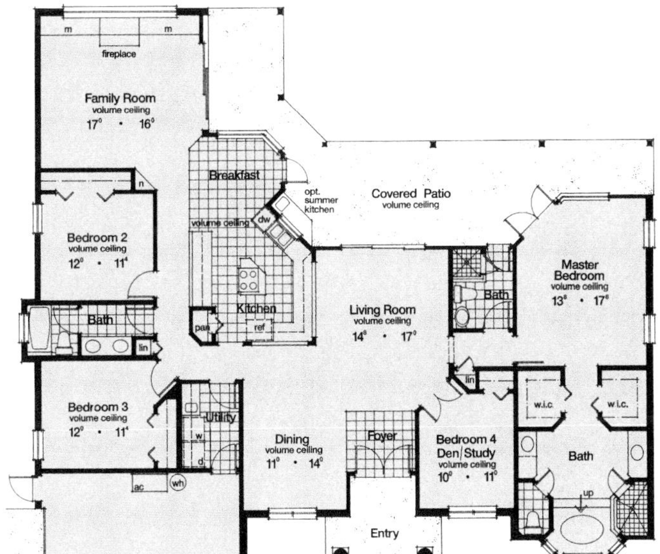
fireplace
Family Room
volume ceiling
17^0 • 16^0
Breakfast
opt. summer kitchen
Covered Patio
volume ceiling
volume ceiling
dw
Bedroom 2
volume ceiling
12^0 • 11^4
Kitchen
ref
pan
Bath
lin
Living Room
volume ceiling
14^0 • 17^0
Bath
Master Bedroom
volume ceiling
13^8 • 17^0
lin
w.i.c.
w.i.c.
Bedroom 3
volume ceiling
12^0 • 11^4
Utility
Dining
volume ceiling
11^0 • 14^0
Foyer
Bedroom 4
Den/Study
volume ceiling
10^0 • 11^0
Bath
up
ac
wh
Entry
Double Garage

THE GRAND ENTRANCE AND FACADE are only the beginning to this well-balanced home. The foyer is centered with the formal living room, with a wall of glass through which to view the outdoor living space. Traffic areas, tiled in marble, add graciousness and practicality as you walk thorugh the home. The master wing has a convenient and versatile den/guest/library adjacent to the master suite entry and poolside bath. The perfectly balanced master bath has a beautiful bay window framing the soaking tub, with matching spaces for the shower and toilet chamber, matching vanities, and walk-in closets.

FIRST FLOOR

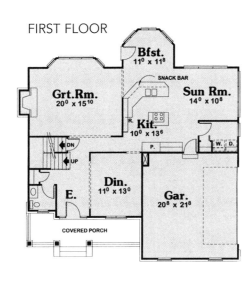

SECOND FLOOR

THIS DELIGHTFUL DESIGN WITH ITS MANY WINDOWS provides a cheerful, sunlit retreat. On the first floor, a great room with a warming fireplace presents a place to relax. The kitchen, with a cooktop island and snack bar, offers easy access to the dining room and connects to the breakfast room and sun room. A powder room, two closets for extra storage, and a handy laundry room complete the first floor. Upstairs, the master suite features a private bath with a spacious walk-in closet and a whirlpool tub. Three secondary bedrooms share another full bath.

HOME PLAN

HPK1200070

Style: Country Cottage

First Floor: 1,256 sq. ft.

Second Floor: 1,108 sq. ft.

Total: 2,364 sq. ft.

Bedrooms: 4

Bathrooms: 2 ½

Width: 46' - 0"

Depth: 48' - 0"

eplans.com

HOME PLAN

HPK1200014

Style: Traditional

Square Footage: 2,365

Bonus Space: 390 sq. ft.

Bedrooms: 4

Bathrooms: 2

Width: 67' - 6"

Depth: 75' - 0"

Foundation: Slab, Crawlspace

eplans.com

AN ELEGANT PALLADIAN ENTRY enhances an inviting covered front porch on this traditional design. Decorative columns, half-round transom windows, and graceful arches will welcome guests; owners will most appreciate the easy-care brick and stucco exterior. The interior blends comfort and privacy with a split-bedroom plan—and a master bedroom so luxurious it deserves its own wing. The private bath is replete with amenities—a windowed whirlpool tub, separate walk-in closets, twin vanities, and a compartmented toilet. Beyond the foyer, a grand-scale living room, warmed by a corner fireplace, spills into an informal eating nook that opens to the rear covered porch. The convenient kitchen easily services both the breakfast area and the formal dining room. Three bedrooms—or make Bedroom 2 a study—share a full bath.

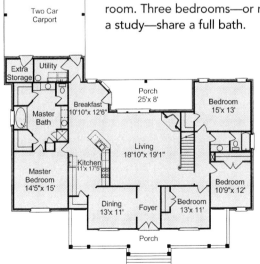

© William E. Poole Designs, Inc.

HOME PLAN

HPK1200019

Style: Country Cottage
First Floor: 1,627 sq. ft.
Second Floor: 783 sq. ft.
Total: 2,410 sq. ft.
Bonus Space: 418 sq. ft.
Bedrooms: 4
Bathrooms: 2 ½
Width: 46' - 0"
Depth: 58' - 6"
Foundation: Crawlspace

FIRST FLOOR

SECOND FLOOR

HOME PLAN

HPK1200071

Style: Craftsman
First Floor: 1,501 sq. ft.
Second Floor: 921 sq. ft.
Total: 2,422 sq. ft.
Bedrooms: 3
Bathrooms: 2 ½
Width: 52' - 0"
Depth: 36' - 0"
**Foundation:
Unfinished Walkout
Basement, Crawl-
space, Finished
Walkout Basement**

FIRST FLOOR

SECOND FLOOR

BASEMENT

HOME PLAN

HPK1200352

Style: Floridian

Square Footage: 2,447

Bedrooms: 4

Bathrooms: 3

Width: 93' - 0"

Depth: 50' - 0"

Foundation: Slab

eplans.com

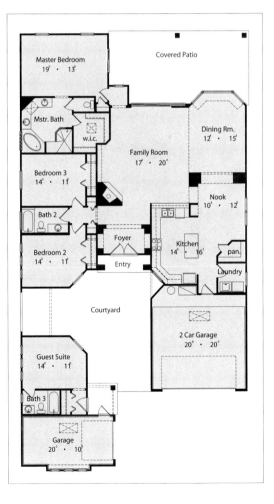

THIS SUN COUNTRY DESIGN PAMPERS VISITORS with its own guest house—including a bath and garage—separated from the main house by a courtyard. Three bedrooms, including the master suite, and two bathrooms comprise the left wing of this one-story masterpiece. The family room is centrally located to be the hub of all activity within, and a covered patio serves the outdoors well. The C-shaped kitchen enjoys a walk-in pantry, an island, access to both the garage and laundry facilities, and proximity to the breakfast nook. The dining room is nearby as well, for more formal occasions.

(#) HPK1200052

Style: Country Cottage

First Floor: 1,333 sq. ft.

Second Floor: 1,129 sq. ft.

Total: 2,462 sq. ft.

Bedrooms: 4

Bathrooms: 2 ½

Width: 69' - 8"

Depth: 49' - 0"

Foundation: Crawlspace, Unfinished Basement

eplans.com

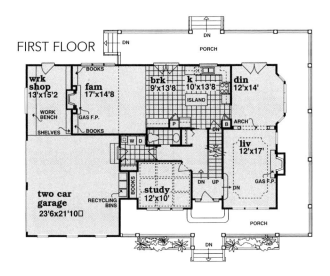

FIRST FLOOR

A LARGE WRAPAROUND PORCH GRACES the exterior of this home and gives it great outdoor livability. The raised foyer spills into a hearth-warmed living room and to the bay-windowed dining room beyond. French doors open from the breakfast and dining rooms to the spacious porch. Built-ins surround another hearth in the family room. The front study is adorned by a beamed ceiling and also features built-ins. Three bedrooms and a master suite are found on the second floor. The master suite features a walk-in closet and a private bath. Don't miss the workshop area in the garage.

SECOND FLOOR

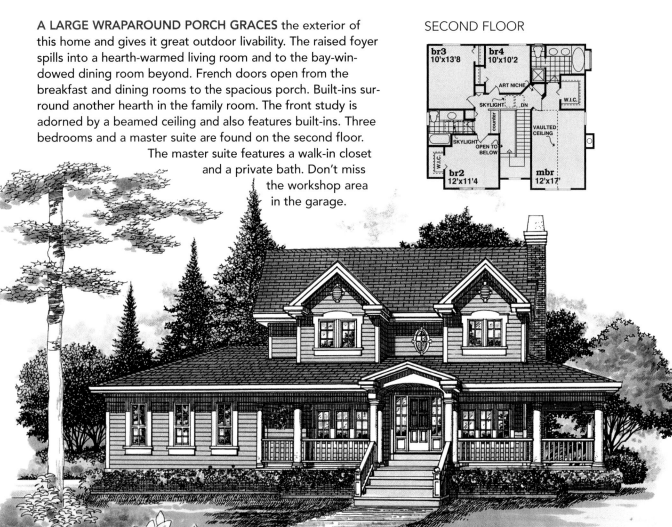

HOME PLAN

HPK1200352

Style: Floridian

Square Footage: 2,447

Bedrooms: 4

Bathrooms: 3

Width: 93' - 0"

Depth: 50' - 0"

Foundation: Slab

eplans.com

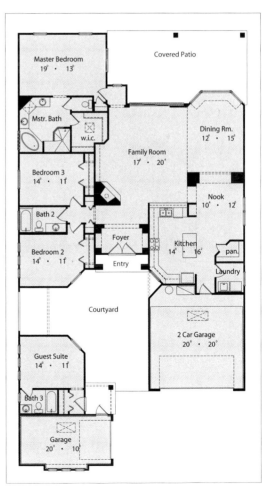

THIS SUN COUNTRY DESIGN PAMPERS VISITORS with its own guest house—including a bath and garage—separated from the main house by a courtyard. Three bedrooms, including the master suite, and two bathrooms comprise the left wing of this one-story masterpiece. The family room is centrally located to be the hub of all activity within, and a covered patio serves the outdoors well. The C-shaped kitchen enjoys a walk-in pantry, an island, access to both the garage and laundry facilities, and proximity to the breakfast nook. The dining room is nearby as well, for more formal occasions.

HOME PLAN

HPK1200052

Style: Country Cottage

First Floor: 1,333 sq. ft.

Second Floor: 1,129 sq. ft.

Total: 2,462 sq. ft.

Bedrooms: 4

Bathrooms: 2 ½

Width: 69' - 8"

Depth: 49' - 0"

Foundation: Crawlspace, Unfinished Basement

eplans.com

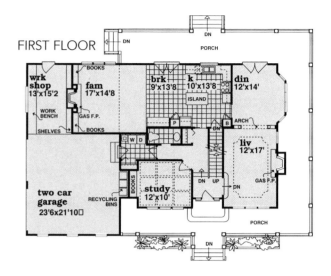

FIRST FLOOR

A LARGE WRAPAROUND PORCH GRACES the exterior of this home and gives it great outdoor livability. The raised foyer spills into a hearth-warmed living room and to the bay-windowed dining room beyond. French doors open from the breakfast and dining rooms to the spacious porch. Built-ins surround another hearth in the family room. The front study is adorned by a beamed ceiling and also features built-ins. Three bedrooms and a master suite are found on the second floor. The master suite features a walk-in closet and a private bath. Don't miss the workshop area in the garage.

SECOND FLOOR

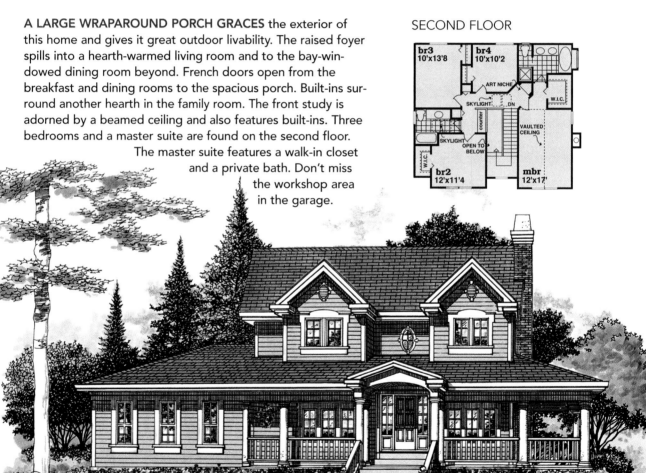

© 1998 Donald A. Gardner, Inc.

THIS FINE THREE-BEDROOM HOME is full of amenities and will surely be a family favorite! A covered porch leads into the great room/dining room. Here, a fireplace reigns at one end, casting its glow throughout the room. A private study is tucked away, perfect for a home office or computer study. The master bedroom suite offers a bayed sitting area, large walk-in closet, and pampering bath. With plenty of counter and cabinet space and an adjacent breakfast area, the kitchen will be a favorite gathering place for casual meal-times. The family sleeping zone is upstairs and includes two bed-rooms, a full bath, a loft/study area, and a huge storage room.

HOME PLAN

HPK1200032

Style: Craftsman
First Floor: 1,896 sq. ft.
Second Floor: 692 sq. ft.
Total: 2,588 sq. ft.
Bedrooms: 3
Bathrooms: 2 1/2
Width: 60' - 0"
Depth: 84' - 10"

eplans.com

HOMES FOR FIRST-TIME BUILDERS

FIRST FLOOR

SECOND FLOOR

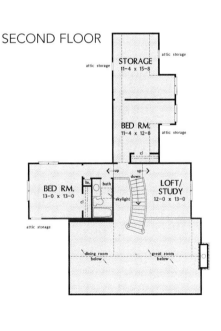

Table for Two—Designs That Let Empty Nesters Rule the Roost

These are homes for people who have earned their chance to relax and enjoy life. Although the size of these designs remains under 2,500 square feet, the master suites are more sumptuous—and located on the first level for easy enjoyment. In place of a third or fourth bedroom the plan designates a study or recreation room. Large kitchens and sunny outdoor areas abound.

Some of our best traditional designs have been collected here—traditional, but with a twist. Classic features such as gables, dormers, wraparound porches, and verandas, let these homes look like they've been in the family for generations. Some favor a country style; others sport a more cosmopolitan attitude.

Take a look at one of our larger empty-nest designs, plan HPK1200100 on page 161, for an example of a home that lives well every day and makes room for visiting children. And there are 72 other plans to consider, arranged by square footage and hand-chosen by our knowledgeable staff.

IN PLACE OF EXTRA BEDROOMS and formal dining rooms, empty-nesters may appreciate more useful spaces. An elegant study or old-fashioned parlor will receive year-round use.

Left to Right: Ted Yarwood, Tony Giammarino

EQUALLY GRACIOUS OUTSIDE AND INSIDE,
this one- or two-bedroom cottage has a post-and-rail covered porch hugging one wing, with convenient access through double doors or pass-through windows in the dining room and kitchen. The columned entry foyer has a sloped ceiling and leads past a second bedroom or media room into a great room with a sloped ceiling, fireplace, and low wall along the staircase that leads to the attic. The master suite fills the right wing and features a plant shelf in the bedroom and a garden tub in the master bath, plus a large walk-in closet and laundry facilities.

HOME PLAN

HPK1200093

Style: Country Cottage

Square Footage: 1,295

Bedrooms: 2

Bathrooms: 2

Width: 48' - 0"

Depth: 59' - 0"

Foundation: Unfinished Basement

eplans.com

A QUIET, AESTHETICALLY PLEASANT, and comfortable one-story country home answers the requirements of modest-income families. The entrance to the house is sheltered by the front porch, which leads to the hearth-warmed living room. The master suite is arranged with a large dressing area that has a walk-in closet plus two linear closets and space for a vanity. The main part of the bedroom contains a media center. The adjoining, fully equipped kitchen includes the dinette, which can comfortably seat six people and leads to the rear terrace through six-foot sliding glass doors.

(#) HPK1200096

Style: Country Cottage

Square Footage: 1,366

Bedrooms: 3

Bathrooms: 2

Width: 71' - 4"

Depth: 35' - 10"

Foundation: Slab, Unfinished Basement, Crawlspace

eplans.com

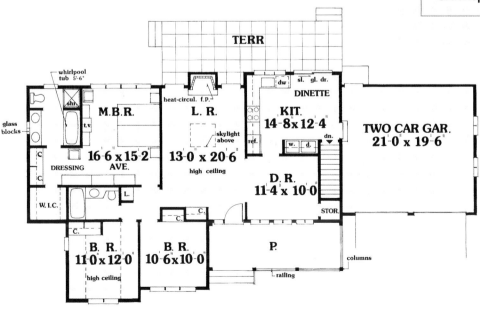

TERR

whirlpool tub 5'-6"

glass blocks

M.B.R.

16-6 x 15-2 AVE.

DRESSING

W.I.C.

heat-circul. f.p.

L. R.

13-0 x 20-6 high ceiling

skylight above

ref.

dw

sl. gl. dr.

DINETTE

KIT. 14-8 x 12-4

w. d.

D. R. 11-4 x 10-0

dn.

TWO CAR GAR. 21-0 x 19-6

STOR.

B. R. 11-0 x 12-0 high ceiling

B. R. 10-6 x 10-0

P.

columns

railing

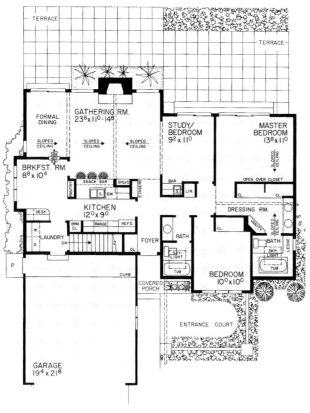

SITUATING THE GARAGE TO THE FRONT OF A HOUSE is very economical in two ways. One, it reduces the required lot size; and two, it will help protect the interior from street noise. Many other characteristics of this design deserve mention, too. The kitchen has an adjacent breakfast room and a snack bar. The study contains a wet bar, and the nearby master suite enjoys a lavish bath with a dressing area. Sliding glass doors in three rooms open to the rear terrace.

HPK1200086

Style: Farmhouse

Square Footage: 1,387

Bedrooms: 3

Bathrooms: 2

Width: 49' - 8"

Depth: 50' - 0"

Foundation: Unfinished Basement

eplans.com

(#) HPK1200124

Style: Contemporary

Square Footage: 1,414

Bedrooms: 3

Bathrooms: 3

Width: 44' - 8"

Depth: 54' - 4"

Foundation: Slab

eplans.com

THIS COZY COTTAGE features a front-facing office/guest suite, which provides privacy for the entry courtyard. With its separate entrance, it offers the perfect haven for an in-home office or for those with live-in parents. The remainder of the house is designed with the same level of efficiency. It contains a large living area with access to a covered patio and a three-sided fireplace that shares its warmth with a dining room featuring built-ins. A unique kitchen provides garage access. The bedrooms include a comfortable master suite with a whirlpool tub, a double-bowl vanity, and twin closets.

THIS COZY COTTAGE OFFERS THE CHOICE OF A THREE- or four-bedroom plan. The design features a front-facing office/guest suite which provides privacy for the entry courtyard. With its separate entrance it offers the perfect haven for an in-home office or a separate suite for live-in parents. The remainder of the house is designed with the same level of efficiency. It contains a large living area with access to a covered patio and a three-sided fireplace that shares its warmth with a dining room featuring built-ins. A unique kitchen provides garage access. The bedrooms include a comfortable master suite with a whirlpool tub, a double-bowl vanity, and twin closets.

HOME PLAN

HPK1200123

Style: Country Cottage

Square Footage: 1,418

Bedrooms: 4

Bathrooms: 3

Width: 44' - 8"

Depth: 52' - 4"

Foundation: Slab

eplans.com

HPK1200101

Style: Country Cottage

Square Footage: 1,549

Bonus Space: 247 sq. ft.

Bedrooms: 3

Bathrooms: 2

Width: 52' - 4"

Depth: 49' - 0"

Foundation: Crawlspace, Unfinished Walkout Basement

eplans.com

THE COZY COMFORT OF THE COVERED PORCH invites visitors through a short foyer and into the vault-ceilinged family room, complete with a central fireplace. The open floor plan allows the fireplace to warm the adjoining dining room, kitchen, and breakfast nook. A serving bar conveniently serves the area. Access to the rear covered porch is available from the breakfast nook. A short hallway leads to the master suite, two additional family bedrooms, and a full bath. French doors lead from the master bedroom into the master bath. Options include a bonus room/office and an additional full bath. The two-car garage offers convenient extra storage space.

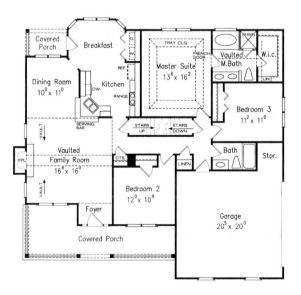

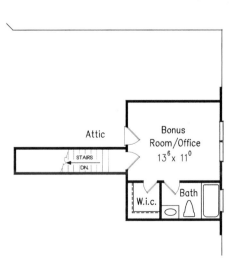

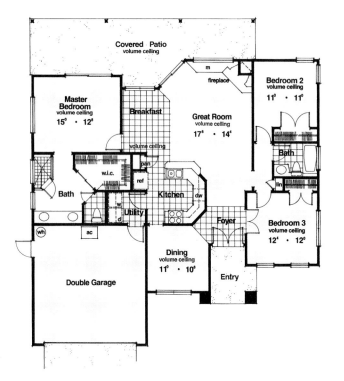

THIS COZY COTTAGE OFFERS ALL OF THE COM-FORTS of a first home in a one-story, efficient design. The bedrooms sit to either side of the plan, with the master suite on the left, and two additional family bedrooms on the right. The great room is at the heart of the home, outfitted with a corner fireplace. The U-shaped kitchen with serving bar offers added convenience. The breakfast nook enjoys a pleasant view of the rear covered patio. A two-car garage completes this plan.

HPK1200353

Style: Mediterranean

Square Footage: 1,550

Bedrooms: 3

Bathrooms: 2

Width: 50' - 0"

Depth: 55' - 0"

Foundation: Slab

eplans.com

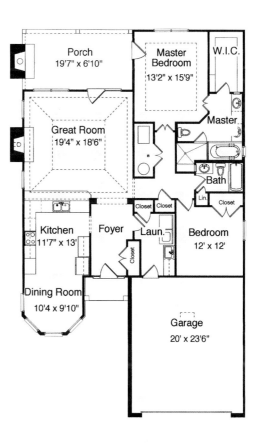

HPK1200080

Style: European Cottage

Square Footage: 1,612

Bedrooms: 2

Bathrooms: 2

Width: 42' - 0"

Depth: 67' - 4"

Foundation: Slab, Unfinished Basement

eplans.com

HOME PLAN

A BRICK-AND-STONE EXTERIOR WITH SHAKE SIDING decorates the front of this delightful home. The large great room enjoys an 11-foot ceiling, gas fireplace, and access to the rear porch. The master bedroom suite offers a luxury bath with a dual-bowl vanity, whirlpool tub, and large walk-in closet. Access to the rear porch from the master suite is an unexpected feature. This home, designed for a narrow lot, offers spaciousness and luxurious living.

Porch 19'7" x 6'10"

Master Bedroom 13'2" x 15'9"

W.I.C.

Great Room 19'4" x 18'6"

Master

Bath

Kitchen 11'7" x 13'

Foyer

Laun.

Bedroom 12' x 12'

Dining Room 10'4" x 9'10"

Garage 20' x 23'6"

HOMES FOR EMPTY NESTERS

HPK1200129

Style: Country Cottage

Square Footage: 1,580

Bedrooms: 3

Bathrooms: 2 ½

Width: 50' - 0"

Depth: 48' - 0"

Foundation: Crawlspace

eplans.com

THIS CHARMING ONE-STORY PLAN FEATURES A FACADE that is accented by a stone pediment and a shed-dormer window. Inside, elegant touches grace the efficient floor plan. Vaulted ceilings adorn the great room and master bedroom, and a 10-foot tray ceiling highlights the foyer. One of the front bedrooms makes a perfect den; another accesses a full hall bath with a linen closet. The great room, which opens to the porch, includes a fireplace and a media niche. The dining room offers outdoor access and built-ins for ultimate convenience.

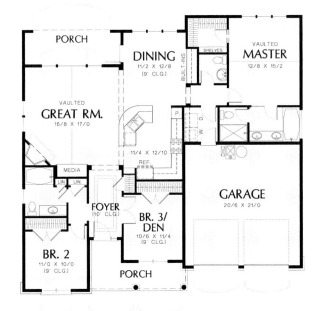

(#) HPK1200082

Style: Southern Colonial

First Floor: 1,136 sq. ft.

Second Floor: 464 sq. ft.

Total: 1,600 sq. ft.

Bedrooms: 3

Bathrooms: 2

Width: 58' - 0"

Depth: 42' - 0"

Foundation: Crawlspace, Slab

eplans.com

FIRST FLOOR

porch 14 x 12

dining 13 x 12

util 9x6

w d

storage 22 x 5

garage 22 x 21

ref

rng 11x9 kit

pan

dw

brm

lin

living 24 x 14

shv

a/c

clo

mbr 15 x 14

vanity

ent

porch 36 x 6

SECOND FLOOR

attic

clo

dn

shvs

attic

br 2 12 x 11

clo

clo

br 3 14 x 12

clo

lin

ATTRACTIVE YET VERY AFFORDABLE, this three-bedroom home is perfect for every family. A raised porch views the front yard. The entry introduces the large living room with a warming fireplace and views front and back. Stairs to the second floor are set privately between the living room and the dining area. The U-shaped kitchen opens to the dining area. A first-floor master suite features private access to the entry and a full bath. Tucked on the second floor, two family bedrooms share a full bath and attic access.

LOVELY COLUMNS AND OPEN GABLES
define Southern style on this welcoming country design. A single-level floor plan makes intelligent use of space. The C-shaped kitchen sits between the formal dining room and a large, open family room and adjoining eating nook. A corner fireplace draws attention to the covered patio just beyond the family room. Two secondary bedrooms split to the right of the plan and share a full hall bath. The private master suite sits off the nook and enjoys a super bath and walk-in closet.

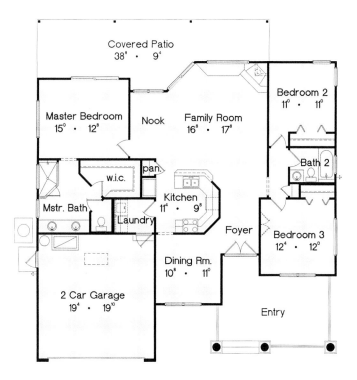

HOME PLAN

HPK1200354

Style: Country Cottage

Square Footage: 1,550

Bedrooms: 3

Bathrooms: 2

Width: 50' - 0"

Depth: 55' - 0"

Foundation: Slab

eplans.com

HPK1200099

Style: Country Cottage

First Floor: 1,046 sq. ft.

Second Floor: 572 sq. ft.

Total: 1,618 sq. ft.

Bedrooms: 3

Bathrooms: 2 ½

Width: 44' - 0"

Depth: 39' - 0"

Foundation: Slab, Crawlspace

eplans.com

A DEEP WRAPAROUND PORCH TRIMMED WITH SQUARE PILLARS, a wood balustrade, and traditional lattice add character and interest to this Cape Cod design. Floor-to-ceiling double-hung windows and dormers complete the rustic look. The main level includes a fireplace in the living room, a bay window in the dining room, and a master suite with a walk-in closet. The dining room and kitchen are divided by a peninsula with seating for informal dining. Upstairs, two bedrooms, each with a walk-in closet, share a bath.

FIRST FLOOR

SECOND FLOOR

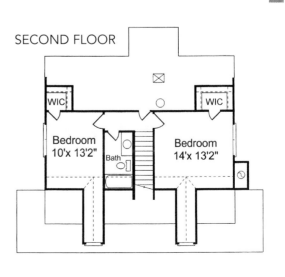

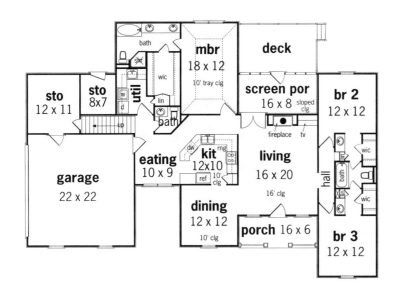

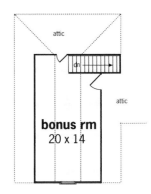

A TOUCH FRENCH AND A TOUCH COLONIAL, this home showcases an elegant exterior and a beautiful floor plan. Guests will feel welcome at the entry, which provides a great view of the warming fireplace in the spacious living room. Offset to the left of the foyer is the dining room. An unobtrusive kitchen entrance keeps the mess out of view. A cozy casual eating nook just off the kitchen enjoys front views and natural light. The master suite features a tray ceiling and a full private bath with dual-sink vanity and a walk-in closet. Two family bedrooms are split to the right of the plan and share a Jack-and-Jill bath.

HPK1200103

HOME PLAN

Style: Colonial

Square Footage: 1,704

Bonus Space: 364 sq. ft.

Bedrooms: 3

Bathrooms: 2 ½

Width: 71' - 0"

Depth: 50' - 0"

Foundation: Crawlspace, Slab

eplans.com

HPK1200119

Style: Traditional

First Floor: 1,230 sq. ft.

Second Floor: 477 sq. ft.

Total: 1,707 sq. ft.

Bonus Space: 195 sq. ft.

Bedrooms: 3

Bathrooms: 2 1/2

Width: 40' - 0"

Depth: 52' - 10"

Foundation: Crawlspace

eplans.com

FIRST FLOOR

NOOK
8/8 X 8/10

DINING
9/10 X 10/4

VAULTED
MASTER
16/0 X 11/10

TWO STORY
GREAT RM.
15/10 X 19/8

SPA

LINEN

UP

GARAGE
19/4 X 21/8

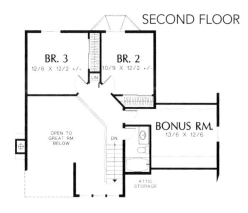

SECOND FLOOR

BR. 3
12/6 X 12/2 +/-

BR. 2
10/9 X 12/2 +/-

LIN

OPEN TO
GREAT RM
BELOW

DN

BONUS RM.
13/6 X 12/6

ATTIC
STORAGE

WITH SUNNY WINDOWS THROUGHOUT and a wonderfully open living space, this plan appears larger than its modest square footage. The great room is highlighted with a corner window, fireplace, and soaring ceiling. The dining room continues the open feeling and is easily served from the kitchen. A bayed nook complements the island kitchen that also has a stylish wraparound counter. The master bedroom suite has a lofty vaulted ceiling. Upstairs, two family bedrooms share a full hall bath; a bonus room can be developed as needed.

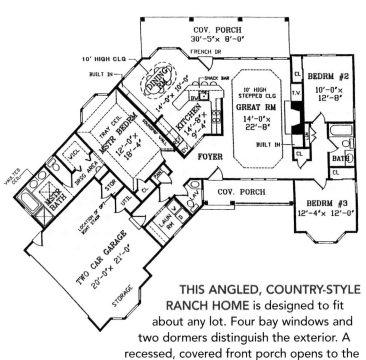

THIS ANGLED, COUNTRY-STYLE RANCH HOME is designed to fit about any lot. Four bay windows and two dormers distinguish the exterior. A recessed, covered front porch opens to the foyer, which is visually connected to the adjoining great room. The great room features a fireplace and built-ins for media. The great room is a "pavilion-style" area with windows at the front and rear. A dramatic angled kitchen with a snack bar faces the rear porch. A private master suite contains a tray ceiling, a dressing area, two closets, and a compartmented five-fixture bath. Two other bedrooms, one set into an attractive front bay, share a full bath. The unusual-shaped kitchen, which looks out over the covered porch, is easily served by the kitchen. A convenient half-bath is located off the foyer.

HOME PLAN

HPK1200104

Style: Country Cottage

Square Footage: 1,709

Bedrooms: 3

Bathrooms: 2 ½

Width: 70' - 1"

Depth: 60' - 7"

Foundation: Unfinished Basement, Slab, Crawlspace

eplans.com

HOME PLAN

HPK1200137

Style: Farmhouse

First Floor: 1,356 sq. ft.

Second Floor: 405 sq. ft.

Total: 1,761 sq. ft.

Bedrooms: 3

Bathrooms: 2 ½

Width: 61' - 5"

Depth: 47' - 8"

Foundation: Crawlspace, Slab, Unfinished Basement

eplans.com

PRECISE DETAILING MAKES THIS HOME AN INVITING and interesting one. Sunburst windows with decorative lintels, two front-facing bay windows, a wraparound porch, and varying rooflines are just some of the elements that accent this home. The foyer leads to the great room, which boasts a large fireplace and French-door access to the master suite—complete with a garden tub an walk-in closet. French doors also lead to the island kitchen and nook with rear-property views. The second floor holds two additional bedrooms, a full bath, and a balcony open to the great room below.

FIRST FLOOR

Mstr Ste 14-0x12-5
wic
Porch
Grt Rm 17-0x16-0
Kitch 13-0x12-4
Nook 10-0x10-0
Util
Foy
Dining 11-0x12-5
Garage 19-5x24-7
Porch

SECOND FLOOR

Open to Below
Bedrm 10-0x9-7
Bedrm 10-0x10-7
balc

HOMES FOR EMPTY NESTERS

ARCHED WINDOWS AND AN ARCHED PORCH ENTRY complement the gabled peaks on the front of this traditional one-story home. Welcome guests into the dining area as they enter or usher them to the comfortable family room at the end of the hallway, with its cozy fireplace. The compact, well-organized kitchen includes built-in bookshelves and a sunny breakfast alcove. The vaulted ceilings and lavish amenities make the master suite a dream come true. Two more bedrooms, both with spacious closets, share a bathroom on the other side of the house. Especially appealing is the rear veranda that stretches the full-length of the house.

HPK1200102

Style: Country Cottage

Square Footage: 1,775

Bedrooms: 3

Bathrooms: 2

Width: 52' - 0"

Depth: 52' - 0"

Foundation: Slab, Crawlspace

eplans.com

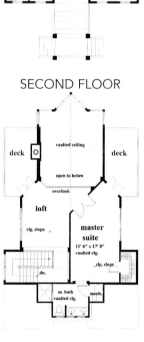

FIRST FLOOR

deck

great room
15' 0" x 16' 0"
2-story clg.
fireplace
built-in cabinetry

ver.

ver.

pass-thru

dining
9' 4" x 12' 8"
9' 4"h. clg.

kitchen
pantry
8' 8" x 14' 0"

up

foyer

bedroom 2
11' 0" x 11' 0"
9' 4" ceiling

ut.

p.

entry

SECOND FLOOR

deck

vaulted ceiling

deck

open to below

overlook

loft
clg. slope

master suite
11' 6" x 17' 8"
vaulted clg.

clg. slope

dn.

m. bath
vaulted clg.

mech.

BASEMENT

storage/ bonus room
14' 8" x 20' 0"
8' 8"h. ceiling

lanai

lanai

2 car garage
22' 0" x 25' 6" avg.
8' 8"h. ceiling

up

storage
10' 8" x 9' 4"
8' 8"h. clg.

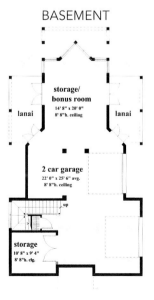

HOME PLAN

HPK1200111

Style: Italianate

First Floor: 1,143 sq. ft.

Second Floor: 651 sq. ft.

Total: 1,794 sq. ft.

Bonus Space: 476 sq. ft.

Bedrooms: 2

Bathrooms: 2 ½

Width: 32' - 0"

Depth: 57' - 0"

Foundation: Slab

eplans.com

ITALIAN COUNTRY ELEGANCE GRACES THE EXTERIOR of this casa bellisima, swept in Mediterranean enchantment. The covered entryway extends into the foyer, where straight ahead the two-story great room spaciously enhances the interior. This room features a warming fireplace and offers built-in cabinetry. The open dining room extends through double doors to the veranda on the left side of the plan. The adjacent kitchen features efficient pantry space. A family bedroom with a bath, a powder room, and a utility room also reside on this main floor. Upstairs, a vaulted master suite with a vaulted private bath and deck share the floor with a loft area, which overlooks the great room. Downstairs, the basement-level bonus room and storage area share space with the two-car garage. Two lanais open on either side of the bonus room for additional outdoor patio space.

HOMES FOR EMPTY NESTERS

FIRST FLOOR

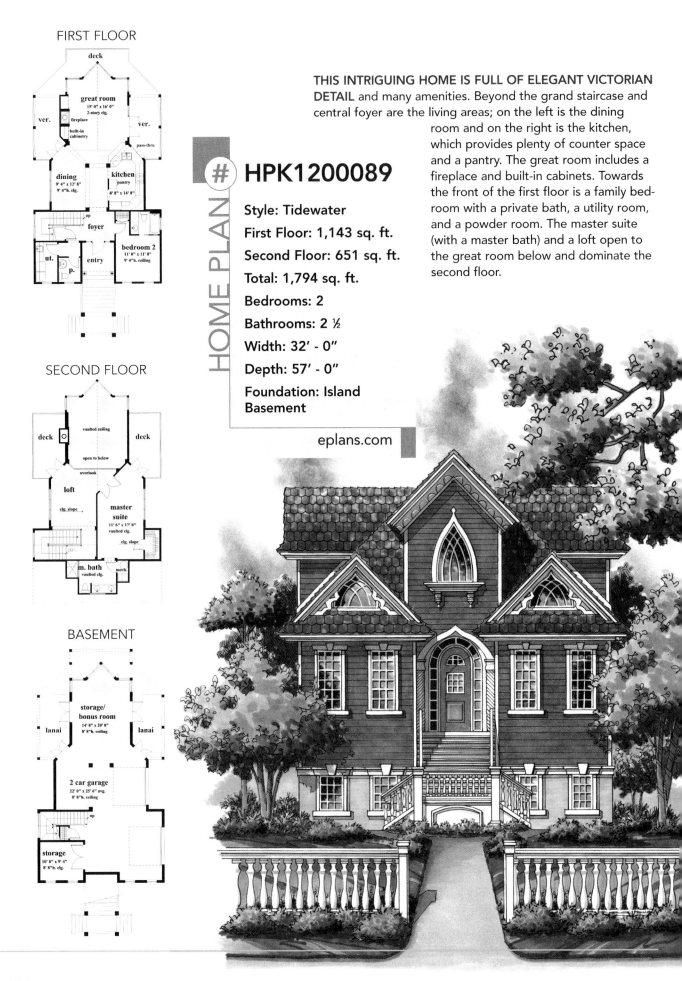

deck

great room
15' 0" x 16' 0"
2-story clg.

ver.

fireplace

built-in
cabinetry

ver.

pass-thru

dining
9' 4" x 12' 8"
9' 4"h. clg.

kitchen
pantry
8' 8" x 14' 0"

up

foyer

ut.

p.

entry

bedroom 2
11' 0" x 11' 0"
9' 4" ceiling

SECOND FLOOR

deck

vaulted ceiling

deck

open to below

overlook

loft

clg. slope

master
suite
11' 6" x 17' 8"
vaulted clg.

clg. slope

m. bath
vaulted clg.

mech.

BASEMENT

storage/
bonus room
14' 8" x 20' 0"
8' 8"h. ceiling

lanai

lanai

2 car garage
22' 0" x 25' 6" avg.
8' 8"h. ceiling

up

storage
10' 8" x 9' 4"
8' 8"h. clg.

HOME PLAN

HPK1200089

Style: Tidewater

First Floor: 1,143 sq. ft.

Second Floor: 651 sq. ft.

Total: 1,794 sq. ft.

Bedrooms: 2

Bathrooms: 2 ½

Width: 32' - 0"

Depth: 57' - 0"

Foundation: Island Basement

eplans.com

THIS INTRIGUING HOME IS FULL OF ELEGANT VICTORIAN DETAIL and many amenities. Beyond the grand staircase and central foyer are the living areas; on the left is the dining room and on the right is the kitchen, which provides plenty of counter space and a pantry. The great room includes a fireplace and built-in cabinets. Towards the front of the first floor is a family bedroom with a private bath, a utility room, and a powder room. The master suite (with a master bath) and a loft open to the great room below and dominate the second floor.

HPK1200131

Style: Lakefront

First Floor: 1,290 sq. ft.

Second Floor: 548 sq. ft.

Total: 1,838 sq. ft.

Bedrooms: 3

Bathrooms: 2 ½

Width: 38' - 0"

Depth: 51' - 0"

Foundation: Crawlspace

eplans.com

A ROMANTIC AIR FLIRTS WITH THE CLEAN, SIMPLE LINES of this seaside getaway, set off by stunning shingle accents and sunburst transom. Horizontal siding complements an insulated metal roof to create a charming look that calls up a sense of 19th-Century style. Inside, an unrestrained floor plan harbors cozy interior spaces and offers great outdoor views through wide windows and French doors. At the heart of the home, the two-story great rooms features a corner fireplace, an angled entertainment center, and an eating bar shared with the gourmet kitchen. Columns and sweeping archways define the formal dining room, and French doors open to the veranda, inviting dreamy ocean breezes inside.

FIRST FLOOR

SECOND FLOOR

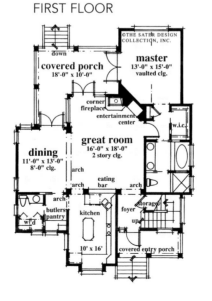

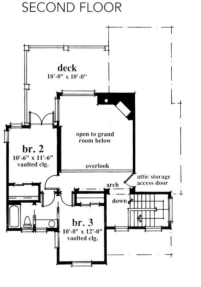

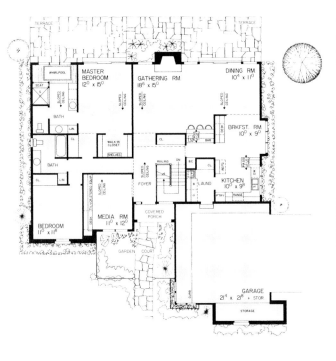

THIS GRAND PLAN IS NOT ONLY AFFORDABLE, but is also loaded with amenities. Sloped ceilings dominate the living areas and the master suite. Notice also the abundance of windows and window walls that allow a burst of natural light to warm the home. The media room contains a full wall of built-ins, the gathering room features its own fireplace, and the master suite pampers with a luxurious whirlpool spa. A garden court in the front and a terrace to the rear enhance outdoor livability. The garage contains a large storage area that could also allow room for a workshop.

 # HPK1200140

HOME PLAN

Style: Traditional

Square Footage: 1,842

Bedrooms: 2

Bathrooms: 2

Width: 58' - 2"

Depth: 59' - 9"

Foundation: Unfinished Basement

eplans.com

HPK1200090

Style: Country Cottage

First Floor: 1,320 sq. ft.

Second Floor: 554 sq. ft.

Total: 1,874 sq. ft.

Bonus Space: 155 sq. ft.

Bedrooms: 4

Bathrooms: 2 ½

Width: 54' - 6"

Depth: 42' - 4"

Foundation: Crawlspace, Unfinished Walkout Basement

eplans.com

THIS PLAN COMBINES A TRADITIONAL, STATELY EXTERIOR with an updated floor plan to create a house that will please the entire family. The heart of the plan is surely the wide-open living space consisting of the vaulted family room, breakfast area, and gourmet kitchen. Highlights here are a full-length fireplace, a French door to the rear yard, and an island cooktop. The master suite has a tray ceiling and a vaulted master bath with a garden tub and walk-in closet. The family sleeping area on the upper level gives the option of two bedrooms and a loft overlooking the family room or three bedrooms.

FIRST FLOOR

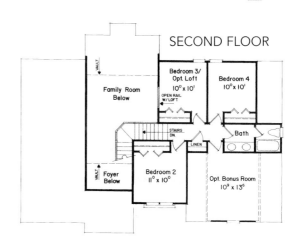

SECOND FLOOR

MAIN LEVEL

HERE'S A MOUNTAIN CABIN WITH PLENTY OF SPACE for entertaining. Three levels include a loft with space for computers, books, and games. The main level features an open living area set off with views from tall windows. The kitchen embraces a casual eating space and provides sliding glass doors that lead to the wraparound deck. Double doors open from the living room to a master bedroom. The lower level creates a thoughtful arrangement of secondary sleeping quarters and a sitting room with a fireplace.

UPPER LEVEL

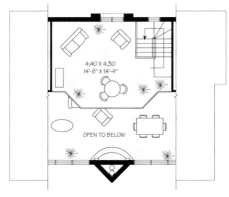

LOWER LEVEL

HOME PLAN

HPK1200132

Style: Cabin

Main Level: 790 sq. ft.

Upper Level: 299 sq. ft.

Lower Level: 787 sq. ft.

Total: 1,876 sq. ft.

Bedrooms: 3

Bathrooms: 2

Width: 32' - 4"

Depth: 24' - 4"

Foundation: Unfinished Walkout Basement

eplans.com

HOME PLAN

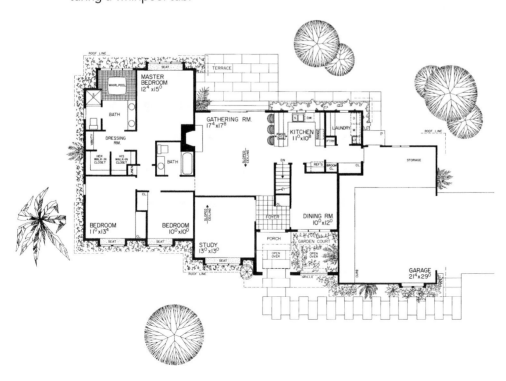

 # HPK1200141

Style: Contemporary

Square Footage: 1,913

Bedrooms: 3

Bathrooms: 2

Width: 77' - 10"

Depth: 46' - 4"

Foundation: Unfinished Basement

eplans.com

THIS ELEGANT SPANISH DESIGN incorporates excellent indoor/outdoor living relationships for modern families who enjoy the sun. Note the overhead openings for rain and sun to fall upon a front garden, and a twin-arched entry leads to the front porch and foyer. Inside, this floor plan features a modern kitchen with pass-through to a large gathering room with fireplace. Other features include a dining room, laundry room, a study off the foyer, plus three bedrooms, including a master suite with its own private bath featuring a whirlpool tub.

HOMES FOR EMPTY NESTERS

(#) HPK1200087

Style: NW Contemporary

Square Footage: 1,951

Bedrooms: 3

Bathrooms: 2

Width: 56' - 0"

Depth: 48' - 8"

Foundation: Unfinished Basement

eplans.com

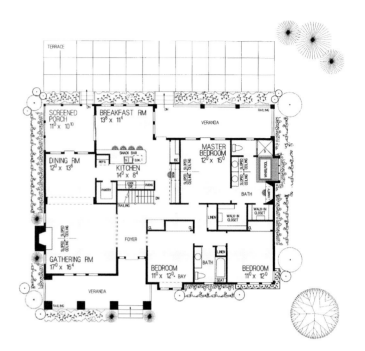

CONTEMPORARY WITH A COUNTRY TWIST, this modern vacation home has it all. Two verandas and a screened porch enlarge the plan and enhance indoor/outdoor livability. The sloped ceiling in the gathering room gives this area an open, airy quality. The breakfast room, with its wealth of windows, will be a cheerful and bright space to enjoy a cup of morning coffee. Added extras provide a thoughtful touch: abundant storage space, walk-in pantry, built-in planning desk, and pass-through snack bar. The master suite features a pampering whirlpool tub to soak your cares away.

HPK1200355

Style: Country Cottage

Square Footage: 1,963

Bedrooms: 3

Bathrooms: 2

Width: 58' - 0"

Depth: 66' - 8"

Foundation: Crawlspace, Slab

eplans.com

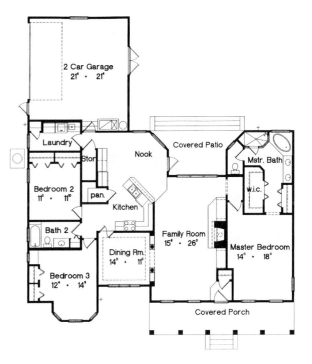

THICK COLUMNS SUPPORTING THE PORCH, plenty of multipaned windows, and a turret create a lovely country retreat. A large family room opens from the covered porch, complete with a warming fireplace. The master suite is tucked to the right of the family room and features a walk-in closet and a sumptuous bath. Columns decorate the entry to the dining room, which views the fireplace in the family room. Conveniently located between the dining room and the garage, the kitchen includes a serving bar, breakfast nook, and walk-in pantry. Two family bedrooms share a full bath to the left of the plan. Note the enchanting bay window in Bedroom 3.

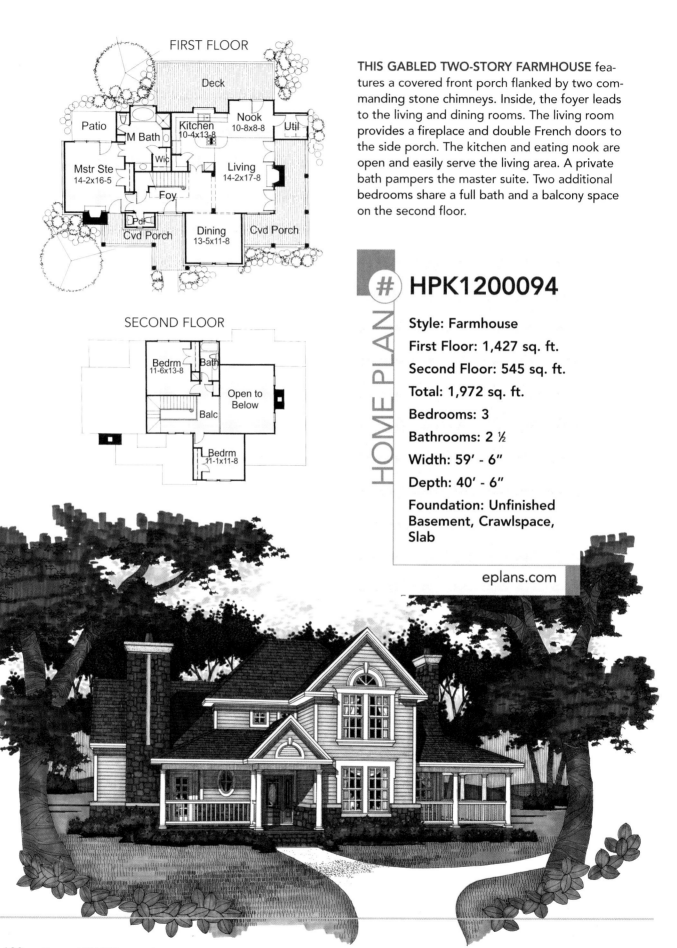

FIRST FLOOR

Deck

Patio

Nook
10-8x8-8

Util

M Bath

Kitchen
10-4x13-8

Wic

Living
14-2x17-8

Mstr Ste
14-2x16-5

Foy

Pdr

Cvd Porch

Dining
13-5x11-8

Cvd Porch

SECOND FLOOR

Bedrm
11-6x13-8

Bath

Open to Below

Balc

Bedrm
11-1x11-8

THIS GABLED TWO-STORY FARMHOUSE features a covered front porch flanked by two commanding stone chimneys. Inside, the foyer leads to the living and dining rooms. The living room provides a fireplace and double French doors to the side porch. The kitchen and eating nook are open and easily serve the living area. A private bath pampers the master suite. Two additional bedrooms share a full bath and a balcony space on the second floor.

HPK1200094

Style: Farmhouse

First Floor: 1,427 sq. ft.

Second Floor: 545 sq. ft.

Total: 1,972 sq. ft.

Bedrooms: 3

Bathrooms: 2 ½

Width: 59' - 6"

Depth: 40' - 6"

Foundation: Unfinished Basement, Crawlspace, Slab

eplans.com

A WRAPAROUND PORCH AND SHUTTERED WIN-
DOWS establish the country character of this mid-size
home. To the left of the foyer, columns define the formal dining room; just beyond the dining room is the
large living room, where French doors open to the rear
covered porch. Built-in bookshelves and a fireplace also
enhance this room. To the right of the plan, the master
suite, also with porch access, provides a lavish private
bath. Two family bedrooms and a full bath, located
upstairs, complete the plan.

(#) HPK1200117

Style: Traditional

First Floor: 1,521 sq. ft.

Second Floor: 473 sq. ft.

Total: 1,994 sq. ft.

Bedrooms: 3

Bathrooms: 2 ½

Width: 60' - 0"

Depth: 55' - 6"

Foundation: Unfinished
Basement, Crawlspace,
Slab

eplans.com

FIRST FLOOR

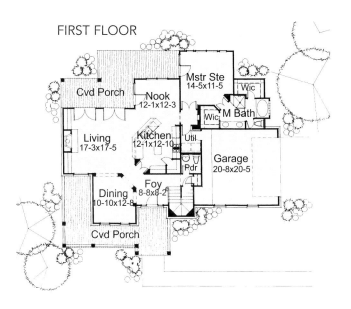

SECOND FLOOR

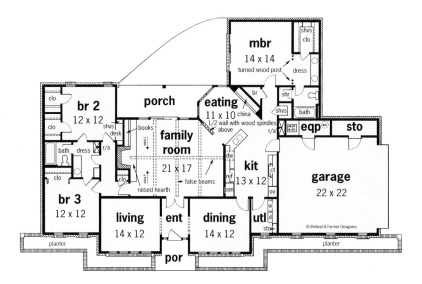

A BEAUTIFUL TAKE ON THE TRADITIONAL RANCH HOUSE, this brick plan is graced by romantic flower boxes that run the width of the home. Floor-to-ceiling glass lights up the interior, beginning with formal living and dining rooms framing the foyer. Decorative beams in the hearth-warmed family room add a vintage touch—or leave the wood unfinished for a rustic look. A modified galley kitchen lives to serve, with easy access to the dining room and bayed nook. At the rear, the master suite enjoys delicate details, like turned-wood posts and abundant natural light. The secondary bedrooms are separated to the left and share a full bath.

HPK1200133

Style: Traditional

Square Footage: 2,009

Bedrooms: 3

Bathrooms: 2

Width: 74' - 6"

Depth: 50' - 0"

Foundation: Crawlspace, Slab

eplans.com

THE CHARM OF THIS COUNTRY DESIGN BEGINS WITH THE COVERED PORCH and continues as you step through the front door. The foyer leads to decorative columns that welcome visitors to the heart of the home, the family room. To the left of the family room is the immense kitchen, complete with an island serving bar and a bay-windowed view of the backyard. To the right of the family room sits the luxurious master suite. French doors lead to the vaulted master bath which features dual vanities, a compartmented toilet, a separate shower, and a large walk-in closet. Upstairs, two additional family bedrooms share a full bath. Optional bonus space completes the second floor.

HOME PLAN (#)

HPK1200125

Style: Country Cottage

First Floor: 1,480 sq. ft.

Second Floor: 544 sq. ft.

Total: 2,024 sq. ft.

Bonus Space: 253 sq. ft.

Bedrooms: 3

Bathrooms: 2 ½

Width: 52' - 0"

Depth: 46' - 4"

Foundation: Crawlspace, Unfinished Walkout Basement, Slab

eplans.com

FIRST FLOOR

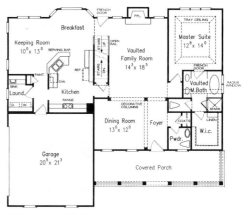

SECOND FLOOR

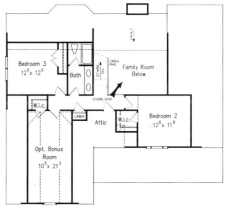

WITH ITS CLEAN LINES AND SYMMETRY, this home radiates grace and style. Inside, cathedral and tray ceilings add volume and elegance. The L-shaped kitchen includes an angled snack bar to the breakfast bay and great room. Secluded at the back of the house, the vaulted master suite includes a skylit bath. Of the two secondary bedrooms, one acts as a "second" master suite with its own private bath, and an alternate bath design creates a wheelchair-accessible option. The bonus room makes a great craft room, playroom, office, or optional fourth bedroom with a bath. The two-car garage loads to the side.

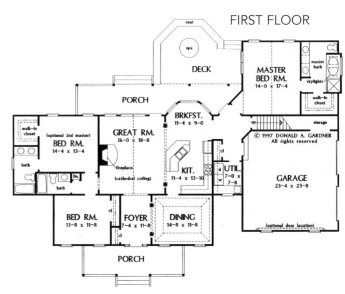

FIRST FLOOR

OPTIONAL LAYOUT

HPK1200115

HOME PLAN

Style: Country Cottage

Square Footage: 2,057

Bonus Space: 444 sq. ft.

Bedrooms: 3

Bathrooms: 3

Width: 80' - 10"

Depth: 61' - 6"

eplans.com

COLUMNS, SHUTTERS, AND FRENCH DOORS give this New Orleans-style home great appeal. The living room features plenty of windows and French-door access to the rear porch. The modified galley kitchen easily serves the bay-windowed informal dining area and the formal dining room. Access to the garage is available from the kitchen through the utility area. The master suite enjoys seclusion on the first floor and has private access to a beautiful atrium. Two bedrooms sharing a full bath are tucked upstairs.

(#) HPK1200110

Style: Country Cottage

First Floor: 1,546 sq. ft.

Second Floor: 512 sq. ft.

Total: 2,058 sq. ft.

Bedrooms: 3

Bathrooms: 2 ½

Width: 46' - 0"

Depth: 65' - 0"

Foundation: Unfinished Basement, Crawlspace, Slab

eplans.com

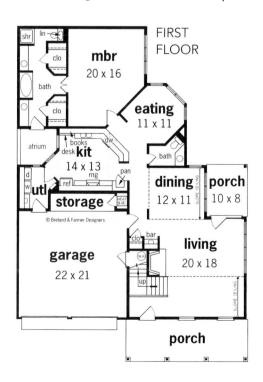

FIRST FLOOR

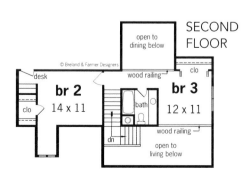

SECOND FLOOR

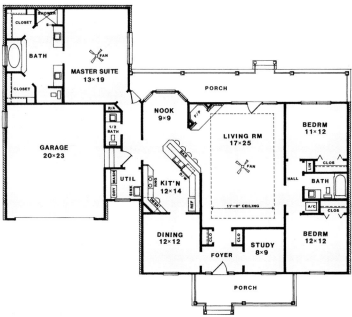

HPK1200091

Style: Farmhouse

Square Footage: 2,069

Bedrooms: 3

Bathrooms: 2 ½

Width: 70' - 0"

Depth: 58' - 8"

Foundation: Slab, Crawlspace

eplans.com

TWIN DORMERS AND A COVERED PORCH add to the relaxed country exterior of this home. The foyer opens to a study on the right and the dining room on the left, with coat closets on the way to the spacious living room with a fireplace and porch access. The galley-style kitchen with an eating bar services the dining room, breakfast nook, and living room. The nook enjoys a bay window that overlooks the rear porch and yard. Two family bedrooms found to the right of the plan share a full bath. The master suite enjoys seclusion at the left rear of the home with an amenity-filled bath with His and Hers walk-in closets.

A MAJESTIC FACADE makes this home pleasing to view. This home provides dual-use space in the wonderful sunken sitting room and media area. The kitchen has a breakfast bay and overlooks the snack bar to the sunken family area. A few steps from the kitchen is the formal dining room, which functions well with the upper patio. Two family bedrooms share a full bath. The private master suite includes a sitting area and French doors that open to a private covered patio.

HPK1200106

Style: SW Contemporary

Square Footage: 2,086

Bedrooms: 3

Bathrooms: 2

Width: 82' - 0"

Depth: 58' - 4"

Foundation: Slab

eplans.com

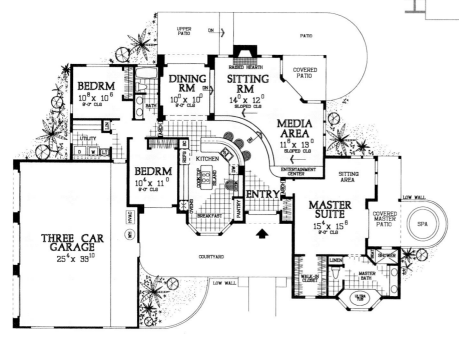

FIRST FLOOR

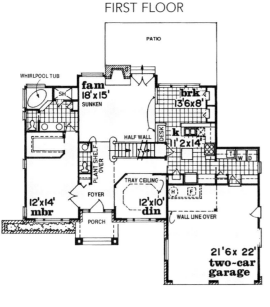

SECOND FLOOR

A PORTICO ENTRY, GRACEFUL ARCHES, and brick detailing provide appeal and a low-maintenance exterior for this design. A half-circle transom over the entry lights the two-story foyer, and a plant shelf lines the hallway to the sunken family room. This living space holds a vaulted ceiling, masonry fireplace, and French-door access to the railed patio. The nearby kitchen has a center prep island, built-in desk overlooking the family room, and extensive pantries in the breakfast area. The formal dining room has a tray ceiling and access to the foyer and the central hall. The master suite is on the first level for privacy and convenience. It features a walk-in closet and lavish bath with twin vanities, a whirlpool tub, and separate shower. Three family bedrooms, two of which feature built-in desks, are on the second floor.

HOME PLAN

 # HPK1200122

Style: Traditional

First Floor: 1,445 sq. ft.

Second Floor: 652 sq. ft.

Total: 2,097 sq. ft.

Bedrooms: 4

Bathrooms: 2 ½

Width: 56' - 8"

Depth: 48' - 4"

Foundation: Crawlspace, Unfinished Basement

eplans.com

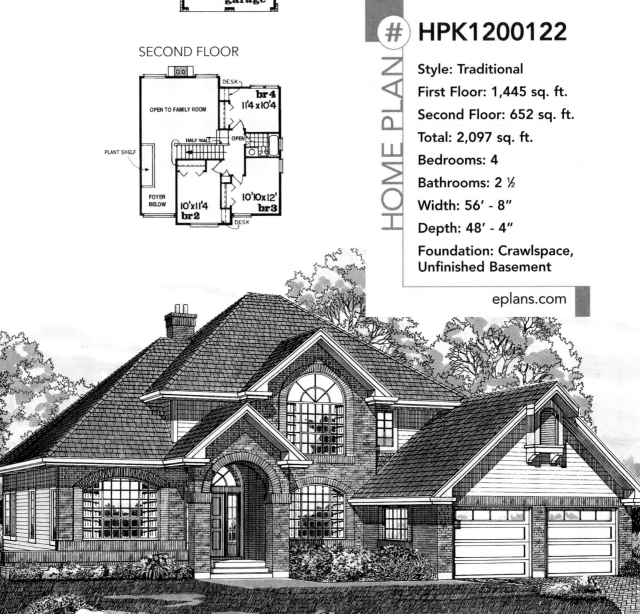

HPK1200120

Style: Country Cottage

First Floor: 1,606 sq. ft.

Second Floor: 496 sq. ft.

Total: 2,102 sq. ft.

Bedrooms: 3

Bathrooms: 3

Width: 40' - 0"

Depth: 64' - 2"

Foundation: Slab, Unfinished Basement

eplans.com

OWNERS WILL LOVE THE CONVENIENCE OF A TWO-CAR GARAGE and a first-floor master suite. The great room and semi-formal dining room work well with the peninsula kitchen, providing a good amount of everyday space at the center of the home. Take advantage of the nearby covered porch—complete with wood-burning fireplace—for larger gatherings and outdoor entertaining. On the first floor, an additional bedroom is available to guest. The second floor's bonus space can become a third bedroom, but might better serve as a library or recreation area.

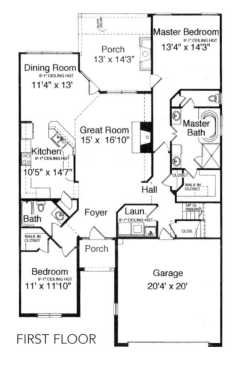

FIRST FLOOR

SECOND FLOOR

HOMES FOR EMPTY NESTERS

FIRST FLOOR

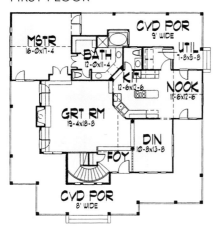

SECOND FLOOR

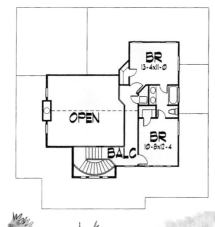

THIS HOME IS THE EPITOME OF COUNTRY CHARM with a little extra pizazz thrown in! A sweeping wrap-around porch, a Palladian window, and an interesting variation in rooflines spice up this spacious, well-lit country plan. The foyer opens to a winding staircase and to the spacious great room. The formal dining room is set off by graceful columns and features a pocket door to the kitchen for convenience and privacy. The secluded master suite is a sumptuous affair with a full bath. Two family bedrooms complete the second floor.

HPK1200138

Style: Victorian

First Floor: 1,598 sq. ft.

Second Floor: 514 sq. ft.

Total: 2,112 sq. ft.

Bedrooms: 3

Bathrooms: 2 ½

Width: 52' - 0"

Depth: 53' - 0"

Foundation: Slab, Unfinished Basement, Crawlspace

HOME PLAN

eplans.com

FIRST FLOOR

SECOND FLOOR

(#) HPK1200097

Style: Country Cottage

First Floor: 1,581 sq. ft.

Second Floor: 534 sq. ft.

Total: 2,115 sq. ft.

Bonus Space: 250 sq. ft.

Bedrooms: 3

Bathrooms: 2 ½

Width: 53' - 0"

Depth: 43' - 4"

Foundation: Crawlspace, Unfinished Walkout Basement

eplans.com

BEHIND THE GABLES AND ARCHED WINDOWS of this fine traditional home lies a great floor plan. The two-story foyer leads past a formal dining room defined by decorative pillars to a vaulted family room with a fireplace. The L-shaped kitchen is open to the sunny breakfast nook and provides access to the rear property. The lavish master suite is separated from the two upper-level bedrooms. Optional bonus space on the second floor invites the possibility of a recreation room, exercise room, or media room.

ARCHED-TOP WINDOWS ACT AS GRACE-FUL ACCENTS for this wonderful design. Inside, the floor plan is compact but commodious. The family room serves as the center of activity. It has a fireplace and connects to a lovely sunroom with rear-porch access. The formal dining room to the front of the plan is open to the entry foyer. A private den also opens off the foyer with double doors. It has its own private, cozy fireplace. The kitchen area opens to the sunroom, and it contains an island work counter. Bedrooms are split, with the master suite to the right side of the design and family bedrooms to the left. There are three full baths in this plan.

HOME PLAN

HPK1200112

Style: Traditional

Square Footage: 2,120

Bedrooms: 3

Bathrooms: 3

Width: 62' - 0"

Depth: 62' - 6"

Foundation: Unfinished Walkout Basement

eplans.com

AMENITIES ABOUND IN THIS CONTEMPORARY FARMHOUSE. The great room sports a fireplace and lots of natural light. Grab a snack at the kitchen island snack bar or the breakfast room. The vaulted foyer grandly introduces the dining room and parlor—the master bedroom is just off this room. Inside it: a fireplace, a luxury bath and a walk-in closet. Stairs lead up to a loft/bedroom, a full bath and an additional bedroom.

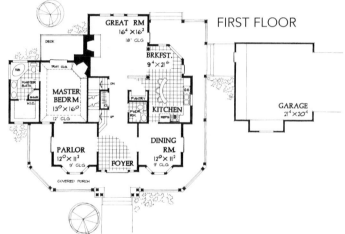

FIRST FLOOR

HPK1200113

Style: Farmhouse

First Floor: 1,618 sq. ft.

Second Floor: 510 sq. ft.

Total: 2,128 sq. ft.

Bedrooms: 3

Bathrooms: 2 ½

Width: 85' - 2"

Depth: 49' - 2"

Foundation: Unfinished Basement

HOME PLAN

eplans.com

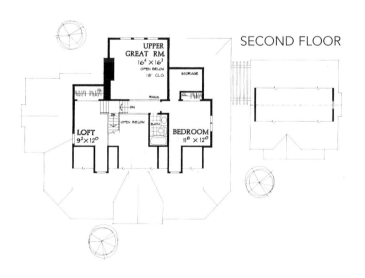

SECOND FLOOR

THIS CLASSIC COTTAGE BOASTS A STONE-AND-WOOD EXTERIOR with a welcoming arch-top entry that leads to a columned foyer. An extended-hearth fireplace is the focal point of the family room, and a nearby sunroom with covered porch access opens up the living area to the outdoors. The gourmet island kitchen opens through double doors from the living area; the breakfast area looks out to a porch. Sleeping quarters include a master wing with a spacious, angled bath and a sitting room or den that has its own full bath—perfect for a guest suite. On the opposite side of the plan, two family bedrooms share a full bath.

HPK1200092

HOME PLAN

Style: Country Cottage

Square Footage: 2,170

Bedrooms: 4

Bathrooms: 3

Width: 62' - 0"

Depth: 61' - 6"

Foundation: Finished Walkout Basement

eplans.com

TWIN DORMERS FRAME AN IMPRESSIVE ENTRANCE to this fine three-bedroom home. The covered front porch leads to a foyer flanked by formal living and dining rooms. The spacious family room—complete with a warming fireplace and built-ins—opens to the breakfast bay. The well-positioned kitchen, with an island, easily serves the formal and informal areas. The master suite has a tray ceiling in the sleeping area and a vaulted ceiling in the bath. The other two bedrooms flank a full bath with a double-bowl vanity.

HOME PLAN

HPK1200126

Style: Country Cottage

Square Footage: 2,170

Bedrooms: 3

Bathrooms: 2 ½

Width: 63' - 6"

Depth: 61' - 0"

Foundation: Crawlspace, Unfinished Walkout Basement

eplans.com

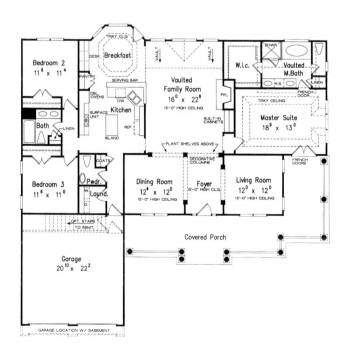

THIS ORIGINAL DESIGN TAKES ITS CUE FROM TRADITION-AL FLORIDIAN SUN COUNTRY HOMES, with a touch of the Southwest. A detailed, columned front porch leads to the grand foyer; a creative floor plan proves to be the ultimate in convenience and privacy. The living room views the rear patio and opens to the gourmet kitchen, rife with island and counter workspace and abundant natural light from the bayed nook. The dining room serves formal occasions while the family room kicks back for casual fun. Twin bedrooms share a full bath on the right side of the home. The left wing is entirely devoted to the comforts of the master suite. A bayed sitting area, French doors to the patio, and a glorious spa bath are sure to please.

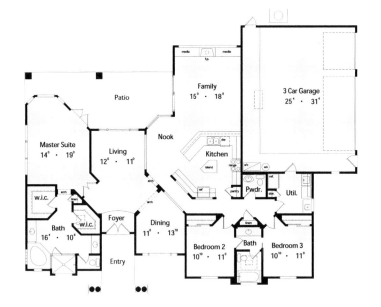

HOME PLAN

HPK1200356

Style: Floridian

Square Footage: 2,173

Bedrooms: 3

Bathrooms: 2 ½

Width: 74' - 4"

Depth: 56' - 0"

Foundation: Slab

eplans.com

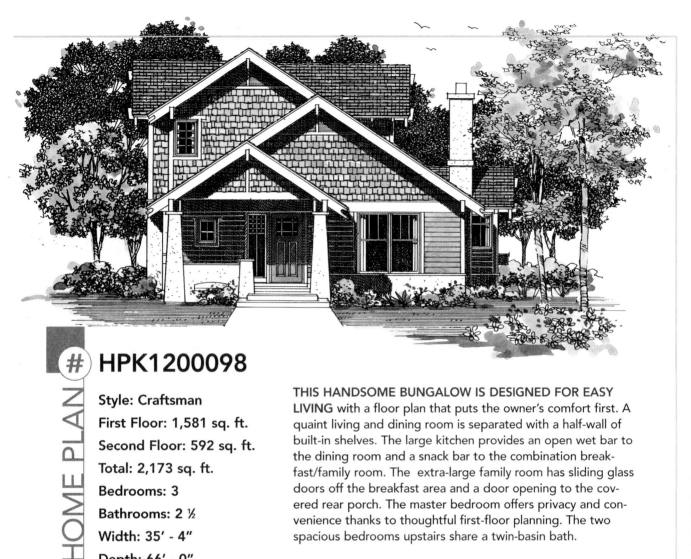

HOME PLAN

HPK1200098

Style: Craftsman

First Floor: 1,581 sq. ft.

Second Floor: 592 sq. ft.

Total: 2,173 sq. ft.

Bedrooms: 3

Bathrooms: 2 ½

Width: 35' - 4"

Depth: 66' - 0"

Foundation: Unfinished Basement

eplans.com

THIS HANDSOME BUNGALOW IS DESIGNED FOR EASY LIVING with a floor plan that puts the owner's comfort first. A quaint living and dining room is separated with a half-wall of built-in shelves. The large kitchen provides an open wet bar to the dining room and a snack bar to the combination breakfast/family room. The extra-large family room has sliding glass doors off the breakfast area and a door opening to the covered rear porch. The master bedroom offers privacy and convenience thanks to thoughtful first-floor planning. The two spacious bedrooms upstairs share a twin-basin bath.

FIRST FLOOR

COVERED PORCH

MASTER BEDRM
13⁴ x 18⁰

FAMILY ROOM
15⁴ x 11⁶

MASTER BATH

BREAKFAST ROOM
15⁴ x 11⁸

DESK

DINING RM
13⁴ x 11⁰

KIT
13⁰ x 11⁴

WET BAR

5' HIGH SHELVES

UP
OPEN ABOVE

LIVING RM
13⁴ x 11⁴

PDR

FOYER

COVERED PORCH

SECOND FLOOR

BEDRM
15⁴ x 11⁸

BATH

BEDRM
11⁶ x 11⁰

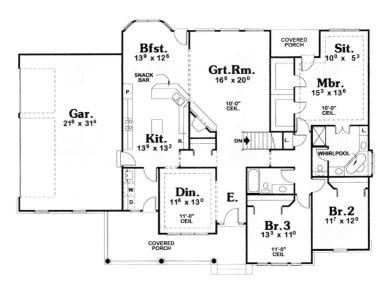

HPK1200084

Style: Traditional

Square Footage: 2,188

Bedrooms: 3

Bathrooms: 2

Width: 74' - 0"

Depth: 49' - 4"

eplans.com

THIS ENCHANTING COUNTRY DESIGN IS PERFECT FOR ANY FAMILY. Mini-dormers shed light onto the dining room and add elegance to the facade. The covered porch shelters from the rain and sun. Two entrances are available from the porch: the front entry opens directly to the great room, while the side entry leads through a convenient laundry to the kitchen. The kitchen offers maneuverability and a convenient snack bar. A bay window brings in natural light and brightens the breakfast nook for morning meals.

© 1994 Donald A. Gardner Architects, Inc.

THIS QUAINT FOUR-BEDROOM HOME WITH FRONT AND REAR PORCHES reinforces its beauty with arched windows and dormers. The pillared dining room opens on the right, and a study that could double as a guest room is available on the left. Straight ahead lies the massive great room with its cathedral ceiling, enchanting fireplace, and access to the private rear porch. Within steps of the dining room is the efficient kitchen and the sunny breakfast nook. The master suite enjoys a cathedral ceiling, rear-deck access, and a master bath with a skylit whirlpool tub. Three additional bedrooms located at the opposite end of the house share a full bath.

HOME PLAN

HPK1200127

Style: Farmhouse
Square Footage: 2,207
Bonus Space: 435 sq. ft.
Bedrooms: 4
Bathrooms: 2 ½
Width: 76' - 1"
Depth: 50' - 0"

eplans.com

HOMES FOR EMPTY NESTERS

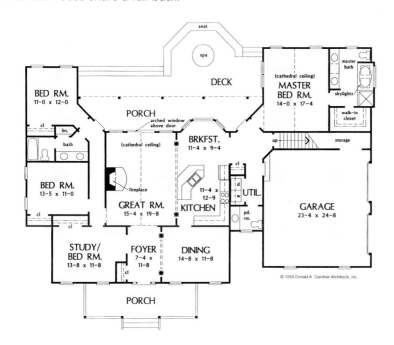

© 1994 Donald A. Gardner Architects, Inc.

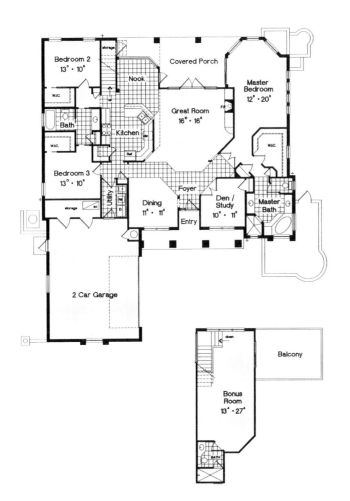

THE ELEGANCE AND GRACE OF THIS SPLIT-LEVEL PLAN are apparent at first sight. Impressive arches open into the foyer, with the wide-open great room beyond, opening to a covered porch through French doors. Enter both the master suite and the adjacent den/study through French doors. A private courtyard keeps the master bath shielded from the front yard. From the nook, near two good-sized bedrooms with a shared bathroom, stairs lead up to a bonus room, which includes a large balcony to take advantage of your lot with a view.

(#) HPK1200081

HOME PLAN

Style: Contemporary

Square Footage: 2,237

Bonus Space: 397 sq. ft.

Bedrooms: 3

Bathrooms: 2

Width: 60' - 0"

Depth: 70' - 0"

Foundation: Slab

eplans.com

THIS ALLURING DESIGN BLENDS A SPECTACULAR FLOOR PLAN WITH A LOVELY FACADE to create a home that's simply irresistible. The efficient house design yields spacious rooms and soaring spaces defying its affordable square footage. You're quickly welcomed inside by an inviting front porch, and greeted by a beautiful leaded glass door that leads to a two-story entryway. To the right, an elegant dining room is adorned with a tray ceiling. Beyond the stairs, the dramatic family room is accented with a corner fireplace and a window wall with arched transoms. The sumptuous master suite includes a double tray ceiling, sitting area, and His and Hers walk-in closets. Upstairs, two bedrooms share a Jack-and-Jill bath.

HPK1200118

Style: Traditional

First Floor: 1,719 sq. ft.

Second Floor: 534 sq. ft.

Total: 2,253 sq. ft.

Bonus Space: 247 sq. ft.

Bedrooms: 4

Bathrooms: 3

Width: 57' - 0"

Depth: 51' - 0"

Foundation: Unfinished Walkout Basement

eplans.com

FIRST FLOOR

SECOND FLOOR

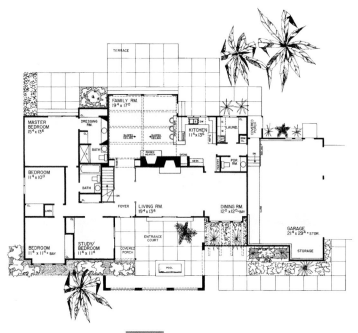

HOME PLAN

HPK1200085

Style: Contemporary

Square Footage: 2,261

Bedrooms: 4

Bathrooms: 2 ½

Width: 85' - 8"

Depth: 46' - 0"

Foundation: Unfinished Basement

eplans.com

A PRIVACY WALL AROUND THE COURTYARD WITH A POOL and trellised planter area is a gracious way by which to enter this one-story design. The Spanish flavor is accented by the grillwork and the tiled roof. The front living room has sliding glass doors that open to the entrance court. The adjacent dining room features a bay window. Informal activities will be enjoyed in the rear family room with a sloped, beamed ceiling, a raised-hearth fireplace, sliding glass doors to the terrace, and a snack bar. The sleeping wing can remain quiet away from the plan's activity centers. Notice the three-car garage with extra storage space.

INSIDE THIS CHARMING COTTAGE YOU'LL FIND A SPACIOUS, open floor plan that is perfect for entertaining. Fireplaces in the family room and keeping room combine to warm the adjoining kitchen and breakfast area. The practical design is ideal for family interaction. French doors lead to a covered porch, an option for outdoor dining or socializing. The master suite features tray ceilings and French-door entry into the master bath. Once inside, the master bath boasts a dual sink vanity, a garden tub, a compartmented shower and toilet, and a large walk-in closet. Two additional family bedrooms share a full bath. Upstairs houses a bonus room with a full bath and a walk-in closet. Two window seats make this a quiet retreat for a visiting guest.

HOME PLAN

HPK1200078

Style: Traditional

Square Footage: 2,275

Bonus Space: 407 sq. ft.

Bedrooms: 3

Bathrooms: 2 ½

Width: 59' - 4"

Depth: 69' - 0"

Foundation: Crawlspace, Unfinished Walkout Basement

eplans.com

HOMES FOR EMPTY NESTERS

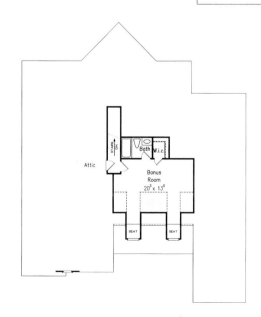

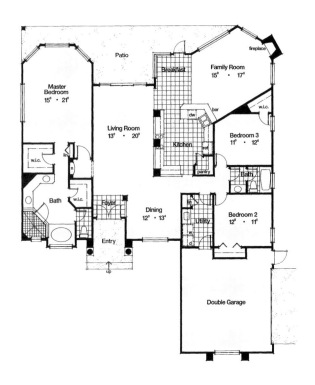

THE GRAND ENTRANCE OF THIS ONE-STORY HOME OFFERS A FINE INTRODUCTION to an open, spacious interior. A welcoming formal living/dining room sized for large get-togethers extends from the foyer. To the left, a decorative niche distinguishes the master wing. The bayed master bedroom wall creates a sitting area with panoramic views. Amenities found in the master bath include a luxurious soaking tub, His and Hers walk-in closets, and a compartmented toilet. The family wing boasts a large kitchen with a walk-in pantry, a nook, and a uniquely angled family room crowned by a fireplace wall. Two family bedrooms of ample size complete this home.

HOME PLAN

HPK1200357

Style: Contemporary

Square Footage: 2,278

Bedrooms: 3

Bathrooms: 2

Width: 57' - 9"

Depth: 71' - 8"

Foundation: Slab

eplans.com

YOU'LL LOVE COMING HOME TO THIS CHARMING COLONIAL COTTAGE! With porches front and back and a relaxing sun room, this home was designed for easy living. The unique kitchen design allows for fluid service to the bayed dinette and the dining room, separated from the living room by a fireplace and pantry corner wall, as well as by decorative columns. The expansive living room includes a built-in entertainment center. The master suite relishes a soothing bath and accesses a study/home office for work or play. Two family bedrooms and a bonus room finish off this home.

HPK1200135

Style: Traditional

Square Footage: 2,299

Bonus Space: 352 sq. ft.

Bedrooms: 3

Bathrooms: 2

Width: 68' - 0"

Depth: 64' - 0"

Foundation: Crawlspace, Slab, Unfinished Walkout Basement

eplans.com

sto 18 x 6

garage 22 x 22

porch 20 x 8

dinette

study / home off 16 x 13

sun rm 16 x 10

living 20 x 20

kit

wic

br 3 12 x 12

fireplace

built-in entertainment ctr

pan

dining 13 x 12

mbr 22 x 13

br 2 12 x 12

foy

porch 20 x 6

wic

bonus rm 21 x 16

dn

FIRST FLOOR

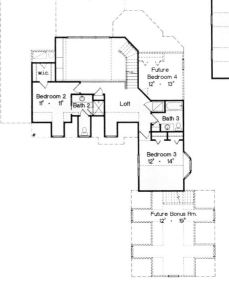

SECOND FLOOR

YOU CAN ALMOST SEE THE HORSE CARRIAGE COMING THROUGH THE PORTE COCHERE in this very delightful country classic. As you enter the home, before you lies a large family room with a direct view through to the covered patio beyond. Turn to the right to see the huge dining room with bay window. Imagine a formal dinner or buffet luncheon set out for your guests. Next to the dining room is a powder room for the use of your guests. Beyond the powder room is a large family kitchen with plenty of counter and cabinet space. Enjoy your morning coffee in the breakfast nook as you take in the views of your back yard. The huge master bedroom shares the same view of the back yard from the other side of the house and features a large walk-in closet. Enjoy the master bath with a double vanity and large shower and tub.

HOME PLAN

HPK1200358

Style: Farmhouse

First Floor: 1,530 sq. ft.

Second Floor: 777 sq. ft.

Total: 2,307 sq. ft.

Bonus Space: 361 sq. ft.

Bedrooms: 3

Bathrooms: 3 ½

Width: 61' - 4"

Depth: 78' - 0"

Foundation: Slab

eplans.com

HOME PLAN

HPK1200107

Style: Country Cottage

Square Footage: 2,329

Bedrooms: 3

Bathrooms: 2 ½

Width: 72' - 0"

Depth: 73' - 4"

Foundation: Crawlspace

eplans.com

RUSTIC IN NATURE, THIS CHARMING HOME OFFERS A REFINED INTERIOR that is accented by the multiple ceiling treatments throughout. The dining room and study flank the foyer and open to the great room where French doors lead to the rear property. Family bedrooms reside on the right and the master suite finds seclusion on the left with His and Hers walk-in closets and a lavish bath. The kitchen is smartly situated between the dining room and the breakfast nook which, in turn, opens to the covered rear porch.

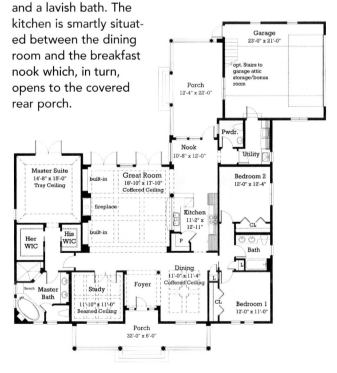

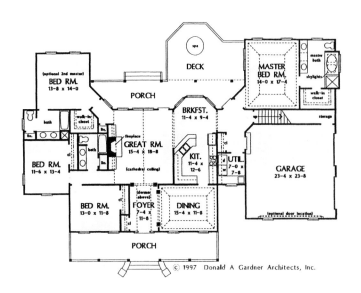

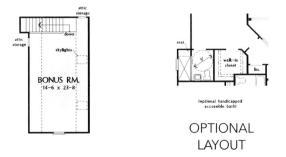

BONUS RM.
14-6 x 23-8

OPTIONAL
LAYOUT

© 1997 Donald A Gardner Architects, Inc.

THIS PLAN'S WIDE FRONT PORCH SAYS "WEL-COME HOME." Inside, its comfortable design encourages relaxation. A center dormer lights the foyer, as columns punctuate the entry to the dining room and the great room. The spacious kitchen offers an angled countertop and is open to the breakfast bay. A roomy utility area is nearby. Tray ceilings add elegance to the dining room and master bedroom. A possible second master suite is located opposite and features an optional arrangement for wheelchair accessibility. Two additional bedrooms share a third full bath that includes a linen closet.

HPK1200128

HOME PLAN

Style: Country Cottage

Square Footage: 2,349

Bonus Space: 435 sq. ft.

Bedrooms: 4

Bathrooms: 3

Width: 83' - 2"

Depth: 56' - 4"

eplans.com

© 1997 Donald A. Gardner Architects, Inc.

(#) HPK1200359

Style: Mediterranean

Square Footage: 2,367

Bedrooms: 3

Bathrooms: 2

Width: 76' - 0"

Depth: 71' - 4"

Foundation: Slab

eplans.com

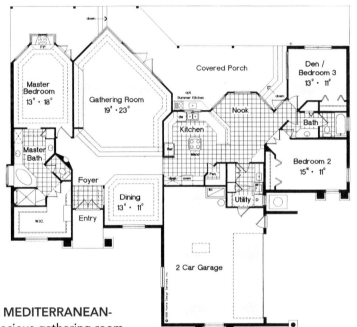

THE IMPRESSIVE ENTRY INTO THIS MEDITERRANEAN-STYLE HOME leads directly into a spacious gathering room, with unique angles and a mitered glass window. This is the perfect home for the family that entertains. The large gathering room and covered porch with summer kitchen are ready for a pool party! Elegance and style grace this split floor plan, with large bedrooms and a very spacious kitchen/breakfast nook area. The kitchen includes a center island and a walk-in pantry. The master suite showcases a fireplace next to French doors which lead onto the covered porch at the rear, sweetly arranged for romantic evenings.

FIRST FLOOR

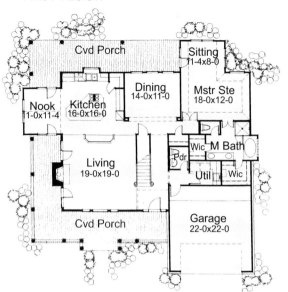

SECOND FLOOR

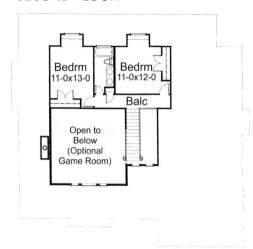

THIS COUNTRY HOME DISPLAYS FOLK VICTORIAN FLAIR, with the large front gable decorated by fish-scale shingles. A wraparound porch and Palladian window topped by a keystone also highlight the home's exterior. Inside, notable features include a two-story living room warmed by a fireplace and a spacious master suite with a private sitting area, walk-in closet, and master bath. The kitchen serves the breakfast nook and formal dining room with ease. Upstairs, two additional bedrooms share a hall bath. An optional game room offers extra space.

HOME PLAN

HPK1200139

Style: Traditional

First Floor: 1,848 sq. ft.

Second Floor: 537 sq. ft.

Total: 2,385 sq. ft.

Bonus Space: 361 sq. ft.

Bedrooms: 3

Bathrooms: 2 ½

Width: 61' - 3"

Depth: 59' - 6"

Foundation: Unfinished Basement, Crawlspace, Slab

eplans.com

SPLIT-BEDROOM FLOOR PLANNING HIGHLIGHTS THIS VOLUME-LOOK home. The master suite on the first floor is completely private and perfectly pampering with a huge walk-in closet, double vanity, and separate tub and shower. The great room and hearth room share a through-fireplace and are complemented by a breakfast area and island kitchen. Formal entertaining is enhanced by the dining room with hutch space and boxed window. A guest half bath just off the hearth room will be appreciated by visitors. Three family bedrooms upstairs share a full bath that has a double vanity.

(#) HPK1200083

Style: Traditional
First Floor: 1,733 sq. ft.
Second Floor: 672 sq. ft.
Total: 2,405 sq. ft.
Bedrooms: 4
Bathrooms: 2 ½
Width: 60' - 0"
Depth: 55' - 4"

eplans.com

FIRST FLOOR

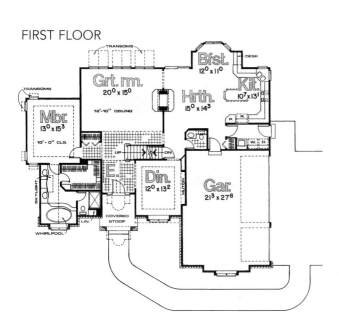

SECOND FLOOR

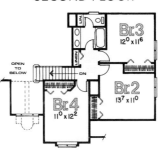

FIRST FLOOR

Porch
13'9" x 14'10"

Master Bedroom
13'4" x 14'3"

Breakfast
9'-1" CEILING HGT.
11'4" x 14'1"

WALK IN CLOSET

Great Room
13'11" x 20'2"

Bath

Kitchen
9'-1" CEILING
11'4" x 14'7"

WALK IN CLOSET

STORAGE

Den/Dining Rm
9'-1" CEILING HGT.
10'4" x 10'7"

Foyer

Laun.

Bath

WALK IN CLOSET

Bedroom
9'-1" CEILING HGT.
11' x 11'10"

Porch

Two-Car Garage
20'4" x 20'

A STYLISH ANGLED ENTRY AT THE FRONT DOOR leads to a well-lit foyer. At right, an optional dining room or den opens to great room, which features a delightful fireplace. The master bedroom, conveniently located on the first floor, provides a luxury bath with all the trimmings. Differently abled individuals will appreciate the roomy master bath. The kitchen offers bar-style seating and also opens to the great room. Rear porch features an outdoor wood-burning fireplace. The plan offers a slab foundation or a basement foundation with eight-or nine-foot basement ceiling.

HOME PLAN

HPK1200136

Style: European Cottage

First Floor: 1,820 sq. ft.

Second Floor: 592 sq. ft.

Total: 2,412 sq. ft.

Bedrooms: 2

Bathrooms: 3

Width: 42' - 0"

Depth: 70' - 8"

Foundation: Slab, Unfinished Basement

eplans.com

SECOND FLOOR

Upper Great Room

Loft
9' X 13'2"

WOOD RAIL

Upper Foyer

Mech

Bath

Bonus Room

A NEAT ROW OF CLASSIC FRONT-PORCH PILLARS opens this beautiful one-story plan. The bay window in the master suite offers a front-row seat to views. Favorite foods will be the order of the day in the step-saving kitchen, with a central island in a unique diamond shape. The pentagonal dining room is large enough for special occasions. A double-sided fireplace lights the great room and adjacent study. To the right of the entry is an angled hallway that leads to two bedrooms and a hall bath. A bonus room with a full bath sits above the double garage.

HOME PLAN

HPK1200114

Style: Farmhouse

Square Footage: 2,454

Bonus Space: 256 sq. ft.

Bedrooms: 3

Bathrooms: 2

Width: 80' - 6"

Depth: 66' - 6"

Foundation: Crawlspace

eplans.com

HOMES FOR EMPTY NESTERS

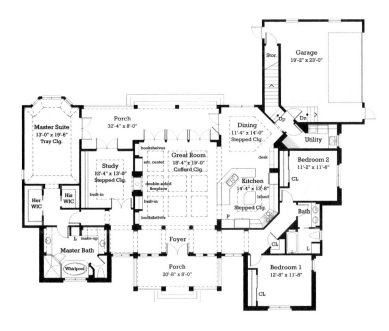

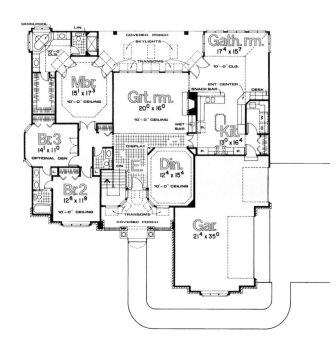

GENTLY TAPERED COLUMNS SET OFF AN ELEGANT ARCHED ENTRY framed by multi-pane windows. Inside, an open great room features a wet bar, fireplace, tall transom windows, and access to a covered porch with skylights. The gourmet kitchen boasts a food-preparation island and a snack bar and overlooks the gathering room. Double doors open to the master suite, where French doors lead to a private bath with an angled whirlpool tub and a sizable walk-in closet. One of two nearby family bedrooms could serve as a den, with optional French doors opening from a hall central to the sleeping wing.

HOME PLAN

HPK1200108

Style: Traditional

Square Footage: 2,456

Bedrooms: 3

Bathrooms: 2 ½

Width: 66' - 0"

Depth: 68' - 0"

eplans.com

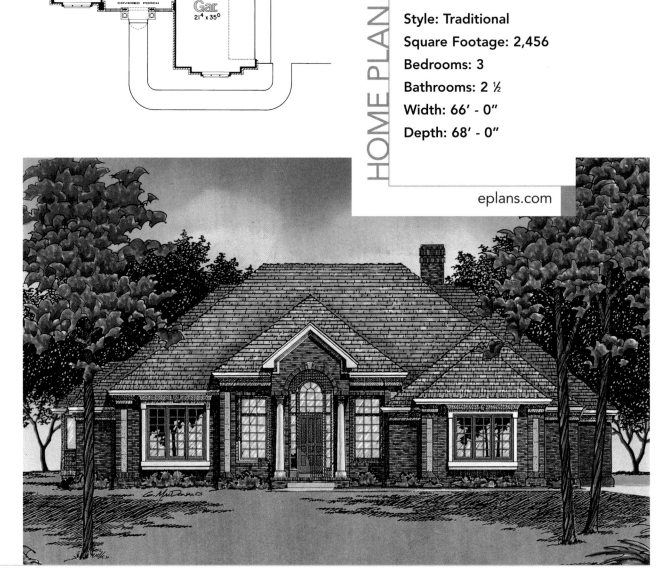

HOME PLAN

HPK1200095

Style: Transitional
First Floor: 1,737 sq. ft.
Second Floor: 727 sq. ft.
Total: 2,464 sq. ft.
Bonus Space: 376 sq. ft.
Bedrooms: 4
Bathrooms: 2 ½
Width: 65' - 6"
Depth: 53' - 0"
Foundation: Unfinished Basement, Crawlspace

eplans.com

THE BEAUTY AND WARMTH OF A BRICK FACADE ADDS STATELY ELEGANCE to this traditional design. Its open floor plan is highlighted by a two-story living room and open dining room. The kitchen includes a central cooking island and opens to a bright breakfast area. The master suite offers an ample walk-in closet/dressing area and a bath featuring an exquisite double vanity and a tub with corner windows. A bonus room over the two-car garage offers room for expansion.

FIRST FLOOR

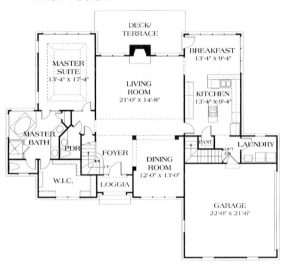

SECOND FLOOR

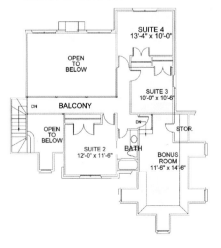

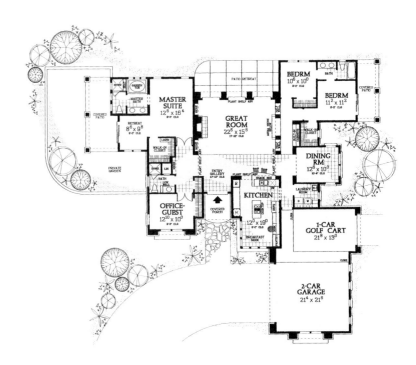

HPK1200130

Style: Traditional

Square Footage: 2,471

Bedrooms: 4

Bathrooms: 3

Width: 86' - 4"

Depth: 80' - 2"

Foundation: Slab

eplans.com

CAPSTONES, QUOINS, AND GENTLE ARCHES LEND AN UNPRETENTIOUS SPIRIT to this European-style plan. A vaulted entry reveals classic instincts and introduces an unrestrained floor plan designed for comfort. The tiled gallery opens to a sizable great room that invites casual entertaining and features a handsome fireplace with an extended hearth, framed with decorative niches. The kitchen features a cooktop island and a built-in desk, and opens to a windowed breakfast bay, which lets in natural light. For formal occasions, a great dining room permits quiet, unhurried evening meals. Relaxation awaits the homeowner in a sensational master suite, with an inner retreat and a private patio. Two family bedrooms share a private bath, and one room opens to a covered patio. A golf cart will easily fit into a side garage, which adjoins a roomy two-car garage.

FIRST FLOOR

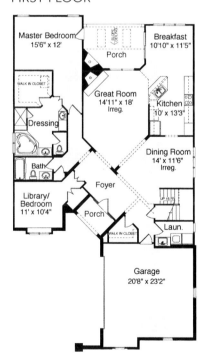

Master Bedroom
15'6" x 12'

Porch

Breakfast
10'10" x 11'5"

WALK IN CLOSET

Great Room
14'11" x 18'
Irreg.

Kitchen
10' x 13'3"

Dressing

Dining Room
14' x 11'6"
Irreg.

Bath

Foyer

Library/
Bedroom
11' x 10'4"

Porch

Laun.

WALK IN CLOSET

Garage
20'8" x 23'2"

SECOND FLOOR

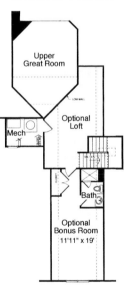

Upper
Great Room

Mech

Optional
Loft

LOW WALL

Optional
Bonus Room
11'11" x 19'

Bath

HPK1200079

Style: European Cottage

First Floor: 1,832 sq. ft.

Second Floor: 651 sq. ft.

Total: 2,483 sq. ft.

Bedrooms: 2

Bathrooms: 3

Width: 42' - 0"

Depth: 75' - 0"

Foundation: Unfinished Basement, Slab

eplans.com

THIS HOME WAS DESIGNED TO ATTRACT THE EMPTY-NESTER MARKET with a first-floor master, rooms with optional uses, and an open floor plan. An angled entry introduces the foyer offering views to the great room and formal dining room. Grand openings between rooms provide a large spacious effect. The kitchen offers an oven cabinet and snack bar with seating. The master bedroom suite boasts a luxury bath, large walk-in closet, and access to the rear porch.

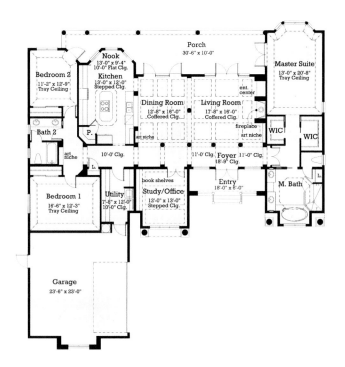

Nook
13'-0" x 9'-4"
10'-0" Flat Clg.

Porch
30'-6" x 10'-0"

Master Suite
13'-0" x 20'-8"
Tray Ceiling

Bedroom 2
11'-2" x 12'-9"
Tray Ceiling

Kitchen
13'-0" x 12'-0"
Stepped Clg.

ent.
center

Bath 2

Dining Room
12'-8" x 16'-0"
Coffered Clg.

Living Room
17'-8" x 16'-0"
Coffered Clg.

fireplace
art niche

WIC

WIC

art niche

P.

art niche

10'-0" Clg.

11'-0" Clg.

Foyer
18'-9" Clg.

11'-0" Clg.

L.

Bedroom 1
16'-6" x 12'-3"
Tray Ceiling

Utility
7'-8" x 12'-0"
10'-0" Clg.

book shelves

Study/Office
12'-0" x 13'-0"
Stepped Clg.

Entry
18'-0" x 6'-0"

M. Bath

L.

Garage
23'-6" x 23'-0"

THE MODERN RUSTIC LOOK OF THIS COTTAGE LENDS A UNIQUE CHARM to the overall plan. Inside, the foyer faces a formal area made up of the combined living and dining rooms. The island kitchen expands into a bayed nook. The study/office is placed just off the entry. Two family bedrooms share a hall bath. Double doors open into the master suite, which offers two walk-in closets and a private bath.

HPK1200116

HOME PLAN

Style: Farmhouse
Square Footage: 2,487
Bedrooms: 3
Bathrooms: 2
Width: 70' - 0"
Depth: 72' - 0"
Foundation: Crawlspace

eplans.com

ELEGANT ARCHES AT THE COVERED ENTRY of this home announce an exquisite floor plan. The tiled entry opens to the formal living and dining rooms, which enjoy open, soaring space defined by arches and a decorative column. A gourmet kitchen offers an island cooktop counter and serves a bayed breakfast nook and a convenient snack bar. The sleeping wing includes a master suite with a whirlpool bath, a sizable walk-in closet, two vanities, and a box-bay window. Two family bedrooms share a full bath nearby, while a secluded den offers the possibility of a fourth bedroom.

HOME PLAN

 # HPK1200100

Style: Traditional
Square Footage: 2,498
Bedrooms: 3
Bathrooms: 2 ½
Width: 76' - 0"
Depth: 55' - 4"

eplans.com

HOMES FOR EMPTY NESTERS

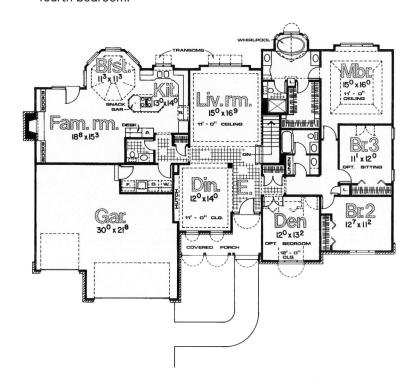

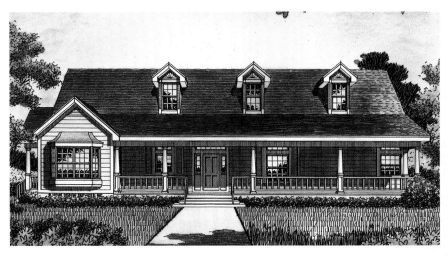

HOME PLAN #

HPK1200360

Style: Traditional

Square Footage: 2,500

Bedrooms: 3

Bathrooms: 3

Width: 64' - 0"

Depth: 52' - 0"

Foundation: Unfinished Basement

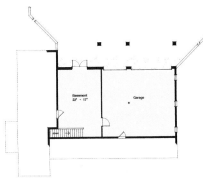

HOME PLAN #

HPK1200134

Style: European Cottage

First Floor: 1,953 sq. ft.

Second Floor: 652 sq. ft.

Total: 2,605 sq. ft.

Bedrooms: 2

Bathrooms: 3

Width: 50' - 0"

Depth: 75' - 0"

Foundation: Unfinished Basement, Slab

FIRST FLOOR

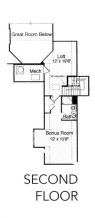

SECOND FLOOR

HOME PLAN
HPK1200109

Style: Country Cottage

First Floor: 2,037 sq. ft.

Second Floor: 596 sq. ft.

Total: 2,633 sq. ft.

Bedrooms: 2

Bathrooms: 3

Width: 42' - 0"

Depth: 75' - 0"

Foundation: Unfinished Basement, Slab

FIRST FLOOR

SECOND FLOOR

HOME PLAN
HPK1200121

Style: European Cottage

First Floor: 2,096 sq. ft.

Second Floor: 651 sq. ft.

Total: 2,747 sq. ft.

Bedrooms: 2

Bathrooms: 3

Width: 47' - 8"

Depth: 75' - 0"

Foundation: Unfinished Basement, Slab

FIRST FLOOR

SECOND FLOOR

Complete Retreat—Cottages and Vacation Plans

Dreaming of a cozy cabin in the woods, a lakeshore cottage, or a small home perched on a hilltop? Rustic retreats beckon us with the promise of regeneration and respite from our world of rush hour commutes and cubicles. Frank Lloyd Wright said that living deep in nature called our democratic spirit out of the confusion of the city and planted it in terra firma. Let us answer that call.

The homes collected in this section provide large gathering spaces, usually centered around the kitchen, with overflow capacity in nearby porches and decks. But most of all, these designs work to maximize views of the surrounding landscape, either from bedroom retreats and soaking tubs or private balconies and sun rooms. Imagine, for instance, the view at night of the ocean from the upper-level balcony of plan HPK1200203 on page 235. Or picture yourself having a late-morning brunch in the kitchen of home HPK1200150 on page 223.

So linger in the shade of a cool front porch, light a fire in the hearth, or sit down with a good book. In one of these attractive vacation plans, you've already escaped the everyday.

Kraftmaid

Photo by Mark Samu

A DRAMATIC WINDOW WALL is the perfect backdrop to this gorgeous cottage-style family room. But first, clear the way for larger rooms by implementing space-reclaiming strategies in the working areas of the home.

THIS CHARMING HOME is ideal for waterfront property with a generous wraparound porch. The porch features a corner gazebo that's perfect for outdoor living. The vestibule offers an energy- and space-efficient pocket door that opens to the island kitchen and dining room where sliding glass doors open to the gazebo. The living room views in three directions, bringing the outside in. A bedroom and lavish bath complete the floor plan.

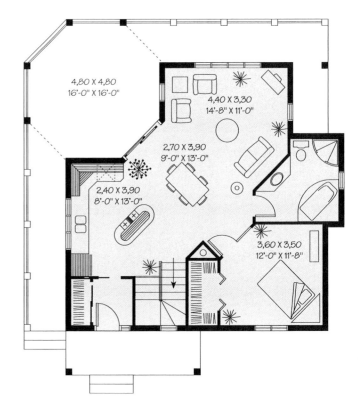

4,80 X 4,80
16'-0" X 16'-0"

4,40 X 3,30
14'-8" X 11'-0"

2,70 X 3,90
9'-0" X 13'-0"

2,40 X 3,90
8'-0" X 13'-0"

3,60 X 3,50
12'-0" X 11'-8"

HOME PLAN

HPK1200209

Style: Victorian

Square Footage: 840

Bedrooms: 1

Bathrooms: 1

Width: 33' - 0"

Depth: 31' - 0"

Foundation: Unfinished Walkout Basement

eplans.com

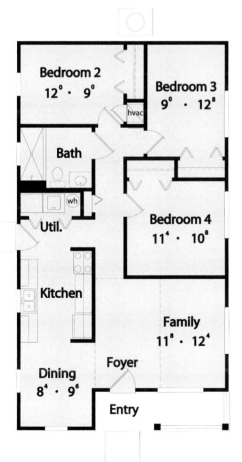

Bedroom 2
12⁰ · 9⁰

Bedroom 3
9⁰ · 12⁸

hvac

Bath

wh

Util.

Bedroom 4
11⁴ · 10⁸

Kitchen

Family
11⁸ · 12⁴

Dining
8⁴ · 9⁶

Foyer

Entry

HPK1200361

Style: Country Cottage

Square Footage: 996

Bedrooms: 3

Bathrooms: 1

Width: 24' - 4"

Depth: 43' - 8"

Foundation: Crawlspace

eplans.com

THIS BUDGET-FRIENDLY and low-maintenance plan takes a direct approach to functional design. Gathering and dining spaces occupy the front of the plan, including a galley-style kitchen and a laundry area that can double as a mud room. Three bedrooms at the back of the plan share a full-sized bath. Convert one of the bedrooms to become a home office or den. Homeowners should also consider modifying the plan to accommodate a second bathroom. This design is perfectly suited for narrower lots.

THIS CHARMING AND
ROMANTIC COTTAGE
DESIGN is great as a second
home or for a growing family.
A quaint, covered porch wraps
around one side of the home—
perfect for rocking chairs on
lazy summer days. Double
doors open directly into the
kitchen/dining area. A staircase
to the second floor overlooks
the open family room. The
first-floor bedroom is located
close to the hall shower bath.
Upstairs, two additional
family bedrooms share a full
hall bath.

FIRST FLOOR

3,30 X 3,30
11'-0" X 11'-0"

3,50 X 4,20
11'-8" X 14'-0"

3,30 X 4,20
11'-0" X 14'-0"

SECOND FLOOR

3,60 X 3,30
12'-0" X 11'-0"

3,30 X 3,30
11'-0" X 11'-0"

HPK1200145

HOME PLAN

Style: Country Cottage

First Floor: 680 sq. ft.

Second Floor: 388 sq. ft.

Total: 1,068 sq. ft.

Bedrooms: 3

Bathrooms: 2

Width: 24' - 0"

Depth: 30' - 0"

Foundation: Unfinished
Basement

eplans.com

HPK1200208

HOME PLAN

Style: Lakefront

Square Footage: 1,114

Bedrooms: 2

Bathrooms: 1

Width: 39' - 8"

Depth: 36' - 4"

Foundation: Unfinished Basement

eplans.com

LAKESIDE OR CURBSIDE, THIS 1,114-SQUARE-FOOT DESIGN soars to new heights for relaxed living. A second-story portico and walls of light-loving windows surround the exterior. The master bedroom with full bath and family room with fireplace enjoy lofty cathedral ceilings. A spacious second bedroom, rounded kitchen with sprawling lunch counter, and gracious dining room complement this outstanding space.

11'-0" X 14'-8"
3,30 X 4,40

11'-0" X 11'-0"
3,30 X 3,30

19'-0" X 12'-0"
5,70 X 3,60

9'-4" X 9'-4"
2,80 X 2,80

12'-4" X 10'-0"
3,70 X 3,00

LARGE WINDOWS, A COVERED PORCH, AND AN UPPER BALCONY make this home perfect for waterfront living. Inside, find a very comfortable plan including a family room, a dining room with French-door access to the patio, and an L-shaped kitchen with a breakfast area. A convenient powder room and laundry facilities are also on this floor. Upstairs are the two bedrooms that share a full bath with a separate tub and shower. The larger bedroom has French doors opening to the balcony.

FIRST FLOOR

SECOND FLOOR

(#) HPK1200170

Style: Cape Cod

First Floor: 691 sq. ft.

Second Floor: 555 sq. ft.

Total: 1,246 sq. ft.

Bedrooms: 2

Bathrooms: 1 ½

Width: 28' - 0"

Depth: 40' - 0"

Foundation: Unfinished Basement

eplans.com

THIS DELIGHTFUL COUNTRY HOME IS SURE TO PLEASE WITH THE WELCOMING TOUCH OF THE BROAD WRAP-AROUND PORCH. Once inside, the open floor plan adjoins the living room, dining room, and kitchen areas, rather than designating formal quarters. A raised snack bar in the kitchen offers convenient service to the dining room. The master suite, a second bedroom, and a full bath complete the first floor. Upstairs, there is a loft with a view of the living room below, and an optional full bathroom for a possible future bedroom.

HOME PLAN

(#) HPK1200168

Style: **Country Cottage**

Square Footage: **1,250**

Bonus Space: **341 sq. ft.**

Bedrooms: **2**

Bathrooms: **2**

Width: **52' - 6"**

Depth: **45' - 8"**

Foundation: **Crawlspace, Slab**

eplans.com

COTTAGE AND VACATION HOMES

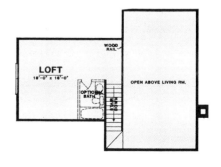

PORCH

BED RM. 2
12'-6" x 12'-0"

KITCH.
12'-0" x 11'-0"

DINING
10'-6" x 12'-0"

RAISED BAR

MASTER SUITE
12'-0" x 16'-0"

STOR.

OPEN ABOVE
LIVING RM.
16'-0" x 16'-0"

B. 1

DESK

PORCH

WOOD RAIL

LOFT
16'-0" x 16'-0"

OPEN ABOVE LIVING RM.

OPTIONAL BATH

FIRST FLOOR

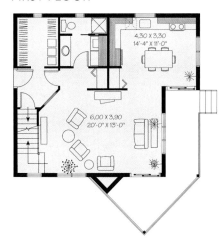

4,30 X 3,30
14'-4" X 11'-0"

6,00 X 3,90
20'-0" X 13'-0"

SECOND FLOOR

3,30 X 3,40
11'-0" X 11'-4"

3,50 X 5,80
11'-8" X 19'-4"

THE MODERN EXTERIOR OF THIS HOME SPORTS A UNIQUELY SHAPED DECK and customized windows. This lovely cottage features a second-floor hall with an overlook to the living room. A spacious secondary bedroom on this floor has a walk-in closet and a private door to the shared bath. On the first floor, a cathedral ceiling highlights the living room, which opens to the dining area and kitchen. A full bath and a storage area complete the plan.

HOME PLAN

HPK1200176

Style: Contemporary

First Floor: 715 sq. ft.

Second Floor: 570 sq. ft.

Total: 1,285 sq. ft.

Bedrooms: 2

Bathrooms: 2

Width: 30' - 8"

Depth: 26' - 0"

Foundation: Unfinished Basement

eplans.com

THE FASCINATING
CLERESTORY WINDOW ABOVE THE FRONT
COVERED PORCH of this home grows on you, beckoning you to find out what wonders are housed inside. Surely, the openness of this plan is its most intriguing quality. The vault-ceiling activity room flows naturally into the kitchen, graced by ample counter and cabinet space, and then into the bayed dining area. Off the kitchen is a handy laundry, a utility room, storage space, and entry to the garage. On the other side of the house reside three bedrooms and two baths. The huge oval bathtub and twin vanities set below a vaulted ceiling make the master suite special. Extra space is available above the garage for another bedroom, study, or whatever you need.

HOME PLAN

HPK1200198

Style: Country Cottage

Square Footage: 1,294

Bonus Space: 374 sq. ft.

Bedrooms: 3

Bathrooms: 2

Width: 64' - 6"

Depth: 29' - 10"

Foundation: Crawlspace, Slab

eplans.com

COTTAGE AND VACATION HOMES

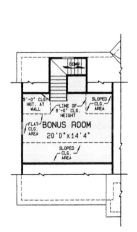

HERE IS A WONDERFULLY ORGANIZED PLAN WITH AN ARCHITECTURAL DESIGN that commands attention, both inside and out. The dramatic rooflines, pointed glass, and gable-end walls bring the outdoors in with beautiful views. The delightful deck echoes the roofline and invites outdoor entertainment. Inside, the spacious living room is crowned by a sloping ceiling with an exposed ridge beam. A free-standing fireplace will make its contribution to a cheerful atmosphere. The family sleeping quarters include two bedrooms, two bunk rooms, two full baths, and lots of closet space.

HPK1200182

Style: Contemporary

Square Footage: 1,312

Bedrooms: 4

Bathrooms: 2

Width: 40' - 0"

Depth: 48' - 0"

Foundation: Crawlspace

eplans.com

HOME PLAN

HPK1200177

Style: European Cottage

First Floor: 756 sq. ft.

Second Floor: 580 sq. ft.

Total: 1,336 sq. ft.

Bedrooms: 2

Bathrooms: 2 ½

Width: 32' - 0"

Depth: 36' - 9"

Foundation: Crawlspace

eplans.com

THIS SWEET TUDOR COTTAGE OFFERS A PETITE DESIGN with plenty of family appeal. Mixed materials enhance the exterior and a quaint covered porch welcomes you inside. The first floor offers a two-sided fireplace that warms the living and dining rooms. The main level is completed by a U-shaped kitchen, powder room, laundry, and plenty of outdoor porch space. Upstairs, the master bedroom features a private bath and walk-in closet, while the guest bedroom also features a private bath and a bayed wall of windows.

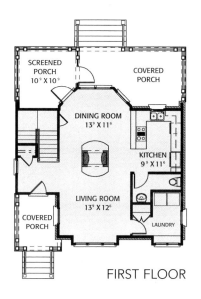

FIRST FLOOR

SECOND FLOOR

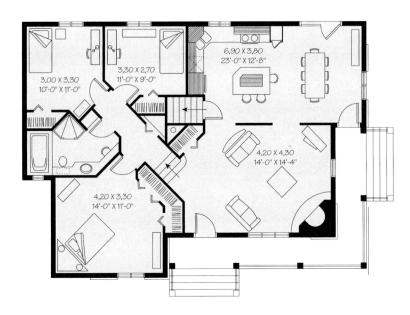

HPK1200166

Style: Country

Square Footage: 1,337

Bedrooms: 3

Bathrooms: 1

Width: 46' - 8"

Depth: 34' - 4"

Foundation: Unfinished Basement

eplans.com

A BEAUTIFUL EXTERIOR PORCH, WHICH WRAPS AROUND SLIGHTLY, enhances the charm of this quaint plan. An enchanting blend of siding and brick create a familial atmosphere. Arched windows decorate the outside and illuminate the living spaces inside. Enter into the living room and relax by the cheerful corner fireplace. Nearby, the kitchen with its island snack bar and adjoining dining room supports both informal and formal occasions. Three family bedrooms share a full hall bath a half-flight of stairs up from the living room.

HPK1200158

Style: SW Contemporary

Square Footage: 1,375

Bedrooms: 3

Bathrooms: 3

Width: 44' - 0"

Depth: 52' - 4"

Foundation: Slab

eplans.com

HERE'S A TRADITIONAL DESIGN THAT WILL BE ECONOMICAL TO BUILD and a pleasure to own. The front door opens into a spacious living room with sloped ceiling, corner fireplace, and sliding glass doors to the covered porch. The nearby L-shaped kitchen easily serves a dining room with coffered ceiling. A few steps away is the cozy media room with built-in space for audiovisual equipment. Down the hall are two bedrooms and two baths; the master bath features a whirlpool and double-sink vanity. The secondary bedroom has a full bath with linen closet. A guest room, completely separate from the main house, is found across the entry court. It includes a fireplace and sloped ceiling.

COTTAGE AND VACATION HOMES

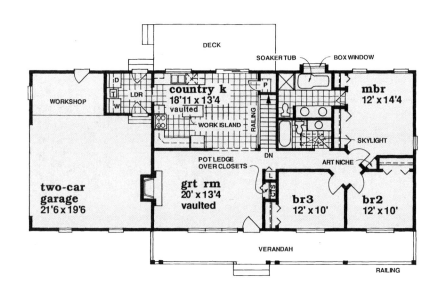

DECK

SOAKER TUB   BOX WINDOW

WORKSHOP

country k
18'11 x 13'4
vaulted

mbr
12' x 14'4

LDR

WORK ISLAND

RAILING

SKYLIGHT

POT LEDGE
OVER CLOSETS

DN

ART NICHE

two-car
garage
21'6 x 19'6

grt rm
20' x 13'4
vaulted

br3
12' x 10'

br2
12' x 10'

VERANDAH

RAILING

OPTIONAL LAYOUT

AN EYEBROW DORMER AND A LARGE VERANDA
give guests a warm country greeting outside; inside,
vaulted ceilings lend a sense of spaciousness to this
three-bedroom home. A bright country kitchen boasts
an abundance of counter space and cupboards. The
front entry is sheltered by a broad veranda. Built-in
amenities adorn the interior, including a pot shelf over
the entry coat closet, an art niche, a skylight, and a
walk-in pantry and island workstation in the kitchen. A
box-bay window and a spa-style tub highlight
the master suite. The two-car garage provides a workshop area.

HOME PLAN

HPK1200164

Style: Ranch

Square Footage: 1,408

Bedrooms: 3

Bathrooms: 2

Width: 70' - 0"

Depth: 34' - 0"

Foundation: Unfinished
Basement, Crawlspace

eplans.com

HPK1200188

HOME PLAN

Style: Country Cottage

Square Footage: 1,477

Bonus Space: 283 sq. ft.

Bedrooms: 3

Bathrooms: 2

Width: 51' - 0"

Depth: 51' - 4"

Foundation: Crawlspace, Unfinished Walkout Basement

eplans.com

THIS ADORABLE THREE-BEDROOM HOME WILL PROVIDE A PLEASANT ATMOSPHERE for your family. The communal living areas reside on the left side of the plan. The L-shaped kitchen includes a serving bar that opens to the dining area. The vaulted family room features a fireplace and leads to the sleeping quarters. A master suite and vaulted master bath will pamper homeowners. Two family bedrooms reside across the hall and share a full hall bath. Upstairs, an optional fourth bedroom and full bath are perfect for guests.

FIRST FLOOR

SECOND FLOOR

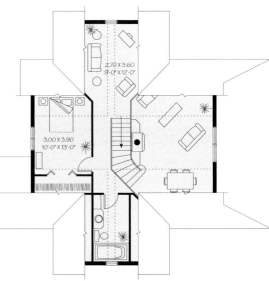

PILLARS, A LARGE FRONT PORCH, AND PLENTY OF WINDOW VIEWS lend a classic feel to this lovely country cottage. Inside, the entry room has a coat closet and an interior entry door to eliminate drafts. The light-filled L-shaped kitchen lies conveniently near the entrance. A large room adjacent to the kitchen serves as a dining and living area where a fireplace adds warmth. A master suite boasts a walk-in closet and full bath. The second floor holds a loft, a second bedroom, and a full bath.

HPK1200167

Style: Cape Cod

First Floor: 1,024 sq. ft.

Second Floor: 456 sq. ft.

Total: 1,480 sq. ft.

Bedrooms: 2

Bathrooms: 2

Width: 32' - 0"

Depth: 40' - 0"

Foundation: Finished Walkout Basement

eplans.com

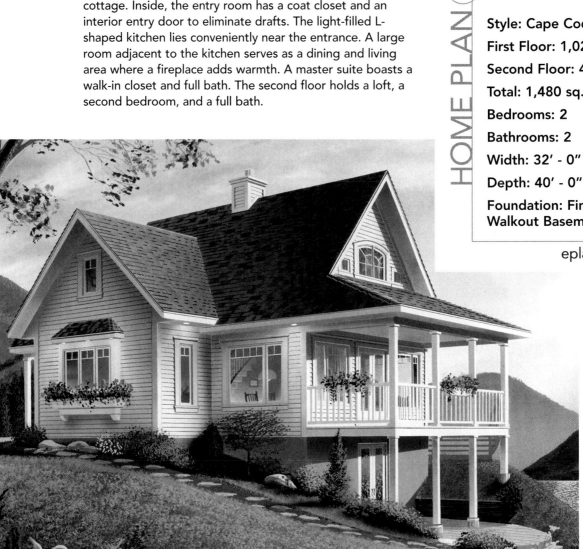

HOME PLAN

(#) HPK1200197

Style: Cape Cod

First Floor: 908 sq. ft.

Second Floor: 576 sq. ft.

Total: 1,484 sq. ft.

Bedrooms: 3

Bathrooms: 2

Width: 26' - 0"

Depth: 36' - 0"

Foundation: Finished Walkout Basement

eplans.com

HERE'S A FAVORITE WATERFRONT HOME WITH PLENTY OF SPACE to kick back and relax. A lovely sunroom opens from the dining room and allows great views. An angled hearth warms the living and dining areas. Three lovely windows brighten the dining space, which leads out to a stunning sunporch. The gourmet kitchen has an island counter with a snack bar. The first-floor master bedroom enjoys a walk-in closet and a nearby bath. Upstairs, a spacious bath with a whirlpool tub is thoughtfully placed between two bedrooms. A daylight basement allows a lower-level portico.

FIRST FLOOR

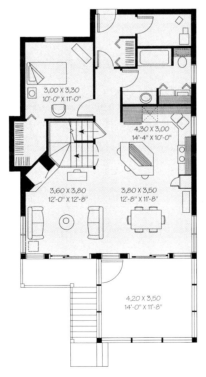

SECOND FLOOR

THIS VACATION HOME ENJOYS A SCREENED PORCH and sits on stilts to avoid any water damage. Truly a free-flowing plan, the dining room, living room, and kitchen share a common space with no walls separating them. An island snack counter in the kitchen provides plenty of space for food preparation. A family bedroom and full bath complete the first level. Upstairs, two additional bedrooms—with ample closet space—share a lavish bath that includes a whirlpool tub and separate shower.

FIRST FLOOR

SECOND FLOOR

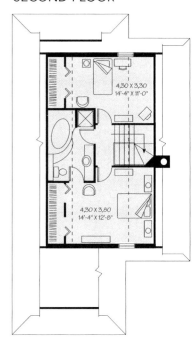

HPK1200199

Style: Resort Lifestyles

First Floor: 908 sq. ft.

Second Floor: 576 sq. ft.

Total: 1,484 sq. ft.

Bedrooms: 3

Bathrooms: 2

Width: 26' - 0"

Depth: 36' - 0"

Foundation: Unfinished Walkout Basement

eplans.com

THIS MODEST-SIZED HOUSE WITH ITS 1,499 SQUARE FEET, could hardly offer more in the way of exterior charm and interior livability. Measuring only 60 feet in width means it will not require a huge, expensive piece of property. The orientation of the garage and the front drive court are features which promote an economical use of property. In addition to the separate formal living and dining rooms, there is the informal kitchen/family room area. Note the beam ceiling, fireplace, sliding glass doors, and eating area in the family room.

HPK1200183

Style: European Cottage

Square Footage: 1,499

Bedrooms: 3

Bathrooms: 2 ½

Width: 60' - 0"

Depth: 58' - 0"

Foundation: Crawlspace, Unfinished Basement

eplans.com

OPTIONAL BASEMENT

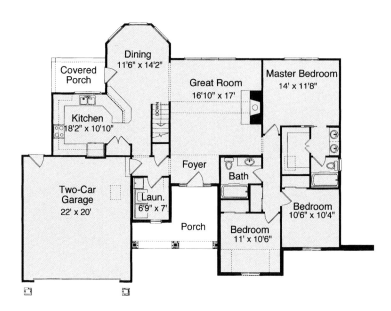

Dining
11'6" x 14'2"

Covered
Porch

Great Room
16'10" x 17'

Master Bedroom
14' x 11'8"

DOWN

Kitchen
18'2" x 10'10"

Two-Car
Garage
22' x 20'

Laun.
6'9" x 7'

Foyer

Bath

Bedroom
10'6" x 10'4"

Porch

Bedroom
11' x 10'6"

SIDING AND STONE WITH AN ARCHED WINDOW AND CEDAR SIDING create a charming exterior on this one-level home. A sloped ceiling in the great room rises two-and-a-half feet above the standard eight-foot ceiling height while a grand opening between the great room and dining area visually expands the living space. A spacious kitchen with an abundance of counter space, a pantry, and snack bar create a delightful place to prepare meals. The master bedroom enjoys a private bath with a double-bowl vanity and large walk-in closet. Two additional bedrooms and a full basement complete this delightful home.

HOME PLAN

 # HPK1200195

Style: Country Cottage

Square Footage: 1,509

Bedrooms: 3

Bathrooms: 2

Width: 59' - 4"

Depth: 46' - 4"

Foundation: Unfinished Basement

eplans.com

HOME PLAN

HPK1200156

Style: Traditional

First Floor: 1,047 sq. ft.

Second Floor: 467 sq. ft.

Total: 1,514 sq. ft.

Bonus Space: 518 sq. ft.

Bedrooms: 3

Bathrooms: 2 ½

Width: 45' - 0"

Depth: 55' - 0"

eplans.com

A TRADITIONAL EXTERIOR WITH A BEAUTIFUL PALLADIAN WINDOW on the second level gives this home a layer of elegance. A covered porch invites guests in to the living room featuring a corner fireplace. Down the hall the large walk-through kitchen services the multi-windowed dining area. The master bedroom takes up the entire right wing and enjoys access to the rear porch. A laundry room and half bath are conveniently located. Two family bedrooms, a bath, and two unfinished storage areas complete the second floor.

FIRST FLOOR

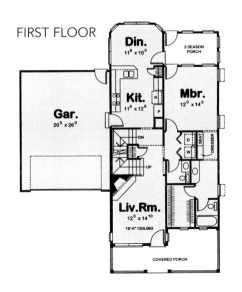

SECOND FLOOR

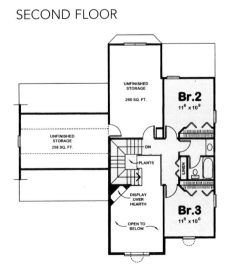

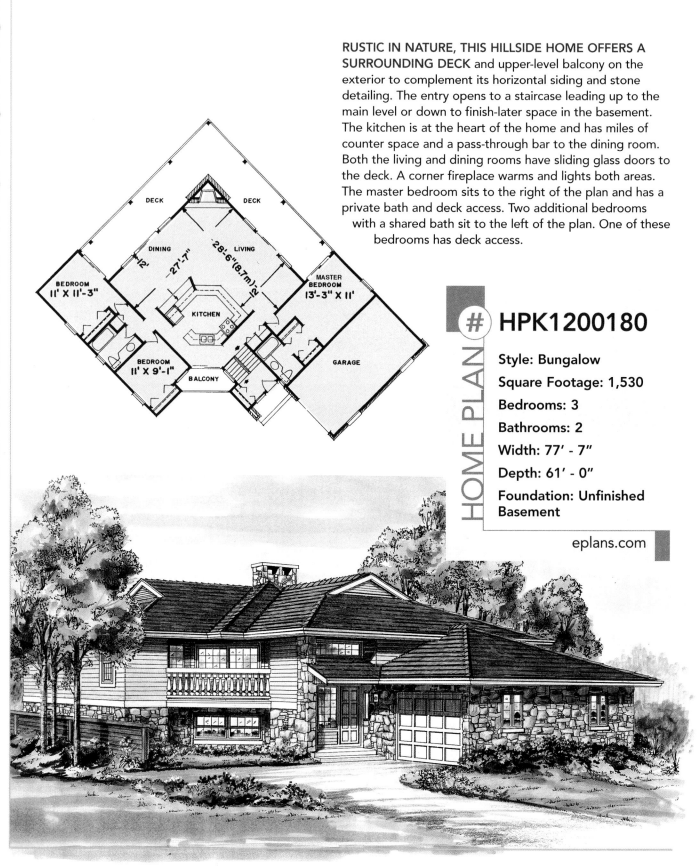

RUSTIC IN NATURE, THIS HILLSIDE HOME OFFERS A SURROUNDING DECK and upper-level balcony on the exterior to complement its horizontal siding and stone detailing. The entry opens to a staircase leading up to the main level or down to finish-later space in the basement. The kitchen is at the heart of the home and has miles of counter space and a pass-through bar to the dining room. Both the living and dining rooms have sliding glass doors to the deck. A corner fireplace warms and lights both areas. The master bedroom sits to the right of the plan and has a private bath and deck access. Two additional bedrooms with a shared bath sit to the left of the plan. One of these bedrooms has deck access.

HOME PLAN

HPK1200180

Style: Bungalow

Square Footage: 1,530

Bedrooms: 3

Bathrooms: 2

Width: 77' - 7"

Depth: 61' - 0"

Foundation: Unfinished Basement

eplans.com

HPK1200148

Style: Contemporary

First Floor: 952 sq. ft.

Second Floor: 604 sq. ft.

Total: 1,556 sq. ft.

Bedrooms: 3

Bathrooms: 2

Width: 37' - 0"

Depth: 30' - 8"

Foundation: Unfinished Basement

HOME PLAN

eplans.com

THIS CONTEMPORARY FOUR-SEASON COTTAGE OFFERS PLENTY OF WINDOWS to take in great views. Excellent for gatherings, the living room boasts a cathedral ceiling and a cozy fireplace. The compartmented entry features a coat closet. The U-shaped kitchen includes a built-in pantry, which opens to a side porch. Upstairs, two family bedrooms share a hall bath. A balcony hall leads to a sitting area with views of the front property.

FIRST FLOOR

SECOND FLOOR

MAIN LEVEL

3,00 X 3,40
10'-0" X 11'-4"

5,40 X 3,40
18'-0" X 11'-4"

3,90 X 3,40
13'-0" X 11'-4"

LOWER LEVEL

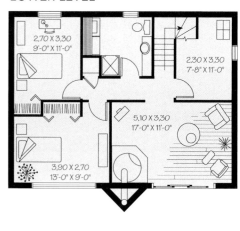

2,70 X 3,30
9'-0" X 11'-0"

2,30 X 3,30
7'-8" X 11'-0"

5,10 X 3,30
17'-0" X 11'-0"

3,90 X 2,70
13'-0" X 9'-0"

HOME PLAN #

HPK1200181

Style: European Cottage

Main Level: 787 sq. ft.

Lower Level: 787 sq. ft.

Total: 1,574 sq. ft.

Bedrooms: 3

Bathrooms: 2

Width: 32' - 4"

Depth: 24' - 4"

Foundation: Unfinished Walkout Basement

eplans.com

THIS MOUNTAIN-TOP CHALET TAKES ADVANTAGE OF VIEWS with tall floor-to-ceiling windows. A central fireplace runs straight up from the lower-level family room to the living/dining room as a visual statement of warmth. A large efficient kitchen, living room, dining area, bedroom, and full bath complete the main level. Downstairs, two bedrooms share a full bath and a laundry room. A family room accesses the patio through sliding glass doors.

STONE-AND-WOOD SIDING ECHO THE GREAT OUTDOORS in this design. A small porch is perfect for dusting off the snow and stargazing on dark winter nights. Inside, a fireplace warms up the living room. The kitchen provides an area for a dining table, plenty of work space, and storage with a corner window sink. The master bedroom enjoys a spacious walk-in closet and is serviced by a full bath with a dual-sink vanity. On the second level, two family bedrooms share a full bath and the loft overlook to the living room.

HOME PLAN

HPK1200210

Style: Resort Lifestyles

First Floor: 1,108 sq. ft.

Second Floor: 517 sq. ft.

Total: 1,625 sq. ft.

Bedrooms: 3

Bathrooms: 2

Width: 36' - 0"

Depth: 36' - 0"

Foundation: Unfinished Basement

eplans.com

COTTAGE AND VACATION HOMES

FIRST FLOOR

4,20 X 3,60
14'-0" X 12'-0"

6,00 X 4,20
20'-0" X 14'-0"

3,90 X 5,10
13'-0" X 17'-0"

SECOND FLOOR

3,00 X 3,50
10'-0" X 11'-8"

3,60 X 3,50
12'-0" X 11'-8"

FIRST FLOOR

BEDROOM 1
11'-10" x 10'-0"

BEDROOM 2
11'-4" x 10'-0"

COATS

LINEN

PANTRY

DECK/PATIO
11'-6" x 18'-8"

GREAT ROOM
27'-4" x 29'-5"
20' HIGH CEILING

VAULT   VAULT

DECK
7'-6" x 36'-0"

PORCH
24'-4" x 7'-6"

SECOND FLOOR

VAULT   LOFT   VAULT
23'-1" x 15'-6"

40" KNEE WALL

OPEN BELOW
20' HIGH CEILING

VAULT   VAULT

WITHIN THIS COMPACT AND SIMPLE DESIGN, you'll find a comfortable and welcome vacation retreat. The handsome exterior is constructed with board and batten siding, standing seam metal roofing, and stone accents on the porch and chimney. From the delightful covered front porch, enter an enormous great room with a 20-foot vaulted ceiling. Within the great room is an open kitchen with an island and breakfast bar. Just beyond, a compartmentalized bath with doors allows wheelchair access. The large pantry area provides space for a stacked washer/dryer unit. Two bedrooms with eight-foot-high ceilings, complete the lower level. Upstairs, an enormous loft with an 11-foot-high ceiling overlooks the great room. This multipurpose area provides an abundance of additional sleeping and recreation space. Three large fixed glass windows provided by each gable lends plenty of light for the loft and great room.

HOME PLAN

HPK1200201

Style: Lakefront

First Floor: 1,288 sq. ft.

Second Floor: 359 sq. ft.

Total: 1,647 sq. ft.

Bedrooms: 2

Bathrooms: 1

Width: 28' - 0"

Depth: 46' - 8"

Foundation: Slab

eplans.com

HOME PLAN

(#) HPK1200165

Style: Seaside

First Floor: 1,122 sq. ft.

Second Floor: 528 sq. ft.

Total: 1,650 sq. ft.

Bedrooms: 4

Bathrooms: 2

Width: 34' - 0"

Depth: 52' - 5"

Foundation: Pier

eplans.com

THIS LOVELY SEASIDE VACATION HOME IS PERFECT FOR SEASONAL FAMILY GETAWAYS or for the family that lives coastal year round. The spacious front deck is great for private sunbathing or outdoor barbecues, providing breathtaking ocean views. The two-story living room is warmed by a fireplace on breezy beach nights, and the island kitchen overlooks the open dining area nearby. Two first-floor family bedrooms share a hall bath. Upstairs, the master bedroom features a walk-in closet, dressing area with a vanity, and access to a whirlpool tub shared with an additional family bedroom.

FIRST FLOOR

Porch 12'x 9'5"

Kitchen 8'8"x 18'

Bedroom 13'x 10'11"

Dining 11'6"x 18'

Living 16'6"x 14'5"

Bedroom 13'x 10'9"

Porch 20'6"x 5'

Deck 34'x 10'

SECOND FLOOR

Bedroom 14'x 11'2"

Open to Below

Master Bedroom 13'x 13'6"

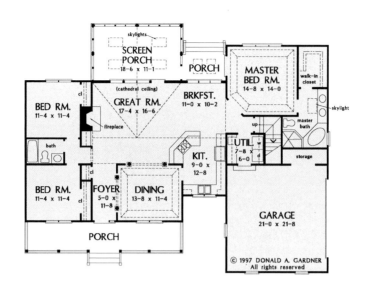

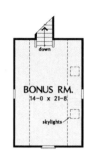

A CLASSIC COUNTRY EXTERIOR ENRICHES THE APPEARANCE of this economical home. A grand front porch and two skylit back porches encourage weekend relaxation. The great room features a cathedral ceiling and a fireplace with adjacent built-ins. The master suite enjoys a double-door entry, back-porch access, and a tray ceiling. The master bath has a garden tub set in the corner, a separate shower, twin vanities, and a skylight. Loads of storage, an open floor plan, and walls of windows make this three-bedroom plan very livable.

HOME PLAN

HPK1200173

Style: Country Cottage
Square Footage: 1,652
Bonus Space: 367 sq. ft.
Bedrooms: 3
Bathrooms: 2
Width: 64' - 4"
Depth: 51' - 0"

eplans.com

HPK1200147

Style: Seaside

First Floor: 731 sq. ft.

Second Floor: 935 sq. ft.

Total: 1,666 sq. ft.

Bedrooms: 3

Bathrooms: 3

Width: 35' - 0"

Depth: 38' - 0"

Foundation: Pier

eplans.com

THIS PIER-FOUNDATION HOME HAS AN ABUNDANCE OF AMENITIES to offer, not the least being the loft lookout. Inside, the living room is complete with a corner gas fireplace. The spacious kitchen features a cooktop island, an adjacent breakfast nook, and easy access to the dining room. From this room, a set of French doors leads out to a small deck—perfect for dining alfresco. Upstairs, the sleeping zone consists of two family bedrooms sharing a full hall bath, and a deluxe master suite. Amenities in this suite include two walk-in closets and a private bath.

FIRST FLOOR

SECOND FLOOR

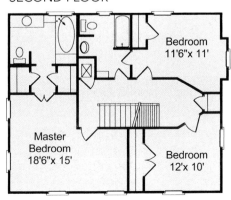

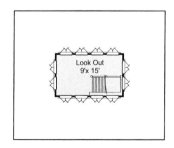

FIRST FLOOR

SECOND FLOOR

HPK1200154

Style: Farmhouse

First Floor: 1,093 sq. ft.

Second Floor: 576 sq. ft.

Total: 1,669 sq. ft.

Bedrooms: 3

Bathrooms: 2

Width: 52' - 0"

Depth: 46' - 0"

Foundation: Crawlspace

eplans.com

HERE'S A GREAT COUNTRY FARMHOUSE with a lot of contemporary appeal. The generous use of windows—including two sets of triple muntin windows in the front—adds exciting visual elements to the exterior as well as plenty of natural light to the interior. An impressive tiled entry opens to a two-story great room with a raised hearth and views to the front and side grounds. The U-shaped kitchen conveniently combines with this area and offers a snack counter in addition to a casual dining nook with rear-porch access. The family bedrooms reside on the main level. An expansive master suite with an adjacent study creates a resplendent retreat upstairs, complete with a private balcony, walk-in closet, and bath.

HOME PLAN

HPK1200175

Style: Vacation

First Floor: 1,094 sq. ft.

Second Floor: 576 sq. ft.

Total: 1,670 sq. ft.

Bedrooms: 3

Bathrooms: 2

Width: 43' - 0"

Depth: 35' - 4"

Foundation: Crawlspace

eplans.com

A COVERED VERANDA WITH COVERED PATIO above opens through French doors to the living/dining area of this vacation cottage. A masonry fireplace with a wood storage bin warms this area. A modified U-shaped kitchen serves the dining room; a laundry is just across the hall with access to a side veranda. The master bedroom is on the first floor and has the use of a full bath. Sliding glass doors in the master bedroom and the living room lead to still another veranda. The second floor has two family bedrooms, a full bath, a family room with a balcony overlooking the living room and dining room, a fireplace, and double doors to a patio. A large storage area on this level adds convenience.

FIRST FLOOR

SECOND FLOOR

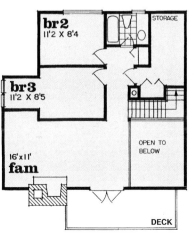

FIRST FLOOR

SECOND FLOOR

BRACKETS AND BALUSTRADES ON FRONT AND REAR COVERED PORCHES spell old-fashioned country charm on this rustic retreat. Warm evenings will invite family and guests outdoors for watching sunsets and stars. In cooler weather, the raised-hearth fireplace will make the great room a cozy place to gather. The nearby kitchen serves both a snack bar and a breakfast nook. Two family bedrooms and a full bath complete the main level. Upstairs, a master suite with a sloped ceiling offers a window seat and a complete bath. The adjacent loft/study overlooks the great room.

HOME PLAN

HPK1200190

Style: **Farmhouse**

First Floor: **1,093 sq. ft.**

Second Floor: **580 sq. ft.**

Total: **1,673 sq. ft.**

Bedrooms: **3**

Bathrooms: **2**

Width: **36' - 0"**

Depth: **52' - 0"**

Foundation: **Crawlspace**

eplans.com

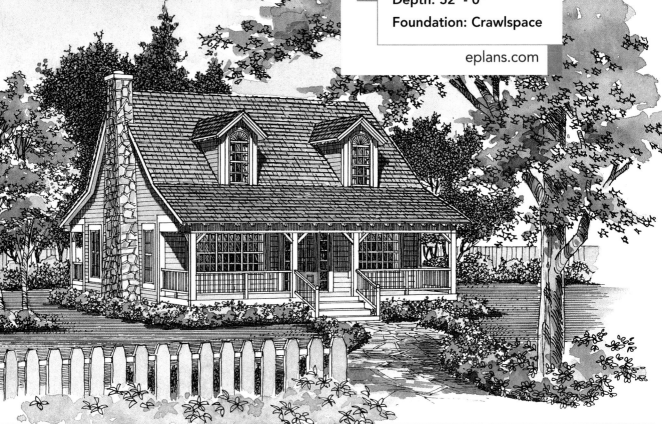

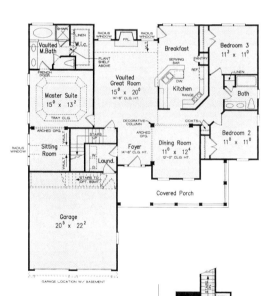

GARAGE LOCATION W/ BASEMENT

Opt. Bonus
12⁵ x 20⁹

OPTIONAL BONUS ROOM PLAN

HPK1200161

Style: Country Cottage

Square Footage: 1,749

Bonus Space: 308 sq. ft.

Bedrooms: 3

Bathrooms: 2

Width: 54' - 0"

Depth: 56' - 6"

Foundation: Crawlspace, Unfinished Walkout Basement

eplans.com

THIS COZY COUNTRY COTTAGE IS ENHANCED with a front-facing planter box above the garage and a charming covered porch. The foyer leads to a vaulted great room, complete with a fireplace and radius windows. Decorative columns complement the entrance to the dining room, as does a decorative arch. On the left side of the plan resides the master suite, which is resplendent with amenities including a vaulted sitting room with an arched opening, tray ceiling, and French doors to the vaulted full bath. On the right side, two additional bedrooms share a full bath.

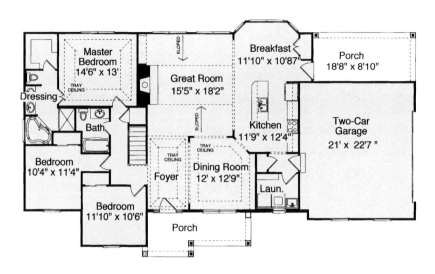

Master Bedroom
14'6" x 13'
TRAY CEILING

Dressing

Bath

Bedroom
10'4" x 11'4"

Bedroom
11'10" x 10'6"

Foyer
TRAY CEILING

Great Room
15'5" x 18'2"
SLOPED

Dining Room
12' x 12'9"
TRAY CEILING

Porch

Breakfast
11'10" x 10'87"

Kitchen
11'9" x 12'4"

Laun.

Porch
18'8" x 8'10"

Two-Car Garage
21' x 22'7"

HOME PLAN (#) HPK1200172

Style: Country Cottage

Square Footage: 1,751

Bedrooms: 3

Bathrooms: 2

Width: 72' - 6"

Depth: 42' - 3"

Foundation: Unfinished Basement

eplans.com

EXCITING CEILING TREATMENTS AND AN OPEN FLOOR PLAN create a feeling of spaciousness in this lovely three-bedroom home. The foyer, dining room, and master bedroom all enjoy nine-foot ceilings; in the great room, a dramatic sloped ceiling soars to 12 feet. A covered porch greets guests and a second porch, off the breakfast area, visually expands the home and enhances outdoor enjoyment. The master suite offers comfort and luxury, with a whirlpool tub, shower, and double vanity. A full basement can be finished at a later date as your family grows.

HOME PLAN

HPK1200362

Style: Farmhouse

Square Footage: 1,782

Bedrooms: 3

Bathrooms: 2

Width: 40' - 0"

Depth: 61' - 0"

Foundation: Slab

eplans.com

THIS DELIGHTFUL ONE-AND-A-HALF STORY PLAN HAS A FORMAL LIVING AND DINING AREA for evening entertainment and boasts a huge family gathering space. Designed for efficiency, the two secondary bedrooms have private entrances off the formal living area. The master suite has all of the features of a larger home including a soaking tub, a large walk-in shower, and a private toilet area. The kitchen is at the heart of the home with a bay-windowed breakfast area adjacent to the efficient laundry room. A loft area on the second floor provides additional space for the growing family. Included in the blueprints are details for two different exteriors.

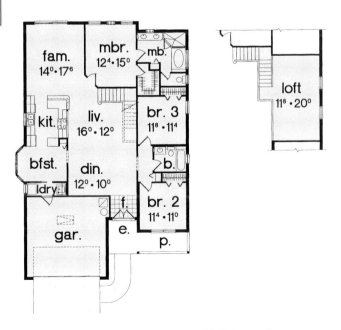

FIRST FLOOR

BASEMENT

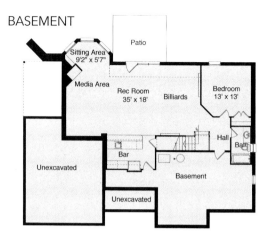

Dining Area
12' x 14'7"

Porch
9' x 14'

Great Room
17'2" x 18'4"

Master Bedroom
15'1" x 13'4"

Kitchen
16'3" x 10'4"

WIC

Two-Car
Garage
20' x 26'6"

Laun.
6' x 8'

Foyer

Bath

Hall

Bedroom
11'8" x 11

Porch

Bedroom
13' x 11'

Sitting Area
9'2" x 5'7"

Patio

Media Area

Rec Room
35' x 18'

Billiards

Bedroom
13' x 13'

Bar

Hall

Bath

Unexcavated

Basement

Unexcavated

HOME PLAN

HPK1200174

Style: Country Cottage

Square Footage: 1,794

Bedrooms: 3

Bathrooms: 2

Width: 59' - 8"

Depth: 48' - 3"

Foundation: Finished
Walkout Basement

eplans.com

MULTIPLE GABLES AND A BRICK-AND-STONE FACADE WITH WOOD TRIM and dormers decorate the exterior of this enchanting one-level home. An open floor plan allows the great room, with sloped ceiling and fireplace, to interact with the kitchen and dining area for everyday enjoyment. Angles, seating at the snack bar, French doors to a covered porch, and a nine-foot ceiling combine to create spectacular surroundings. The master bedroom enjoys a private bath with shower enclosure, double-bowl vanity, and walk-in closet. A finished basement plan comes with these drawings and includes a media area, billiards space, wet bar, and an extra bedroom with bath. All of these wonderful amenities create a home perfect for the first-time buyer, growing family, or empty-nester market.

HPK1200191

Style: NW Contemporary
First Floor: 1,157 sq. ft.
Second Floor: 638 sq. ft.
Total: 1,795 sq. ft.
Bedrooms: 3
Bathrooms: 2 ½
Width: 36' - 0"
Depth: 40' - 0"
Foundation: Crawlspace, Unfinished Basement

eplans.com

WHEN YOU LOOK AT THIS HOUSE YOU CAN'T HELP BUT SEE IT SETTLED DEEP IN A WOODSY RETREAT AREA or nestled by a lake where views through the large expanse of front windows will be fully enjoyed. A sunken spa on the front deck is a treat, but the rear deck will ensure that you don't miss any angle of views. The vaulted living and dining rooms are separated from the kitchen—with a serving/eating counter—by attractive wood columns. The master bedroom is on the first floor with a private bath. The half-bath and laundry room round out the main floor. Upstairs are two more bedrooms—for family or visiting friends—and a full bath. A loft and decorative plant ledges complete the relaxing second floor.

FIRST FLOOR

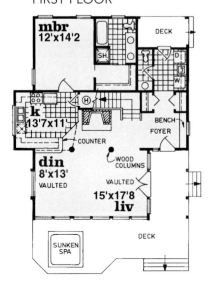

SECOND FLOOR

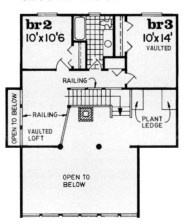

FIRST FLOOR

SECOND FLOOR

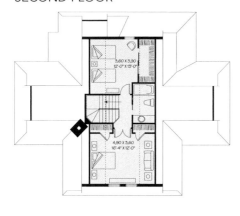

THIS COMFORTABLE VACATION DESIGN PRO-VIDES TWO LEVELS of relaxing family space. The main level offers a spacious wrapping front porch and an abundance of windows, filling interior spaces with the summer sunshine. A two-sided fireplace warms the living room/dining room combination and a master bedroom that features a roomy walk-in closet. Nearby, the hall bath offers a relaxing whirlpool tub. The kitchen is open and features an island snack bar and pantry storage. A cozy sunroom accesses the wrapping deck. Upstairs, two additional bedrooms feature ample closet space and share a second-floor bath.

HOME PLAN

HPK1200144

Style: Lakefront

First Floor: 1,212 sq. ft.

Second Floor: 620 sq. ft.

Total: 1,832 sq. ft.

Bedrooms: 3

Bathrooms: 2

Width: 38' - 0"

Depth: 40' - 0"

Foundation: Unfinished Walkout Basement

eplans.com

HOME PLAN

(#) HPK1200373

Style: Floridian

First Floor: 1,342 sq. ft.

Second Floor: 511 sq. ft.

Total: 1,853 sq. ft.

Bedrooms: 3

Bathrooms: 2

Width: 44' - 0"

Depth: 40' - 0"

Foundation: Pier

eplans.com

AMENITIES ABOUND in this delightful two-story home. The foyer opens directly into the fantastic grand room, which offers a warming fireplace and two sets of double doors to the rear deck. The dining room also accesses this deck and a second deck shared with Bedroom 2. A convenient kitchen and another bedroom also reside on this level. Upstairs, the master bedroom reigns supreme. Entered through double doors, it pampers with a luxurious bath, walk-in closet, morning kitchen, and private observation deck.

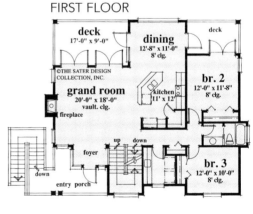

FIRST FLOOR

deck 17'-0" x 9'-0"

dining 12'-8" x 11'-0" 8' clg.

deck

©THE SATER DESIGN COLLECTION, INC.

grand room 20'-0" x 18'-0" vault. clg.

fireplace

kitchen 11' x 12'

br. 2 12'-0" x 11'-8" 8' clg.

up   down

foyer

down

entry porch

br. 3 12'-0" x 10'-0" 8' clg.

SECOND FLOOR

observation deck

master 13'-0" x 14'-0" vault. clg.

am kitchen

open to grand room below

down

BASEMENT

garage 40'-0" x 20'-0" avg.

storage 13'-0" x 18'-0" avg.

stor./bonus 20'-0" x 20'-0"

up   stor.

up

lattice work panel walls

HOME PLAN

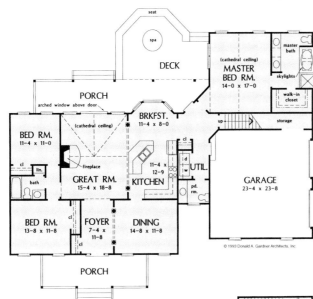

HPK1200193

Style: Farmhouse

Square Footage: 1,864

Bonus Space: 420 sq. ft.

Bedrooms: 3

Bathrooms: 2 ½

Width: 71' - 0"

Depth: 56' - 4"

eplans.com

QUAINT AND COZY ON THE OUTSIDE WITH PORCHES FRONT AND BACK, this three-bedroom country home surprises with an open floor plan featuring a large great room with a cathedral ceiling. A central kitchen with an angled counter opens to the breakfast and great rooms for easy entertaining. The privately located master bedroom enjoys a cathedral ceiling and access to the deck. Two secondary bedrooms share a full hall bath. A bonus room makes expanding easy.

FIRST FLOOR

SECOND FLOOR

THIS CAPTIVATING THREE-BEDROOM HOME COMBINES THE RUSTIC, EARTHY FEEL of cut stone with the crisp look of siding to create a design that will be the hallmark of your neighborhood. From the impressive two-story foyer, the vaulted family room lies straight ahead. The extended-hearth fireplace can be viewed from the kitchen via a serving bar that accesses the breakfast nook. The vaulted dining room is an elegant space for formal occasions. The first-floor master suite includes a pampering bath and dual walk-in closets, one with linen storage. Upstairs, a short hall and family-room overlook separate the bedrooms. Bonus space can serve as a home office, playroom... anything your family desires.

HPK1200187

HOME PLAN

Style: Country Cottage

First Floor: 1,407 sq. ft.

Second Floor: 472 sq. ft.

Total: 1,879 sq. ft.

Bonus Space: 321 sq. ft.

Bedrooms: 3

Bathrooms: 2 ½

Width: 48' - 0"

Depth: 53' - 10"

Foundation: Crawlspace, Unfinished Walkout Basement

eplans.com

FIRST FLOOR

SECOND FLOOR

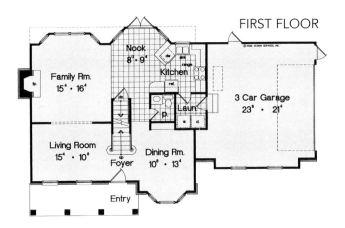

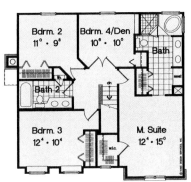

A BAY WINDOW, BRICK-AND-SIDING FACADE, AND CURVED ARCHES BETWEEN COLUMNS at the front porch create the feel of a bright, fresh morning. Inside, bay windows add light and dimension to the family room, breakfast nook, and dining room. The living room has lovely views of the front yard and porch. A fireplace warms the family room for cozy winter evenings. A powder room sits between the kitchen and dining room for the convenience of guests. Upstairs, three family bedrooms sharing a full bath join the master suite and its luxurious bath.

HOME PLAN

HPK1200363

Style: Farmhouse

First Floor: 946 sq. ft.

Second Floor: 933 sq. ft.

Total: 1,879 sq. ft.

Bedrooms: 4

Bathrooms: 2 ½

Width: 55' - 4"

Depth: 35' - 0"

Foundation: Slab, Unfinished Basement

eplans.com

A UNIQUE DESIGN LIKE THIS ONE IS ABSOLUTELY PLEASING TO THE EYE, and the floor plan satisfies livability. The front porch permits room for a rocking chair or even a hammock to enjoy the evening sunsets. Just through the entry is the dining area and a room that may serve as a bedroom or a living area. The family room is the heart of this home, easily serviced by the kitchen and eating area. The master bedroom provides a private bath and a walk-in closet, and two family bedrooms enjoy a balcony and full private baths.

(#) HPK1200206

Style: Traditional

First Floor: 1,320 sq. ft.

Second Floor: 636 sq. ft.

Total: 1,956 sq. ft.

Bedrooms: 3

Bathrooms: 4

Width: 56' - 0"

Depth: 61' - 0"

Foundation: Unfinished Basement, Crawlspace, Slab

eplans.com

FIRST FLOOR

garage 22 x 22

sto 10 x 6

porch 19 x 7

mbr 17 x 13

eat 9 x 9

kit

family 18 x 15

bath

up

util

dining 12 x 11

entry

living /br 4 12 x 11

clo

porch 43 x 7

SECOND FLOOR

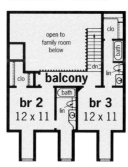

open to family room below

clo

bath

clo

balcony

br 2 12 x 11

bath

br 3 12 x 11

OPTIONAL LAYOUT

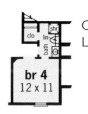

clo

lin

shr

bath

br 4 12 x 11

BALUSTRADES AND BRACKETS, DUAL BAL-CONIES, AND A WRAPAROUND PORCH create a country-style exterior reminiscent of soft summer evenings spent watching fireflies and sipping tea. The tiled foyer opens to the two-story great room filled with light from six windows and a fireplace. The sunny bayed nook shares its natural light with the snack counter and kitchen. A spacious master suite occupies a bay window and offers a sumptuous bath. Upstairs, two family bedrooms—each with a private balcony and a walk-in closet—share a full bath.

FIRST FLOOR

HPK1200196

Style: Farmhouse

First Floor: 1,374 sq. ft.

Second Floor: 600 sq. ft.

Total: 1,974 sq. ft.

Bedrooms: 3

Bathrooms: 2 ½

Width: 51' - 8"

Depth: 50' - 8"

Foundation: Unfinished Basement

eplans.com

SECOND FLOOR

HOME PLAN

#HPK1200204

Style: Country Cottage

Square Footage: 1,991

Bonus Space: 938 sq. ft.

Bedrooms: 3

Bathrooms: 2 ½

Width: 60' - 0"

Depth: 57' - 6"

Foundation: Crawlspace, Slab, Unfinished Basement

eplans.com

THIS CHARMING DESIGN IS ACCENTED WITH AN ARRAY OF COUNTRY COMPLEMENTS. The front porch welcomes you inside to a foyer flanked on either side by a dining room and study. The family room features a fireplace and views of the rear deck. Two family bedrooms sharing a Jack-and-Jill bath are located to the right of the plan. The island kitchen easily serves the breakfast nook. The master bedroom enjoys a private bath and walk-in closet. The garage features extra storage space. The second-floor option provides plans for two more bedrooms, a hall bath, and a game room.

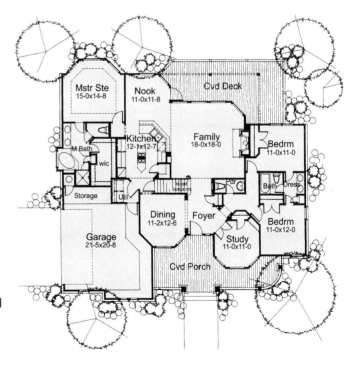

OPTIONAL LAYOUT

opt. Utility

OPTIONAL LAYOUT

opt. Bath

A BRILLIANT USE OF INTERIOR PLANNING AND A STUNNING FACADE challenge this functional home's modest square footage. A triplet of arches begin the inviting porch; from here, enter to a vaulted foyer that continues into the vaulted dining room on the right. Ahead, the great room is lit by radius windows and warmed by a fireplace. The kitchen is efficient, yet spacious, easily serving the breakfast nook and dining room. The master suite is on the left, decked out with a tray ceiling, vaulted bath, and ample walk-in closet. Two additional bedrooms share a full bath to the rear of the plan; a fourth bedroom (or make it a study) is at the front of the home, graced by a Palladian window. Optional space over the garage would make an ideal guest suite.

HPK1200153

Style: Country Cottage

Square Footage: 1,996

Bonus Space: 258 sq. ft.

Bedrooms: 4

Bathrooms: 3

Width: 60' - 0"

Depth: 47' - 6"

Foundation: Crawlspace, Unfinished Walkout Basement

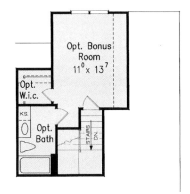

eplans.com

HOME PLAN

 # HPK1200169

Style: Vacation

First Floor: 1,182 sq. ft.

Second Floor: 838 sq. ft.

Total: 2,020 sq. ft.

Bedrooms: 4

Bathrooms: 3

Width: 34' - 0"

Depth: 52' - 0"

Foundation: Pier

eplans.com

THIS TWO-STORY COASTAL HOME FINDS ITS INSPIRATION
in a Craftsman style that's highlighted by ornamented gables. Open planning is the key with the living and dining areas sharing the front of the first floor with the U-shaped kitchen and stairway. Both the dining room and the living room access the second porch. The master suite boasts a walk-in closet, private vanity, and angled tub. The utility room is efficiently placed between the kitchen and bath. Bedrooms 2 and 3 share a bath while Bedroom 4 enjoys a private bath.

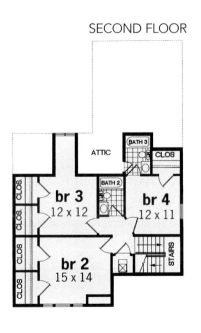

FIRST FLOOR

SECOND FLOOR

A SIX-PANEL DOOR WITH AN ARCHED TRANSOM MAKES AN IMPRESSIVE ENTRY. Upon entering the foyer, the formal dining room resides to the right. The great room comes complete with a cozy fireplace and built-ins. On the far left of the home, two bedrooms share a full bath and a linen closet. The kitchen and breakfast room provide ample space for the family to enjoy meals together. The rear porch is also accessible from a rear bedroom and from an angled door between the great room and breakfast room. In the master bedroom, two walk-in closets provide plenty of space, and two separate vanities make dressing less crowded.

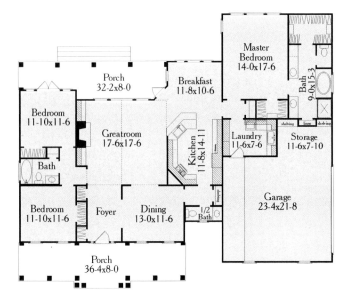

HOME PLAN

(#) HPK1200205

Style: Traditional

Square Footage: 2,046

Bedrooms: 3

Bathrooms: 2 ½

Width: 68' - 2"

Depth: 57' - 4"

Foundation: Crawlspace, Slab, Unfinished Basement

eplans.com

© 1999 Donald A. Gardner, Inc.

HOME PLAN

HPK1200179

Style: Country Cottage

Square Footage: 2,078

Bonus Space: 339 sq. ft.

Bedrooms: 3

Bathrooms: 2 ½

Width: 62' - 2"

Depth: 47' - 8"

eplans.com

©1999 Donald A. Gardner, Inc.

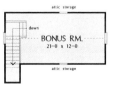

AN ENCHANTING L-SHAPED FRONT PORCH LENDS CHARM AND GRACE to this country home with dual dormers and gables. Bay windows expand both of the home's dining areas; the great room and kitchen are amplified by a shared cathedral ceiling. The generous great room features a fireplace with flanking built-ins, skylights, and access to a marvelous back porch. A cathedral ceiling enhances the master suite, which enjoys a large walk-in closet and a luxurious bath. Two more bedrooms share a generous hall bath that has a dual-sink vanity.

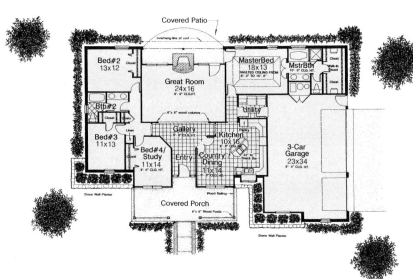

(#) HPK1200189

Style: Farmhouse

Square Footage: 2,078

Bedrooms: 4

Bathrooms: 2

Width: 75' - 0"

Depth: 47' - 10"

Foundation: Slab,
Crawlspace

eplans.com

COLONIAL STYLE MEETS FARMHOUSE CHARM IN THIS PLAN, furnishing old-fashioned charisma with a flourish. From the entry, double doors open to the country dining room and a large island kitchen. Nearby, the spacious great room takes center stage and is warmed by a fireplace flanked by large windows. Tucked behind the three-car garage, the secluded master suite features a vaulted ceiling. The master bath contains a relaxing tub, double-bowl vanity, separate shower, and compartmented toilet. Beyond the bath is a huge walk-in closet with two built-in chests. Three family bedrooms—one doubles as a study or home office—a full bath, and a utility room complete the plan.

FIRST FLOOR

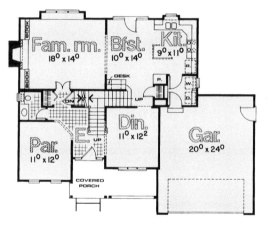

SECOND FLOOR

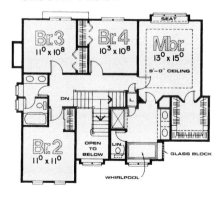

HOME PLAN

 # HPK1200186

Style: Farmhouse

First Floor: 1,082 sq. ft.

Second Floor: 1,021 sq. ft.

Total: 2,103 sq. ft.

Bedrooms: 4

Bathrooms: 2 ½

Width: 50' - 0"

Depth: 40' - 0"

eplans.com

A COVERED PORCH INVITES YOU INTO THIS COUNTRY-STYLE HOME. Handsome bookcases frame the fireplace in the spacious family room. Double doors off the entry provide the family room with added privacy. The kitchen features an island, a lazy Susan, and easy access to a walk-in laundry. The master bedroom features a boxed ceiling and separate entries to a walk-in closet and a pampering bath. The upstairs hall bath is compartmented, allowing maximum usage for today's busy family.

FIRST FLOOR

SECOND FLOOR

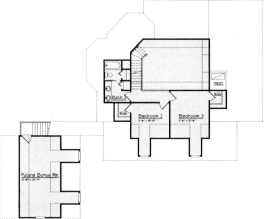

THIS ELEGANT HOME HAS MANY TRADITIONAL ARCHITECTURAL FEATURES that make it a classic. Transoms gently light the foyer and dining room. The great room with a fireplace provides convenient access to the rest of the house. A wraparound front porch and covered porch in the back provide areas for quiet relaxation. This home's most unique feature is the drive-through garage, which allows for both a courtyard and side entry. The secluded master suite resides on the first floor, and the two family bedrooms are upstairs. A bonus area above the garage can be used as an apartment for rental income, an in-law suite, teenager's bedroom, detached office/studio, or storage space.

HOME PLAN

HPK1200364

Style: Country Cottage

First Floor: 1,582 sq. ft.

Second Floor: 536 sq. ft.

Total: 2,118 sq. ft.

Bonus Space: 349 sq. ft.

Bedrooms: 3

Bathrooms: 2 ½

Width: 52' - 8"

Depth: 46' - 5"

Foundation: Slab

eplans.com

NOSTALGIC AND EARTHY, THIS CRAFTSMAN DESIGN has an attractive floor plan and thoughtful amenties. A column-lined covered porch is the perfect welcome to guests. A large vaulted family room, enhanced by a fireplace, opens to the spacious island kitchen and roomy breakfast area. The private master suite is embellished with a vaulted ceiling, walk-in closet, and vaulted super bath with French-door entry. With family in mind, two secondary bedrooms—each with a walk-in closet—share a computer workstation or loft area. A bonus room can be used as bedroom or home office.

HOME PLAN #

HPK1200151

Style: Country Cottage
First Floor: 1,561 sq. ft.
Second Floor: 578 sq. ft.
Total: 2,139 sq. ft.
Bonus Space: 284 sq. ft.
Bedrooms: 3
Bathrooms: 2 ½
Width: 50' - 0"
Depth: 57' - 0"
Foundation: Crawlspace, Finished Walkout Basement

eplans.com

FIRST FLOOR

SECOND FLOOR

THE FANCIFUL VICTORIAN DETAILS, LATTICE WORK, ORNATE COLUMNS AND RAILING, and a cupola perched atop a standing seam metal roof set the character of this charming coastal home. Entering the double front doors into the large columned foyer, one soon realizes the excitement of this floor plan. The family room features a full wall fireplace and entertainment center. The kitchen nook and dining areas offer many opportunities for entertaining with wonderful views to the exterior. The master bedroom, with spacious bath and closet area, provides for a private retreat, with windows overlooking the backyard.

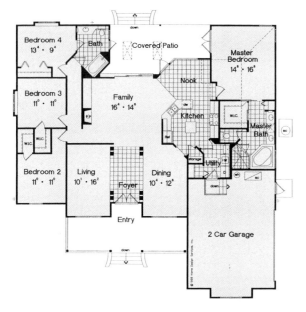

HPK1200365

HOME PLAN

Style: Victorian

Square Footage: 2,151

Bedrooms: 4

Bathrooms: 2

Width: 60' - 4"

Depth: 62' - 0"

Foundation: Slab

eplans.com

HOME PLAN

HPK1200159

Style: Country Cottage

Square Footage: 2,151

Bonus Space: 814 sq. ft.

Bedrooms: 3

Bathrooms: 2

Width: 61' - 0"

Depth: 55' - 8"

Foundation: Crawlspace, Unfinished Basement

eplans.com

COUNTRY FLAVOR IS WELL ESTABLISHED ON THIS FINE THREE-BEDROOM HOME. The covered front porch welcomes friends and family alike to the foyer, where the formal dining room opens off to the left. The vaulted ceiling in the great room enhances the warmth of the fireplace and the wall of windows. An efficient kitchen works well with the bayed breakfast area. The secluded master suite offers a walk-in closet and a lavish bath; on the other side of the home, two family bedrooms share a full bath. Upstairs, an optional fourth bedroom is available for guests or in-laws and provides access to a large recreation room.

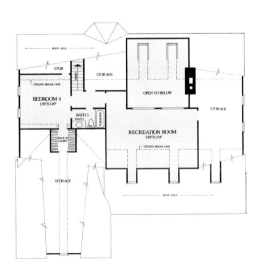

COTTAGE AND VACATION HOMES

PORCHES AND BALCONIES ARE JUST THE BEGINNING OF THE AMENITIES provided by this fine two-story home. The foyer opens to the living room, where a fireplace and built-ins create a warm ambiance. The open kitchen offers a cooktop island and leads to the dining room. Upstairs, a lavish master suite boasts a private wraparound deck, a walk-in closet, a lavish bath, and an adjacent loft—perfect for a computer room or a home office.

HPK1200207

Style: Vacation

First Floor: 1,252 sq. ft.

Second Floor: 920 sq. ft.

Total: 2,172 sq. ft.

Bedrooms: 3

Bathrooms: 2

Width: 37' - 0"

Depth: 46' - 0"

Foundation: Crawlspace, Slab, Pier

eplans.com

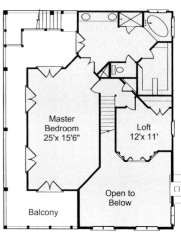

FIRST FLOOR

SECOND FLOOR

HOME PLAN

HPK1200155

Style: Farmhouse

First Floor: 1,186 sq. ft.

Second Floor: 988 sq. ft.

Total: 2,174 sq. ft.

Bedrooms: 4

Bathrooms: 2 ½

Width: 72' - 0"

Depth: 50' - 10"

Foundation: Unfinished Basement

eplans.com

A PALLADIAN WINDOW, FISH-SCALE SHINGLES, AND TUR-RET-STYLE BAYS set off this country-style Victorian exterior. Muntin windows and a quintessential wraparound porch dress up an understated theme and introduce an unrestrained floor plan with plenty of bays and niches. An impressive tile entry opens to the formal rooms, which nestle to the left side of the plan and enjoy natural light from an abundance of windows. The turret houses a secluded study on the first floor and provides a sunny bay window for a family bedroom upstairs. The second-floor master suite boasts its own fireplace, a dressing area with a walk-in closet, and a lavish bath with a garden tub and twin vanities. The two-car garage offers space for a workshop or extra storage and leads to a service entrance to the walk-through utility room.

FIRST FLOOR

SECOND FLOOR

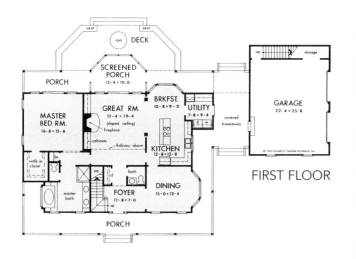

FIRST FLOOR

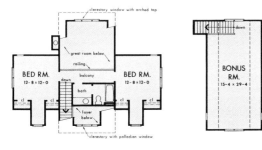

SECOND FLOOR

THE FOYER AND GREAT ROOM IN THIS MAG-NIFICENT FARMHOUSE have Palladian window clerestories to allow natural light to enter, illuminating the whole house. The spacious great room boasts a fireplace, cabinets, and bookshelves. The second-floor balcony overlooks the great room. The kitchen with a cooking island is conveniently located between the dining room and the breakfast room with an open view of the great room. A generous master bedroom has plenty of closet space as well as an expansive master bath. A bonus room over the garage allows for expansion.

HPK1200194

HOME PLAN

Style: Farmhouse

First Floor: 1,618 sq. ft.

Second Floor: 570 sq. ft.

Total: 2,188 sq. ft.

Bonus Space: 495 sq. ft.

Bedrooms: 3

Bathrooms: 2 ½

Width: 87' - 0"

Depth: 57' - 0"

eplans.com

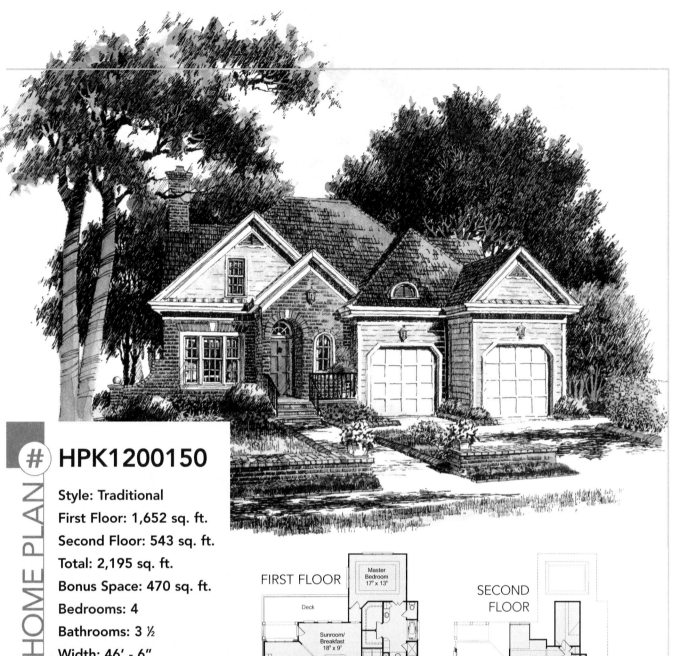

HOME PLAN

(#) HPK1200150

Style: Traditional

First Floor: 1,652 sq. ft.

Second Floor: 543 sq. ft.

Total: 2,195 sq. ft.

Bonus Space: 470 sq. ft.

Bedrooms: 4

Bathrooms: 3 ½

Width: 46' - 6"

Depth: 72' - 0"

Foundation: Unfinished Basement

eplans.com

FIRST FLOOR

SECOND FLOOR

THIS STATELY COLONIAL-STYLE BRICK HOME FEATURES AN ELEGANT RECESSED ENTRY and a ribbon of windows topped by a keystone accent. A paneled door crowned by a fanlight opens to an entry hall with a powder room and coat closet. Double doors open to a versatile, well-lit room that serves as either a study with built-in bookshelves or a formal dining room. The unique great room provides built-in shelves as well as a fireplace. An island kitchen adjoins a breakfast area/sun room with access to the rear deck. The master suite, thoughtfully placed away from traffic flow, includes a spacious bath with two walk-in closets and separate vanities.

FIRST FLOOR

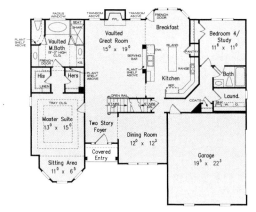

GRACEFUL DETAILS COMBINE WITH A COVERED ENTRYWAY to welcome friends and family to come on in. The canted bay sitting area in the master suite provides sunny respite and quiet solitude. To be the center of attention, invite everyone to party in the vaulted great room, which spills over into the big, airy kitchen. Guests can make use of the optional study/bedroom. Upstairs, secondary bedrooms share a full bath and a balcony overlook. A spacious central hall leads to a bonus room that provides wardrobe space.

SECOND FLOOR

HOME PLAN

HPK1200163

Style: Country Cottage

First Floor: 1,688 sq. ft.

Second Floor: 558 sq. ft.

Total: 2,246 sq. ft.

Bonus Space: 269 sq. ft.

Bedrooms: 4

Bathrooms: 3

Width: 54' - 0"

Depth: 48' - 0"

Foundation: Crawlspace, Slab, Unfinished Walkout Basement

eplans.com

©1998 Donald A. Gardner, Inc.

 # HPK1200146

THE WIDE PORCH ACROSS THE FRONT AND THE DECK OFF THE GREAT ROOM in back allow as much outdoor living as the weather permits. The foyer opens through columns from the front porch to the dining room, with a nearby powder room, and to the great room. The breakfast room is open to the great room and the adjacent kitchen. The utility room adjoins this area and accesses the garage. On the opposite side of the plan, the master suite offers a compartmented bath and two walk-in closets. A staircase leads upstairs to two family bedrooms—one at each end of a balcony that overlooks the great room. Each bedroom contains a walk-in closet, a dormer window, and private access to the bath through a private vanity area.

Style: Country Cottage
First Floor: 1,569 sq. ft.
Second Floor: 682 sq. ft.
Total: 2,251 sq. ft.
Bonus Space: 332 sq. ft.
Bedrooms: 3
Bathrooms: 2 ½
Width: 64' - 8"
Depth: 43' - 4"

eplans.com

FIRST FLOOR

SECOND FLOOR

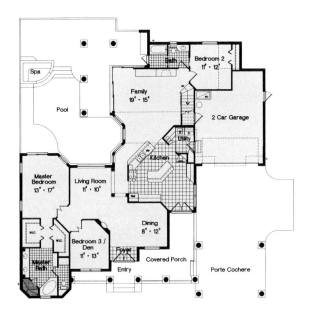

THE CHARM AND ALLURING NATURE OF CLASSIC VICTORIAN ARCHITECTURE comes to new life in this very up-to-date design. Covered porches and a porte cochere drive-through add depth and dimension to the curb appeal of this home. Upon entry, the relationship between the living room area and the formal dining room brings a new twist in traditional layout, by introducing both spaces at an angle. The master suite enjoys living "on the water" with the pool up close. Generous His and Hers walk-in closets cap the well-appointed bath. No home built today would be complete without a home office or den, and this home sports one with French doors and a porch.

HPK1200366

HOME PLAN

Style: Victorian

Square Footage: 2,270

Bonus Space: 461 sq. ft.

Bedrooms: 3

Bathrooms: 2

Width: 70' - 0"

Depth: 70' - 0"

Foundation: Slab

eplans.com

COLUMNS AND KEYSTONE LINTELS LEND A EUROPEAN

AURA to this stone-and-siding home. Arched openings and decorative columns define the formal dining room to the left of the foyer. A ribbon of windows with transoms above draws sunshine into the living room. The master suite opens from a short hallway and enjoys a tray ceiling and a vaulted bathroom with shelving, compartmented toilet, separate shower, and garden tub. Transoms abound in the open informal living areas of this home. A bay-windowed breakfast nook adjoins the kitchen with a central serving bar and the family room with a warming fireplace. Two additional bedrooms share a full bath to the left of the plan.

HPK1200192

Style: Country Cottage

Square Footage: 2,282

Bonus Space: 629 sq. ft.

Bedrooms: 3

Bathrooms: 2 ½

Width: 60' - 0"

Depth: 75' - 4"

Foundation: Unfinished Walkout Basement, Crawlspace

eplans.com

HOME PLAN

COTTAGE AND VACATION HOMES

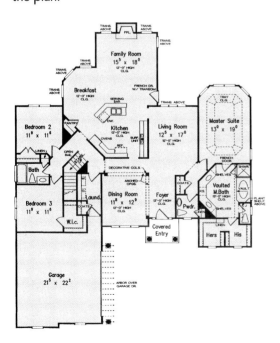

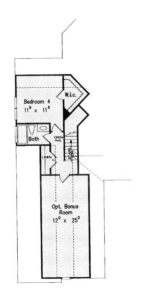

OPTIONAL LAYOUT

HOME PLAN

TAKE A TRADITIONAL COUNTRY COTTAGE AND COMBINE IT WITH AN INGENIOUS FLOOR PLAN for a home that will accommodate in style. From a quaint covered porch, follow an abbreviated hall to the octagonal foyer. Three bedrooms are situated at the front of the home; French doors accent one bedroom, making it an ideal study or formal living room. Just ahead, a tray ceiling defines the dining room, which enjoys direct access to the kitchen. A peninsula serving bar and box-bay nook are perfect for casual meals. Unique angles in the family room create an open, cheerful space. The master bedroom benefits from patio access, a distinctive shape, and a spa bath with a garden tub. Bonus space is available to expand as your needs change.

HPK1200367

Style: Country Cottage

Square Footage: 2,293

Bonus Space: 509 sq. ft.

Bedrooms: 4

Bathrooms: 2

Width: 51' - 0"

Depth: 79' - 4"

Foundation: Slab

eplans.com

HOME PLAN

HPK1200143

Style: Country Cottage

First Floor: 1,743 sq. ft.

Second Floor: 555 sq. ft.

Total: 2,298 sq. ft.

Bonus Space: 350 sq. ft.

Bedrooms: 4

Bathrooms: 3

Width: 77' - 11"

Depth: 53' - 2"

eplans.com

FIRST FLOOR

A LOVELY ARCH-TOP WINDOW AND A WRAPAROUND PORCH set off this country exterior. Inside, formal rooms open off the foyer, which leads to a spacious great room. This living area provides a fireplace and access to a screened porch with a cathedral ceiling. Bay windows allow natural light into the breakfast area and formal dining room. The master suite features a spacious bath and access to a private area of the rear porch. Two second-floor bedrooms share a bath and a balcony hall that offers an overlook to the great room.

SECOND FLOOR

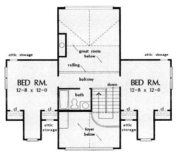

OPTIONAL LAYOUT

Sitting
Area
TRAY CEILING

Master Suite
16⁶ x 14⁰

FRENCH DOOR

Vaulted M. Bath

RAD. WDW

W.i.c.

LINEN

PLANT SHELF ABOVE

Pwdr.

Foyer
14'-0" HIGH CLG.

FRENCH DOORS

Living Room
13⁵ x 14⁰

COVERED ENTRY

ACTIVE DORMER W/ RAD. WDW

Vaulted Family Room
15⁸ x 20²

Kitchen
11'-0" HIGH CLG.

ISLAND

DW

DBL. OVEN

RANGE

REF

PANTRY

DECORATIVE COLUMNS

ARCHED OPENINGS

Dining Room
12⁰ x 14⁰
14'-0" HIGH CLG.

OPT. STAIR TO BSMT.

RAD. WDW

RAD. WDW

RAD. WDW

Breakfast
11'-0" HIGH CLG.

FRENCH DOOR

Bedroom 2
11⁰ x 13⁰

W.i.c.

Bath

LINEN

W.i.c.

Bedroom 3
12¹⁰ x 11⁶

SINK

W.H.

W.

Laund.

Garage
20⁵ x 20⁹

copyright © 1995 frank betz associates, inc.

GARAGE LOCATION WITH BASEMENT

AN ECLECTIC MIX OF BUILDING MATERI-ALS—STONE, STUCCO, AND SIDING—sings in tune with the European charm of this one-story home. Within, decorative columns set off the formal dining room and the foyer from the vaulted family room; the formal living room is quietly tucked behind French doors. The gourmet kitchen provides an angled snack bar and a sunny breakfast room. Two family bedrooms each have a walk-in closet and private access to a shared bath. The mas-ter suite holds an elegant tray ceiling, a bay sitting area, and a lush bath.

HPK1200184

HOME PLAN

Style: Country Cottage

Square Footage: 2,322

Bedrooms: 3

Bathrooms: 2 ½

Width: 62' - 0"

Depth: 61' - 0"

Foundation: Crawlspace, Slab, Unfinished Walkout Basement

eplans.com

THIS SENSIBLE PLAN FLOUTS TRADITION AND DELIVERS HIGH-END AMENITIES in a well-balanced design. A full-sized formal dining room featuring a tray ceiling enables homeowners to host elegant dinners made to perfection in the gourmet kitchen. The combined space of the great room, breakfast nook, and sun room is enhanced even further by the lanai and deck. Homeowners will know just how pleasing this home can be as they retire each night to a deluxe master suite. The bedroom features exclusive access to the deck, and a private garden beautifies the corner whirlpool tub.

HOME PLAN

HPK1200368

Style: Farmhouse

Square Footage: 2,326

Bonus Space: 358 sq. ft.

Bedrooms: 3

Bathrooms: 2 ½

Width: 64' - 0"

Depth: 72' - 4"

Foundation: Finished Walkout Basement

eplans.com

COTTAGE AND VACATION HOMES

APPEARANCES CAN BE DECEIVING IN THIS COUNTRY COTTAGE. Stone accents arched windows topped with fanlights and enhances the turreted bay. Inside, a large, well-thought-out floor plan unfolds. A long dining room sits to the left of the tiled entry hall and is also accessed from the island kitchen and spacious living room. The breakfast nook enjoys the natural light from the turreted bay. At the rear of the plan, the master suite is pampered with a see-through fireplace and elegant double doors to the bath. Two walk-in closets provide ample storage. Three family bedrooms—one enjoys a window seat—sit to the right of the plan and share a full hall bath. A bonus room is perfect for media or a gym.

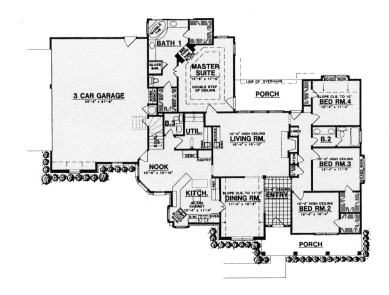

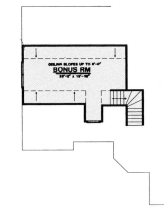

(#) HPK1200162

HOME PLAN

Style: Farmhouse

Square Footage: 2,328

Bonus Space: 384 sq. ft.

Bedrooms: 4

Bathrooms: 2 ½

Width: 81' - 8"

Depth: 61' - 0"

Foundation: Slab, Crawlspace

eplans.com

HPK1200171

Style: Country Cottage

First Floor: 1,482 sq. ft.

Second Floor: 885 sq. ft.

Total: 2,367 sq. ft.

Bedrooms: 3

Bathrooms: 2 ½

Width: 64' - 0"

Depth: 50' - 0"

Foundation: Unfinished Basement

eplans.com

COZY LIVING ABOUNDS IN THIS COMFORTABLE TWO-STORY BUNGALOW. Enter the foyer and find a spacious living room with a fireplace to the left. The bayed family room features a fireplace and entry to a screened porch. Upstairs, secondary bedrooms offer ample closet space and direct access to a shared bath. The master suite contains a large walk-in closet, a double-bowl vanity, and a compartmented shower and toilet.

FIRST FLOOR

SECOND FLOOR

IF YOU ARE LOOKING FOR A HOME THAT GROWS WITH YOUR FAMILY, this is it! Six rounded columns grace the front porch and lend a Colonial feel to this great home plan. Inside, the foyer opens to the formal dining space, which is only a few steps to the kitchen. A walk-in pantry, spacious counters and cabinets, snack bar, adjoining breakfast area, and planning desk make this kitchen efficient and gourmet. A private master suite features a sitting bay, twin walk-in closets, and an amenity-filled bath. Two oversized secondary bedrooms enjoy walk-in closets and share a corner bath. The entire second level is future space that will become exactly what you need. Plenty of storage can be found in the garage.

OPTIONAL LAYOUT

HOME PLAN

HPK1200178

Style: Country Cottage

Square Footage: 2,379

Bonus Space: 367 sq. ft.

Bedrooms: 3

Bathrooms: 2 ½

Width: 61' - 0"

Depth: 81' - 9"

Foundation: Crawlspace, Slab, Unfinished Basement

eplans.com

HOME PLAN

#

HPK1200203

Style: Cape Cod

First Floor: 967 sq. ft.

Second Floor: 1,076 sq. ft.

Third Floor: 342 sq. ft.

Total: 2,385 sq. ft.

Bedrooms: 5

Bathrooms: 3 ½

Width: 39' - 8"

Depth: 36' - 8"

Foundation: Pier

eplans.com

THIS THREE-LEVEL BEACH HOUSE OFFERS SPECTACU-LAR VIEWS all around. With three deck levels accessible from all living areas, the outside sea air will surround you. The first level enjoys a living room, three bedrooms, a full bath, and a laundry area. The second level expands to a family area, a dining room, and a kitchen with an island snack bar and nearby half-bath. The master suite enjoys a walk-through closet and an amenity-filled bath with dual vanities and a separate tub and shower. The third level is a private haven—perfect for another bedroom—complete with a bath, walk-in closet, and sitting area.

FIRST FLOOR

SECOND FLOOR

THIRD FLOOR

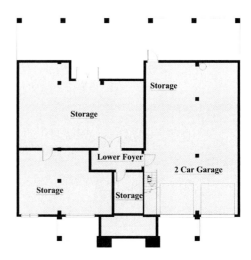

HPK1200200

Style: Italianate

Square Footage: 2,385

Bedrooms: 3

Bathrooms: 3

Width: 60' - 0"

Depth: 52' - 0"

Foundation: Slab

eplans.com

THIS ENTICING EUROPEAN VILLA BOASTS AN ITALIAN CHARM and a distinct Mediterranean feel. The foyer steps lead up to the formal living areas. To the left, a study is expanded by a vaulted ceiling and double doors that open to the front balcony. The island kitchen is conveniently open to a breakfast nook. The guest quarters reside on the right side of the plan—one suite boasts a private bath; the other uses a full hall bath. The secluded master suite features two walk-in closets and a pampering whirlpool master bath. The home is completed by a basement-level garage.

HOME PLAN

HPK1200202

Style: Lakefront

First Floor: 967 sq. ft.

Second Floor: 1,076 sq. ft.

Third Floor: 349 sq. ft.

Total: 2,392 sq. ft.

Bedrooms: 5

Bathrooms: 3 ½

Width: 39' - 8"

Depth: 36' - 8"

Foundation: Pier

FIRST FLOOR

SECOND FLOOR

THIRD FLOOR

HOME PLAN

HPK1200160

Style: Country Cottage

First Floor: 1,805 sq. ft.

Second Floor: 593 sq. ft.

Total: 2,398 sq. ft.

Bonus Space: 255 sq. ft.

Bedrooms: 4

Bathrooms: 3

Width: 55' - 0"

Depth: 48' - 0"

Foundation: Crawlspace, Unfinished Walkout Basement

FIRST FLOOR

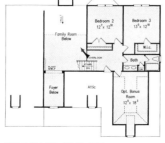

SECOND FLOOR

HOME PLAN #

HPK1200185

Style: Country Cottage
Square Footage: 2,414
Bedrooms: 3
Bathrooms: 2 ½
Width: 65' - 0"
Depth: 62' - 0"
Foundation: Slab

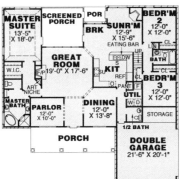

HOME PLAN #

HPK1200152

Style: Country Cottage
First Floor: 1,704 sq. ft.
Second Floor: 734 sq. ft.
Total: 2,438 sq. ft.
Bonus Space: 479 sq. ft.
Bedrooms: 3
Bathrooms: 3 ½
Width: 50' - 0"
Depth: 82' - 6"
Foundation: Crawlspace

FIRST FLOOR

SECOND FLOOR

HOME PLAN
HPK1200157

Style: Italianate

First Floor: 1,293 sq. ft.

Second Floor: 1,154 sq. ft.

Total: 2,447 sq. ft.

Bonus Space: 426 sq. ft.

Bedrooms: 3

Bathrooms: 2 ½

Width: 50' - 0"

Depth: 90' - 0"

Foundation: Slab

FIRST FLOOR

SECOND FLOOR

HOME PLAN
HPK1200142

Style: French

First Floor: 2,019 sq. ft.

Second Floor: 468 sq. ft.

Total: 2,487 sq. ft.

Bonus Space: 286 sq. ft.

Bedrooms: 5

Bathrooms: 3

Width: 59' - 0"

Depth: 58' - 0"

FIRST FLOOR

SECOND FLOOR

COTTAGE AND VACATION HOMES

Sunny Days, Starry Nights— Outdoor Living at Its Best

Porches, balconies, decks, and courtyards can significantly increase the overall living space of a home at a fraction of the cost of adding interior rooms. In addition, outdoor rooms offer attractive ways to bring light to the interior of a plan by way of French doors or full-height windows that open onto the porch or courtyard. In a small home plan, where access to exterior windows and doors is easily achieved, the result is quite dramatic. A properly situated home can receive natural light through most of the day, lowering the demand for artificial lighting and gently heating

the home on colder days. In the summer, blinds and other window treatments will be needed to control the amount of light entering the home and keep down cooling costs.

Furthermore, there's no denying the classic flavor that a wraparound porch—such as for plan HPK1200268 on page 299—can bring to the exterior of a home. Well-designed front porches and street-facing balconies can announce your home's style and establish excellent curb appeal. Consider these 73 plans, arranged in order of square footage, for a home that will always offer a warm reception and can stand out—tastefully—in a crowd.

OUTDOOR SPACES are all about combining the comfort of your home with the beauty of the natural environment. Take cues from the design of your home. Look to where the plan interacts with the landscape.

Clockwise from Left: Fireplace Xtrrordinair, Mark Samu, Milgard, Mark Samu

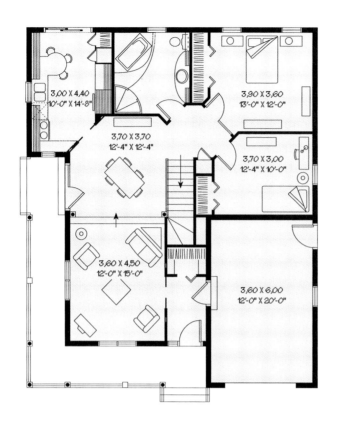

3,00 X 4,40
10'-0" X 14'-8"

3,90 X 3,60
13'-0" X 12'-0"

3,70 X 3,70
12'-4" X 12'-4"

3,70 X 3,00
12'-4" X 10'-0"

3,60 X 4,50
12'-0" X 15'-0"

3,60 X 6,00
12'-0" X 20'-0"

COUNTRY CHARM AND MODERN convenience combine in this lovely home with a wraparound porch. The galley kitchen features acres of counter space and a convenient snack bar. The luxurious bathroom enjoys a corner bathtub and separate angled shower. Adjoining living and dining rooms share access to the side porch—perfect for outdoor grilling. The homeowner is sure to appreciate the spacious master bedroom.

HOME PLAN

HPK1200282

Style: Farmhouse

Square Footage: 1,124

Bedrooms: 2

Bathrooms: 1

Width: 37' - 0"

Depth: 44' - 0"

Foundation: Unfinished Basement

eplans.com

HORIZONTAL SIDING WITH BRICK ACCENTS and multipane windows enhance the exterior of this home. A large living/dining room provides plenty of space for formal and informal activities. A fireplace makes a delightful focal point. Located for efficiency, the kitchen easily serves this area. The centrally located main bath has twin lavatories and a nearby linen closet. One of the two family bedrooms has direct access to the veranda. The master bedroom is flanked by the master bath and its own covered porch.

HOME PLAN **#**

HPK1200284

Style: Contemporary

Square Footage: 1,410

Bedrooms: 3

Bathrooms: 2

Width: 66' - 7"

Depth: 55' - 0"

Foundation: Unfinished Basement

eplans.com

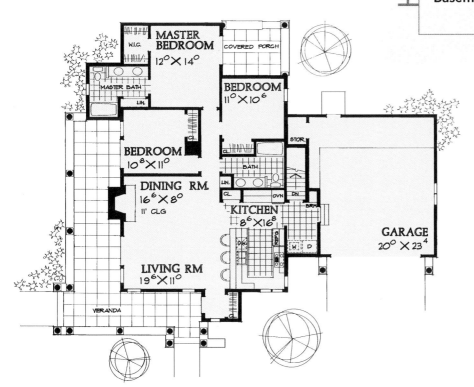

FIRST FLOOR

12'-0" X 9'-0"

7,40 X 3,70
24'-8" X 12'-4"

3,40 X 4,10
11'-4" X 13'-8"

SECOND FLOOR

4,40 X 3,50
14'-8" X 11'-0"

4,40 X 3,70
14'-8" X 12'-4"

THIS FOUR-SEASON CAPE COD COTTAGE is perfect for a site with great views. A sunroom provides wide vistas and easy indoor/outdoor flow. The living area boasts a corner fireplace. A well-organized kitchen serves a snack counter as well as the dining room. A laundry room and petite rear storage area round out this floor. Upstairs, two spacious bedrooms share a lavish bath, which is complete with a window tub and separate shower.

HOME PLAN

HPK1200232

Style: **Cape Cod**
First Floor: **895 sq. ft.**
Second Floor: **587 sq. ft.**
Total: **1,482 sq. ft.**
Bedrooms: **2**
Bathrooms: **1 ½**
Width: **38' - 0"**
Depth: **36' - 0"**
Foundation: **Unfinished Walkout Basement**

eplans.com

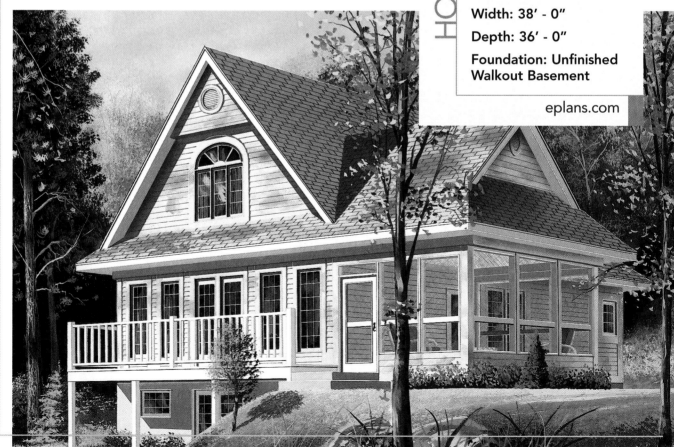

HOME PLAN

HPK1200252

Style: Contemporary

First Floor: 908 sq. ft.

Second Floor: 576 sq. ft.

Total: 1,484 sq. ft.

Bedrooms: 3

Bathrooms: 2

Width: 26' - 0"

Depth: 48' - 0"

Foundation: Unfinished Basement

eplans.com

PICTURE YOURSELF DRIVING UP TO THE LAKE after a long week at work and pulling into the driveway of this gorgeous vacation home. In the foyer, you can hang your coat in the closet and store the toys for the kids. Days are naturally lit by sunlight streaming in through the abundant fenestration throughout the home, but be sure to enjoy the view off the screened porch as well. With a full kitchen at your disposal, you can create a meal to be enjoyed either leisurely at the island or more formally in the dining room. Curl up with a good book and a glass of wine and enjoy the glow of the wood-burning fireplace in the family room, or invite friends over for a movie. They can stay over in the first-floor bedroom with nearby full bath. Then retreat upstairs where you can tuck the kids into their room and fall fast asleep in yours.

FIRST FLOOR

SECOND FLOOR

FIRST FLOOR

3,10 X 3,00
10'-4" X 10'-0"

3,60 X 3,60
12'-0" X 12'-0"

3,60 X 4,90
12'-0" X 16'-4"

SECOND FLOOR

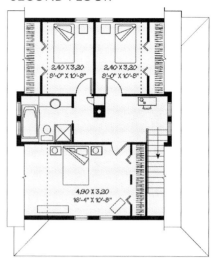

2,40 X 3,20
8'-0" X 10'-8"

2,40 X 3,20
8'-0" X 10'-8"

4,90 X 3,20
16'-4" X 10'-8"

QUAINT DETAILS GIVE THIS COUNTRY HOME a lemonade and porch-swing feel. The foyer leads to the living room with a corner fireplace. Just steps away is the dining room with double French doors to the rear yard. The kitchen provides plenty of space to prepare for large or intimate parties. The laundry room and a half-bath are placed near the kitchen, making chores easier. Upstairs, the master bedroom features plenty of closet space. Across the hall, two secondary bedrooms and a loft round out the upper level.

 # HPK1200297

HOME PLAN

Style: Country

First Floor: 781 sq. ft.

Second Floor: 720 sq. ft.

Total: 1,501 sq. ft.

Bedrooms: 3

Bathrooms: 1 ½

Width: 29' - 4"

Depth: 30' - 0"

Foundation: Unfinished Basement

eplans.com

HPK1200274

Style: Vacation

First Floor: 942 sq. ft.

Second Floor: 571 sq. ft.

Total: 1,513 sq. ft.

Bedrooms: 2

Bathrooms: 2 ½

Width: 32' - 0"

Depth: 53' - 0"

Foundation: Pier

eplans.com

THE MODEST DETAILING OF GREEK REVIVAL STYLE gave rise to this grand home. A mid-level foyer eases the trip from the ground level to the raised living area, while an arched vestibule announces the great room. The formal dining room offers French-door access to the covered porch. Built-ins, a fireplace, and two ways to access the porch make the great room truly great. A well-appointed kitchen serves a casual eating bar as well as the dining room. Upstairs, each of two private suites has a windowed tub, a vanity, and wardrobe space. A pair of French doors opens each of the bedrooms to an observation sun deck through covered porches.

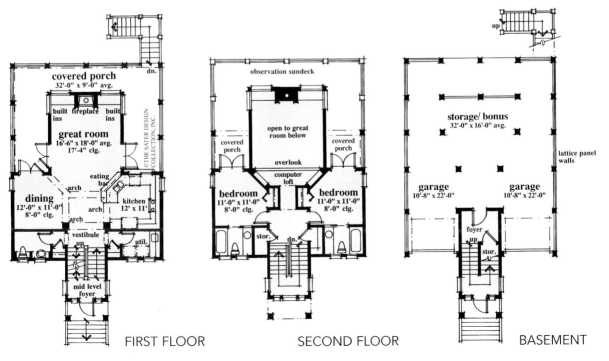

FIRST FLOOR

SECOND FLOOR

BASEMENT

ENJOY RESORT-STYLE LIVING in this striking Sun Country home. Guests will always feel welcome when entertained in the formal living and dining areas, but the eat-in country kitchen overlooking the family room will be the center of attention. Enjoy casual living in the large family room and out on the patio with the help of an optional summer kitchen and a view of the fairway. Built-in shelves and an optional media center provide decorating options. The master suite features a volume ceiling and a spacious master bath.

HOME PLAN

HPK1200369

Style: Floridian

Square Footage: 1,550

Bedrooms: 3

Bathrooms: 2

Width: 43' - 0"

Depth: 59' - 0"

Foundation: Slab

eplans.com

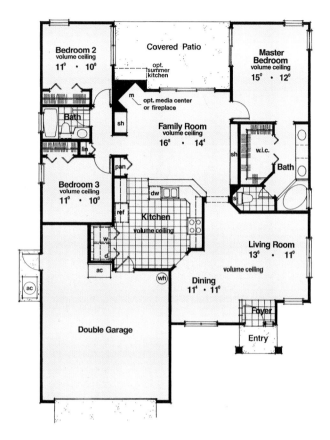

HOME PLAN

#️⃣ HPK1200370

Style: Contemporary

Square Footage: 1,627

Bedrooms: 3

Bathrooms: 2

Width: 46' - 0"

Depth: 70' - 0"

Foundation: Slab

eplans.com

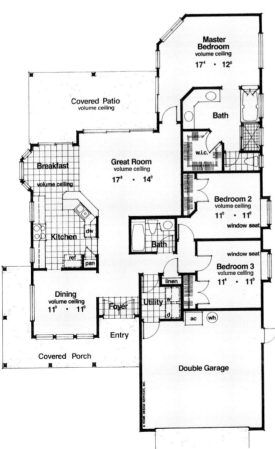

THIS MODERN DESIGN is ideal for a narrow lot. The entry, which is protected by the wraparound covered porch, opens to the dining room and the great room. Here, a window wall leads to the covered patio extending the living areas to the outdoors. The efficient and spacious kitchen adjoins both the formal dining room and the sunny breakfast nook. The sleeping area lies on the right with the generous master suite situated in the rear for privacy.

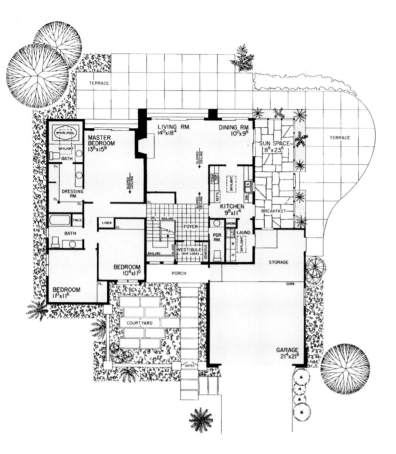

A SUN SPACE HIGHLIGHTS this innovative solar design. It features access from the kitchen, the dining room, and the garage. With abundant natural light, the sun room will be a great place to enjoy casual or formal meals and perfect for entertaining. Three skylights highlight the interior—in the kitchen, laundry, and master bath. An air-locked vestibule reinforces this design's energy efficiency. The living/dining room rises with a sloped ceiling and enjoys a fireplace and two sets of sliding glass doors to the terrace. Three bedrooms are in the sleeping wing. The master bedroom delights in its private bath with a luxurious whirlpool tub.

HOME PLAN # HPK1200234

Style: Contemporary

Square Footage: 1,632

Bedrooms: 3

Bathrooms: 2 ½

Width: 59' - 0"

Depth: 56' - 8"

Foundation: Unfinished Basement

eplans.com

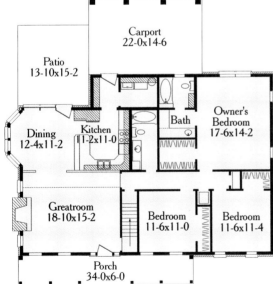

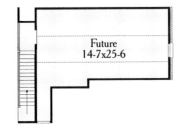

HOME PLAN

HPK1200301

Style: Traditional

Square Footage 1,656

Bonus Space: 427 sq. ft.

Bedrooms: 3

Bathrooms: 2

Width: 52' - 8"

Depth: 54' - 6"

Foundation: Crawlspace, Unfinished Basement, Slab

eplans.com

WELCOME TO COMFORTABLE LIVING! Enter the great room that features a fireplace and open planning. A few steps away, the dining room enjoys access to the patio, walls of windows, and convenient kitchen service. Just around the corner is the utility room and the passageway to the carport. Two family bedrooms located at the front of the home share a hall bath. The spacious master suite features a walk-in closet and lavish bath. Bonus space is available for future expansion.

A CHARMING CUPOLA OVER THE GARAGE and delightful fan windows set the tone for this cozy cottage. A central fireplace and a sloped ceiling highlight the living room's comfortable design, complete with sliding patio doors and an adjoining dining room. The large eat-in kitchen offers a snack bar, planning desk, and patio doors from the breakfast room. An angular hallway leads to the master bedroom featuring a large walk-in closet, twin-sink vanity, and compartmented bath. A secondary bedroom features a lovely window seat. A third bedroom is perfectly situated to be a study. The two-car garage has a separate storage area with a utility entrance.

HOME PLAN

HPK1200275

Style: Colonial

Square Footage: 1,689

Bedrooms: 3

Bathrooms: 2

Width: 58' - 0"

Depth: 52' - 6"

Foundation: Unfinished Basement

eplans.com

GABLES, COLUMNS, AND MULTIPANE WINDOWS

give this ranch-style home great curb appeal. A columned foyer branches off into the great room, formal dining area, and two family bedrooms. A fireplace warms the great room and is visible from the kitchen. The adjoining kitchen and breakfast area enjoy an island/snack bar and a ribbon of windows facing the rear yard. The master suite is privately tucked behind the kitchen and accesses the rear porch.

HOME PLAN

HPK1200280

Style: Transitional

Square Footage: 1,698

Bedrooms: 3

Bathrooms: 2

Width: 66' - 0"

Depth: 49' - 11"

Foundation: Crawlspace, Slab, Unfinished Basement

eplans.com

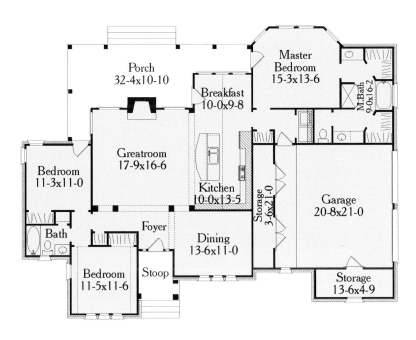

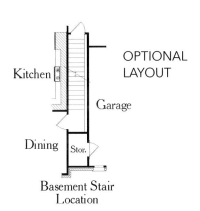

OPTIONAL LAYOUT

Basement Stair Location

FIRST FLOOR

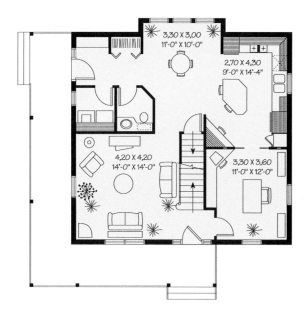

SECOND FLOOR

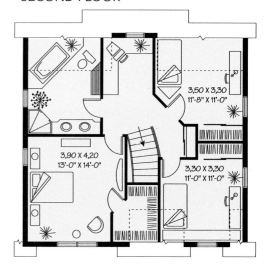

WITH ALL THE INGREDIENTS FOR COUNTRY LIVING, this design gives off its own sweet illumination. Horizontal siding and a wrapping front porch enclose a beautiful floor plan. Inside, the formal living room connects to the more casual areas at the rear of the home. The country kitchen is roomy enough for a small breakfast table. To the left, a coat closet, powder room, and laundry facilities complete the main floor. The master bedroom offers a walk-in closet and shares a full hall bath with two other family bedrooms.

HPK1200235

HOME PLAN

Style: Farmhouse

First Floor: 860 sq. ft.

Second Floor: 840 sq. ft.

Total: 1,700 sq. ft.

Bedrooms: 3

Bathrooms: 1 ½

Width: 30' - 0"

Depth: 28' - 0"

Foundation: Unfinished Basement

eplans.com

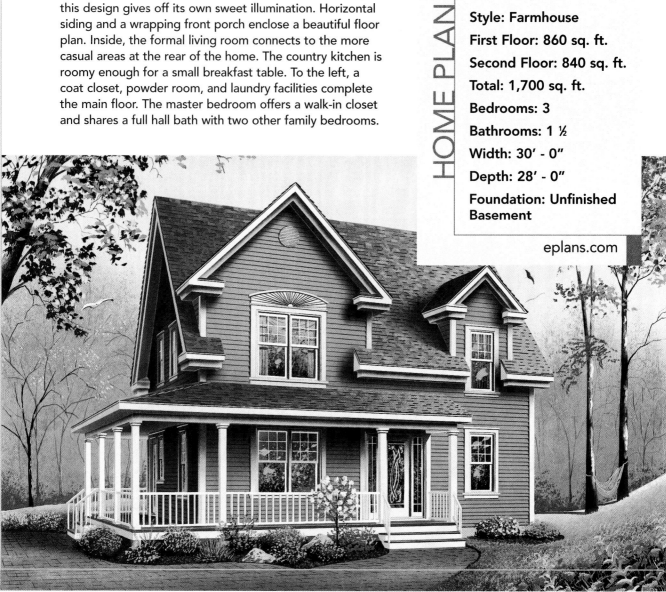

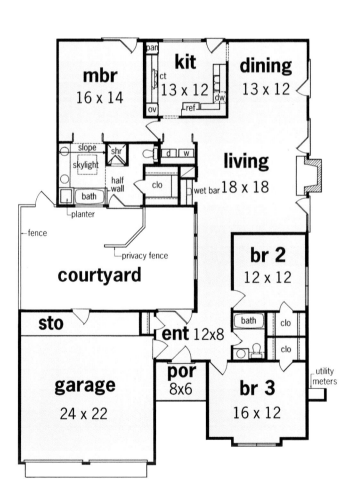

HOME PLAN

HPK1200250

Style: Country Cottage

Square Footage: 1,732

Bedrooms: 3

Bathrooms: 2

Width: 46' - 0"

Depth: 66' - 0"

Foundation: Slab, Crawlspace

eplans.com

SIMPLE VICTORIAN DETAILING marks the exterior of this interesting plan. The interior surrounds a private courtyard. The entry leads to the two-car garage, the courtyard, and two family bedrooms and their shared bath. Each bedroom is equipped with a walk-in closet. French doors accent the remainder of the home; they are found in the master bedroom, the dining area, and on each side of the living-room fireplace. A wet bar in the living room ensures successful entertaining. The master bathroom is a garden retreat with access to the courtyard and a planter inside next to the garden tub. A skylight brings natural light into this incredible room.

screened verandah
20'-0" x 7'-8"

kitchen

great room
21'-0" x 14'-0"
vault. clg.

dining
12'-6" x 9'-0"
8' clg.

sundeck

fireplace

up

down

foyer

study
10'-0" x 13'-0"
8' clg.

br. 2
11'-8" x 11'-6"
8' clg.

© THE SATER DESIGN COLLECTION, INC.

entry porch

down

FIRST FLOOR

master suite
12'-3" x 20'0"
8' clg.

open to below

loft

down

w.i.c.

SECOND FLOOR

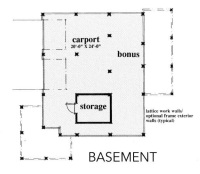

carport
20'-0" X 24'-0"

bonus

storage

lattice work walls/
optional frame exterior
walls (typical)

BASEMENT

THIS TWO-STORY HOME'S PLEASING EXTERIOR is complemented by its warm character and decorative "widow's walk." The covered entry—with its dramatic transom window—leads to a spacious great room highlighted by a warming fireplace. To the right, the dining room and kitchen combine to provide a delightful place for mealtimes, with access to a side sun deck through double doors. A study, bedroom, and full bath complete the first floor. The luxurious master suite on the second floor features an oversized walk-in closet and a separate dressing area. The pampering master bath enjoys a relaxing whirlpool tub, double-bowl vanity, and compartmented toilet.

HPK1200265

Style: Floridian

First Floor: 1,136 sq. ft.

Second Floor: 636 sq. ft.

Total: 1,772 sq. ft.

Bedrooms: 2

Bathrooms: 2

Width: 41' - 9"

Depth: 45' - 0"

Foundation: Slab, Pier

HOME PLAN

eplans.com

© The Sater Group, Inc.

©1991 Donald A. Gardner, Inc.

(#) HPK1200262

Style: Farmhouse

First Floor: 1,325 sq. ft.

Second Floor: 453 sq. ft.

Total: 1,778 sq. ft.

Bedrooms: 3

Bathrooms: 2 ½

Width: 48' - 4"

Depth: 51' - 10"

eplans.com

THIS COMPACT DESIGN has all the amenities available in larger plans with little wasted space. In addition, a wrap-around covered porch, a front Palladian window, dormers, and rear arched windows provide exciting visual elements to the exterior. The spacious great room has a fireplace, a cathedral ceiling, and clerestory windows. A second-level balcony overlooks this gathering area. The kitchen is centrally located for maximum flexibility in layout and features a pass-through to the great room. Besides the generous master suite with a pampering bath, two family bedrooms located on the second level share a full bath.

FIRST FLOOR

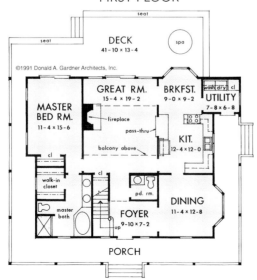

SECOND FLOOR

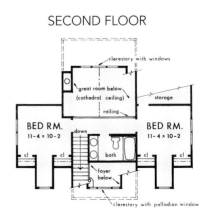

SMALL BUT INVITING, THIS RANCH-STYLE farmhouse is the perfect choice for a small family or empty-nesters. It's loaded with amenities even the most particular homeowner will appreciate. For example, the living room and dining room both have plant shelves, sloped ceilings, and built-in cabinetry to enhance livability. The living room also sports a warming fireplace. The master bedroom contains a well-appointed bath with dual vanities and a walk-in closet. The additional bedroom has its own bath with linen storage. The kitchen is separated from the breakfast nook by a clever bar area. Access to the two-car garage is through a laundry area with washer/dryer hook-up space.

HPK1200236

Style: Contemporary

Square Footage: 1,800

Bedrooms: 2

Bathrooms: 2

Width: 89' - 0"

Depth: 46' - 2"

Foundation: Slab, Crawlspace

HOME PLAN

eplans.com

© 1994 Donald A. Gardner Architects, Inc.

THIS COMFORTABLE COUNTRY home begins with a front porch that opens to a columned foyer. To the right, enter the formal dining room. Decorative columns define the central great room, which boasts wide views of the outdoors. A breakfast nook nearby accommodates casual dining. The master suite and the great room open to the rear porch. Family bedrooms share a full bath with dual lavatories.

HOME PLAN

HPK1200256

Style: Farmhouse
Square Footage: 1,807
Bonus Space: 419 sq. ft.
Bedrooms: 3
Bathrooms: 2
Width: 70' - 8"
Depth: 52' - 8"

eplans.com

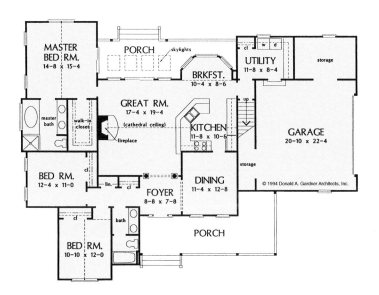

© 1994 Donald A. Gardner Architects, Inc.

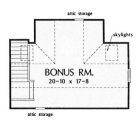

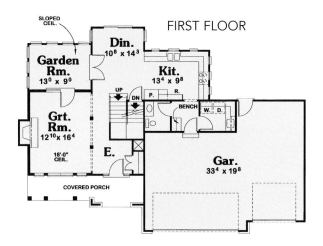

FIRST FLOOR

SLOPED CEIL.

Garden Rm.
13⁰ x 9⁰

Din.
10⁸ x 14³

Kit.
13⁴ x 9⁸

UP

DN

P.

R.

BENCH

W. D.

Grt. Rm.
12¹⁰ x 16⁴

18'-0" CEIL.

E.

Gar.
33⁴ x 19⁸

COVERED PORCH

SECOND FLOOR

Br. 2
10⁷ x 10⁰

SHELVES

Br. 3
11⁰ x 10⁰

DN

L.

OPEN TO BELOW

UNFIN. STORAGE

Br. 4
10⁸ x 10⁶

Mbr.
12⁸ x 14⁰

10'-0" CEIL.

WHIRLPOOL

THIS TRADITIONAL DESIGN FEATURES A GARDEN ROOM with twin skylights, a sloped ceiling, and two walls of windows. The kitchen provides plenty of counter space and easily serves the formal dining room, which opens through double doors to the garden room. A balcony overlooks the great room, which is warmed by a fireplace. All four bedrooms, including the master suite with its full bath and plentiful storage space, are on the upper level.

HOME PLAN

 # HPK1200242

Style: Traditional

First Floor: 837 sq. ft.

Second Floor: 977 sq. ft.

Total: 1,814 sq. ft.

Bedrooms: 4

Bathrooms: 2 ½

Width: 58' - 4"

Depth: 41' - 4"

eplans.com

A GREENHOUSE AREA OFF THE DINING room and living room provides a cheerful focal point for this comfortable three-bedroom home. The spacious living room features a cozy fireplace and a sloped ceiling. In addition to the dining room, there's a less formal breakfast room just off the modern kitchen. The kitchen and breakfast area look out onto a front terrace. Stairs just off the foyer lead down to a recreation room in the basement. The master bedroom suite opens to a terrace. A mudroom and a washroom off the garage allow rear entry to the house during inclement weather.

HPK1200253

Style: NW Contemporary

Square Footage: 1,824

Bedrooms: 3

Bathrooms: 2 ½

Width: 80' - 4"

Depth: 43' - 0"

Foundation: Unfinished Basement

eplans.com

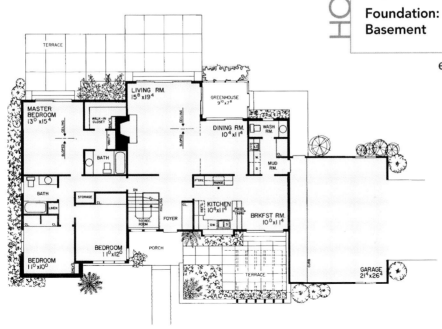

13'-8" X 11'-4"
4,10 X 3,40

14'-2" X 14'-8"
4,25 X 4,40

12'-0" X 16'-0"
3,60 X 4,80

11'-0" X 16'-0"
3,30 X 4,80

13'-8" X 14'-8"
4,10 X 4,40

© 2004 by Designer, All Rights Reserved

SECOND FLOOR

12'-0" X 13'-0"
3,60 X 3,90

16'-4" X 12'-0"
4,90 X 3,60

A CROSS-GABLED DESIGN WITH AN OCEANFRONT view means a bright, airy space at the center of the plan. A dual-facing fireplace also brings warmth to the gathering room as well as to the master bedroom. A walk-in closet and full bath, featuring a corner tub and dual vanities, serve the homeowners. Upstairs, two large bedrooms enjoy spacious closets and comfortably share a full bath. The broad wrap-around porch and sunroom present plenty of opportunities for vacation enjoyment.

(#) HPK1200258

Style: Vacation

First Floor: 1,212 sq. ft.

Second Floor: 620 sq. ft.

Total: 1,832 sq. ft.

Bedrooms: 3

Bathrooms: 2

Width: 38' - 0"

Depth: 40' - 0"

Foundation: Unfinished Basement

eplans.com

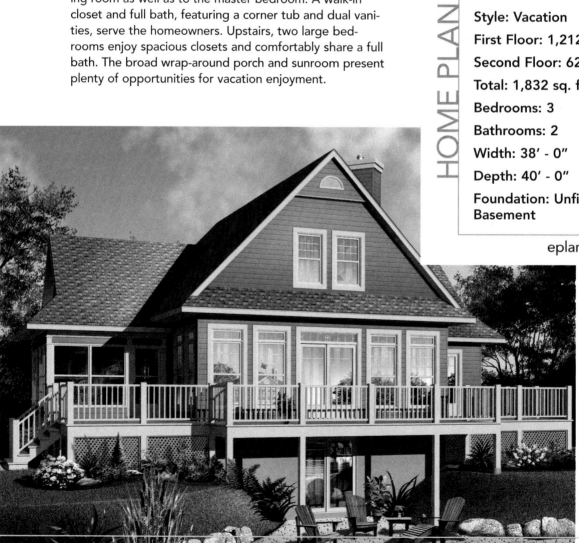

HOME PLAN

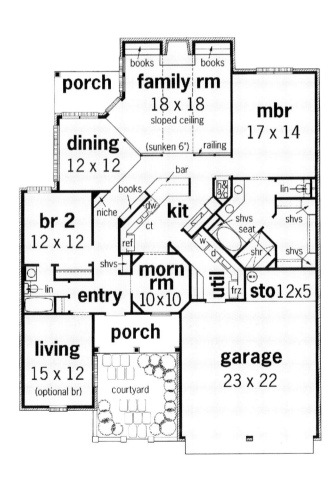

HPK1200291

HOME PLAN

Style: French

Square Footage: 1,891

Bedrooms: 2

Bathrooms: 2

Width: 49' - 0"

Depth: 64' - 0"

Foundation: Crawlspace, Slab

eplans.com

THE GATED COURTYARD ADDS PRIVACY and personality to this charming two-bedroom home. The open interior includes a sunken family room with a sloped ceiling, a gracious fireplace, built-ins, and access to a rear porch. A brilliantly sunny dining room sits opposite an open and cleverly angled kitchen—allowing for ease of service between the dining room and the morning room. The living room could be used as a third bedroom or a study. The master suite includes a dual-bowl vanity, a separate bath and shower, and a large walk-in closet.

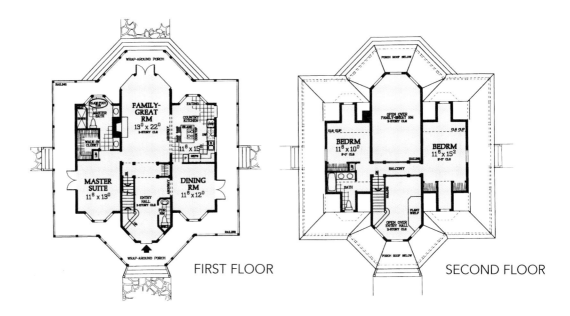

FIRST FLOOR

SECOND FLOOR

HOME PLAN #

HPK1200277

Style: Plantation

First Floor: 1,295 sq. ft.

Second Floor: 600 sq. ft.

Total: 1,895 sq. ft.

Bedrooms: 3

Bathrooms: 2 ½

Width: 50' - 0"

Depth: 55' - 3"

Foundation: Unfinished Basement

eplans.com

THIS SOUTHERN COUNTRY FARMHOUSE extends a warm welcome with a wraparound porch and a bayed entry. An unrestrained floor plan, replete with soaring, open space as well as sunny bays and charming niches, invites traditional festivities and cozy family gatherings. Colonial columns introduce the two-story great room, which boasts an extended-hearth fireplace and French doors to the wraparound porch, and opens through a wide arch to the tiled country kitchen with a cooktop island counter and snack bar. The first-floor master suite enjoys its own bay window, private access to the wraparound porch, and a sumptuous bath with a clawfoot tub and separate vanities. Upstairs, two family bedrooms share a full bath and a balcony hall that overlooks the great room and the entry.

FIRST FLOOR

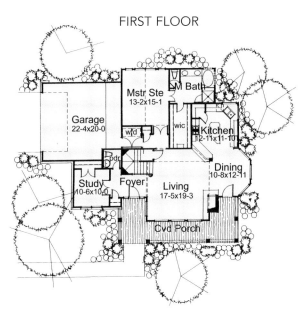

SECOND FLOOR

THIS COUNTRY-STYLE FARMHOUSE features a facade complemented with classic Victorian accents. The wrapping front porch accesses the entry and bayed dining room. The living room and study reside to the front of the plan, and the secluded master bedroom is located at the rear. Master suite amenities include a private bath and roomy walk-in closet. An island kitchen and two-car garage complete the first floor. Upstairs, two additional family bedrooms share a hall bath and balcony overlook to the living room below.

HPK1200293

HOME PLAN

Style: Farmhouse

First Floor: 1,450 sq. ft.

Second Floor: 448 sq. ft.

Total: 1,898 sq. ft.

Bedrooms: 3

Bathrooms: 2 ½

Width: 59' - 11"

Depth: 47' - 6"

Foundation: Crawlspace, Slab, Unfinished Basement

eplans.com

FIRST FLOOR

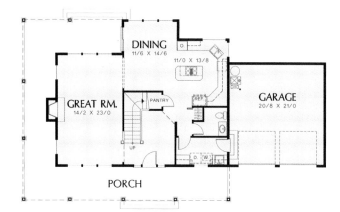

PORCH

SECOND FLOOR

A WRAPAROUND COVERED PORCH and symmetrical dormers produce an inviting appearance to this farmhouse. Inside, the two-story foyer leads directly to the large great room graced by a fireplace and an abundance of windows. The U-shaped island kitchen is convenient to the sunny dining room with a powder room nearby. The utility room offers access to the two-car garage. Upstairs, two family bedrooms share a full hall bath and have convenient access to a large bonus room. The master suite is full of amenities, including a walk-in closet and a pampering bath. A bonus room is also available upstairs near the hall bath.

HPK1200271

HOME PLAN

Style: Farmhouse
First Floor: 1,032 sq. ft.
Second Floor: 870 sq. ft.
Total: 1,902 sq. ft.
Bonus Space: 306 sq. ft.
Bedrooms: 3
Bathrooms: 2 ½
Width: 66' - 0"
Depth: 38' - 0"
Foundation: Crawlspace

eplans.com

THIS EFFICIENT SALTBOX DESIGN includes three bedrooms and two full baths, plus a handy powder room on the first floor. A large great room at the front of the home features a fireplace. The rear of the home is left open, with room for the kitchen with a snack bar, the breakfast area with a fireplace, and the dining room with outdoor access. If you wish, use the breakfast area as an all-purpose dining room and turn the dining room into a library or sitting room. Upstairs, the vaulted master suite accesses its own private sun deck and a full bath, and two additional second-floor bedrooms share a full bath.

SECOND FLOOR

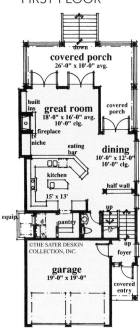

HPK1200283

HOME PLAN #

Style: European Cottage

First Floor: 873 sq. ft.

Second Floor: 1,037 sq. ft.

Total: 1,910 sq. ft.

Bedrooms: 3

Bathrooms: 2 ½

Width: 27' - 6"

Depth: 64' - 0"

Foundation: Crawlspace

eplans.com

FIRST FLOOR

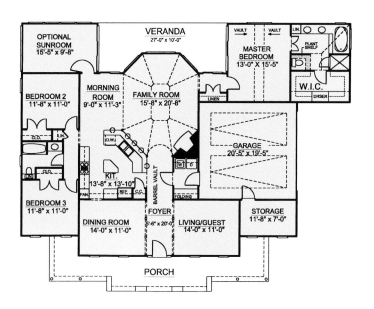

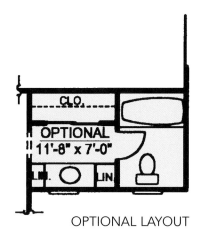

OPTIONAL LAYOUT

STATELY ARCHES TOPPED WITH A PEDIMENT make this home a comfortable fit into an elegant lifestyle. The foyer is flanked by the formal dining and living rooms. A hall with a barrel-vaulted ceiling leads to the vaulted family room, which features a corner fireplace and convenience to the kitchen, morning room, and rear veranda. This area provides a spectacular space for family get-togethers. Two secondary bedrooms with a full bath can be found to the left of the kitchen. An optional sun room is a delight just off the morning room. The master suite accommodates the discerning homeowner. It highlights a vaulted ceiling, dual vanities, a separate tub and shower, and an oversized walk-in closet.

HPK1200237

HOME PLAN

Style: Colonial
Square Footage: 1,928
Bedrooms: 4
Bathrooms: 2
Width: 58' - 0"
Depth: 47' - 0"
Foundation: Slab

eplans.com

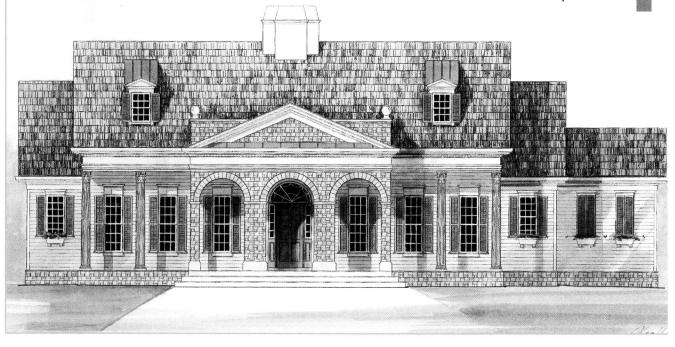

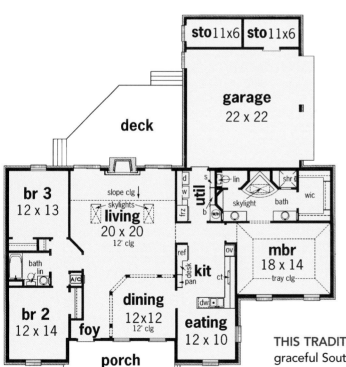

sto 11x6 | sto 11x6

garage
22 x 22

deck

br 3
12 x 13

slope clg ↓

skylights
living
20 x 20
12' clg

util

skylight

bath

wic

shr

lin

d
w
frz

s

b
w/h

bath
lin

A/C

br 2
12 x 14

foy

dining
12x12
12' clg

ref
desk
pan

kit

ct

dw

ov

mbr
18 x 14
tray clg

eating
12 x 10

porch

HPK1200267

HOME PLAN

Style: Traditional

Square Footage: 1,936

Bedrooms: 3

Bathrooms: 2

Width: 62' - 0"

Depth: 68' - 0"

Foundation: Crawlspace, Slab

eplans.com

THIS TRADITIONAL RANCH-STYLE HOME is enhanced by graceful Southern accents. A front covered porch welcomes you inside to a foyer that introduces a formal dining room and living room brightened by skylights. The master suite provides a skylit bath and a roomy walk-in closet. Two additional family bedrooms are located on the opposite side of the home and share a hall bath. The rear deck provides plenty of outdoor entertainment options. A two-car garage with storage and a useful utility room complete this lovely one-story home.

FIRST FLOOR

SECOND FLOOR

HOME PLAN

HPK1200248

Style: Victorian

First Floor: 1,044 sq. ft.

Second Floor: 892 sq. ft.

Total: 1,936 sq. ft.

Bonus Space: 228 sq. ft.

Bedrooms: 3

Bathrooms: 2 ½

Width: 58' - 0"

Depth: 43' - 6"

Foundation: Unfinished Basement

eplans.com

THIS CHARMING COUNTRY TRADITIONAL home provides a well-lit home office, harbored in a beautiful bay with three windows. The second-floor bay brightens the master bath, which has a double-bowl vanity, a step-up tub, and a dressing area. The living and dining rooms share a two-sided fireplace. The gourmet kitchen has a cooktop island counter and enjoys outdoor views through sliding glass doors in the breakfast area. A sizable bonus room above the two-car garage can be developed into hobby space or a recreation room.

COUNTRY LIVING IN A UNIQUE FLOOR PLAN makes this design the perfect choice for just the right family. The covered front porch opens to an angled foyer that leads to a large great room with a sloped ceiling and fireplace. To the right is the formal dining room, defined by columns and plenty of windows overlooking the porch. Two secondary bedrooms share a full bath at the front of the plan. Connecting to the two-car garage via a laundry area, the kitchen provides an island cooktop and a quaint morning room. The master suite offers a retreat with a sloped ceiling, walk-in closet, and a bath with a whirlpool tub.

HPK1200244

HOME PLAN #

Style: Farmhouse

Square Footage: 1,937

Bonus Space: 414 sq. ft.

Bedrooms: 3

Bathrooms: 2

Width: 76' - 4"

Depth: 73' - 4"

Foundation: Crawlspace

eplans.com

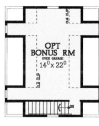

FIRST FLOOR

SECOND FLOOR

HPK1200266

Style: Contemporary

First Floor: 1,301 sq. ft.

Second Floor: 652 sq. ft.

Total: 1,953 sq. ft.

Bonus Space: 372 sq. ft.

Bedrooms: 3

Bathrooms: 2 ½

Width: 58' - 0"

Depth: 55' - 0"

Foundation: Unfinished Basement

SEEING THIS HOME IS BELIEVING in the perfection of vacation-house design. Three sets of French doors provide entrance to three different rooms at the front of the home. Gorgeous sets of stairs surrounding a turreted two-story atrium also lead to a second-level balcony—one of two—so homeowners can truly enjoy the views and atmosphere of their surroundings. Abundant windows allow natural light inside. The master suite and bath are a study in lavishness, and are located on the first floor. Two more bedrooms share a full bath on the second level. Also upstairs are a generous amount of bonus space to finish as you see fit, a two-story office, and a sitting room.

eplans.com

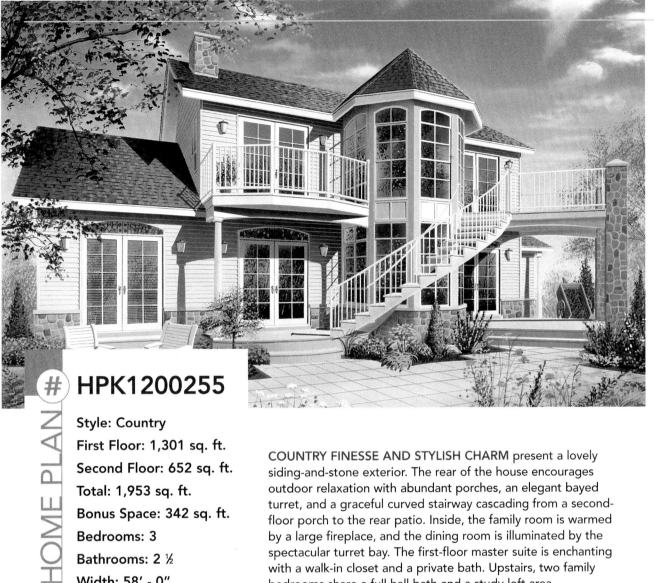

HOME PLAN

 # HPK1200255

Style: Country

First Floor: 1,301 sq. ft.

Second Floor: 652 sq. ft.

Total: 1,953 sq. ft.

Bonus Space: 342 sq. ft.

Bedrooms: 3

Bathrooms: 2 ½

Width: 58' - 0"

Depth: 55' - 0"

Foundation: Unfinished Basement

eplans.com

COUNTRY FINESSE AND STYLISH CHARM present a lovely siding-and-stone exterior. The rear of the house encourages outdoor relaxation with abundant porches, an elegant bayed turret, and a graceful curved stairway cascading from a second-floor porch to the rear patio. Inside, the family room is warmed by a large fireplace, and the dining room is illuminated by the spectacular turret bay. The first-floor master suite is enchanting with a walk-in closet and a private bath. Upstairs, two family bedrooms share a full hall bath and a study loft area.

FIRST FLOOR

SECOND FLOOR

FIRST FLOOR   SECOND FLOOR

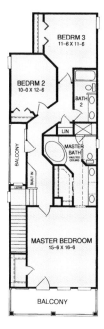

REMINISCENT OF THE POPULAR TOWNHOUSES OF THE PAST, this fine clapboard home is perfect for urban or river-front living. Two balconies grace the second floor—one at the front and one on the side. A two-way fireplace between the formal living and dining rooms provides visual impact. Built-in bookcases flank an arched opening between these rooms. A pass-through from the kitchen to the dining room simplifies serving, and a walk-in pantry provides storage. On the second floor, the master bedroom opens to a large balcony, and the relaxing master bath is designed with a separate shower and an angled whirlpool tub. Two secondary bedrooms and a full bath are located at the rear of the plan.

HPK1200260

Style: Traditional

First Floor: 904 sq. ft.

Second Floor: 1,058 sq. ft.

Total: 1,962 sq. ft.

Bedrooms: 3

Bathrooms: 2 1/2

Width: 22' - 0"

Depth: 74' - 0"

Foundation: Slab, Crawlspace

HOME PLAN

eplans.com

**SIDING
AND STONE AND
TRADITIONAL DORMERS** add country style to this lovely design. A covered front porch welcomes you inside to a foyer flanked by an octagonal study and a formal dining room. The family room is warmed by a fireplace and overlooks the back deck. The island kitchen easily serves the breakfast room. The master suite is secluded for privacy and includes a pampering bath and walk-in closet. Two additional family bedrooms are located on the opposite side of the plan and share a Jack-and-Jill bath. The two-car garage provides extra storage space. Upstairs, the bonus room easily converts to a home office or fourth bedroom and accesses the second-floor attic space.

HOME PLAN

HPK1200279

Style: Country Cottage

Square Footage: 1,991

Bonus Space: 462 sq. ft.

Bedrooms: 3

Bathrooms: 2 ½

Width: 60' - 0"

Depth: 57' - 6"

Foundation: Crawlspace, Slab, Unfinished Basement

eplans.com

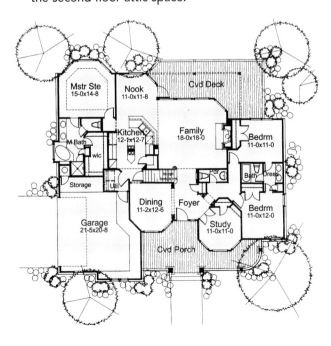

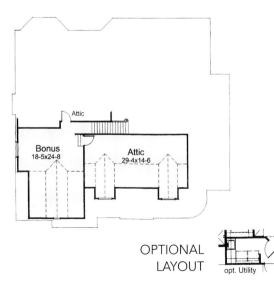

OPTIONAL LAYOUT

opt. Utility

FRENCH ACCENTS INSPIRE this European-influenced creation. A quaint courtyard introduces guests to this family compound. Inside, the central kitchen opens to the morning room. A sunken family room with sloped ceilings features a fireplace and access to the rear porch. The master bedroom, with a private bath and walk-in closet, is placed on the right side of the plan. Two additional family bedrooms reside on the left and share a full bath.

HPK1200300

Style: French

Square Footage: 1,994

Bedrooms: 3

Bathrooms: 2

Width: 49' - 0"

Depth: 68' - 0"

Foundation: Crawlspace, Slab

HOME PLAN

eplans.com

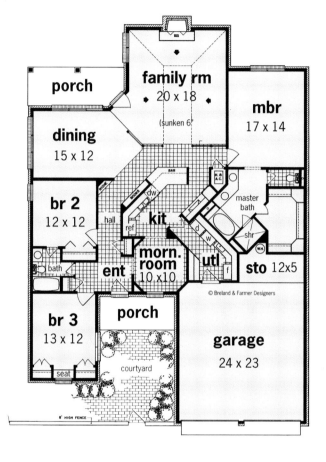

porch

family rm
20 x 18

(sunken 6')

mbr
17 x 14

dining
15 x 12

master
bath

br 2
12 x 12

hall   kit
ref

morn.
room
10 x10

utl

sto 12x5

ent

bath

br 3
13 x 12

porch

courtyard

garage
24 x 23

seat

© Breland & Farmer Designers

8' HIGH FENCE

COVERED PORCHES FRONT AND REAR are the first signal that this is a fine example of Folk Victorian styling. Complementing the exterior is a grand plan for family living. A formal living room and attached dining room provide space for entertaining guests. The large family room with a fireplace is a gathering room for everyday activities. Both areas access outdoor spaces. Four bedrooms occupy the second floor. The master suite features a window seat, three closets, and a bath with two sinks. One of the family bedrooms has its own private balcony and could be used as a study. Note the open staircase and convenient linen storage.

HOME PLAN

HPK1200264

Style: Farmhouse

First Floor: 1,096 sq. ft.

Second Floor: 900 sq. ft.

Total: 1,996 sq. ft.

Bedrooms: 4

Bathrooms: 2 ½

Width: 56' - 0"

Depth: 44' - 0"

Foundation: Unfinished Basement

eplans.com

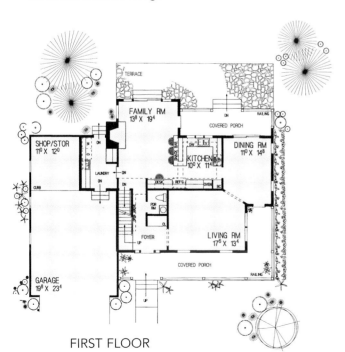

FIRST FLOOR

SECOND FLOOR

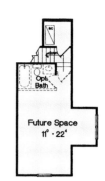

THE HUB OF THIS CHARMING PLAN IS THE SPACIOUS KITCHEN

with an island and serving bar. The nearby breakfast nook accesses the greenhouse with its wall of windows and three large skylights. A built-in media center beside a warming fireplace is the focal point of the family room. Bedroom 2 shares a full bath with the den/study, which might also be a third bedroom. The master suite features large His and Hers vanity sinks, a corner tub with an open walk-in shower, and a supersized walk-in closet. Future space over the garage can expand the living space as your family grows.

HOME PLAN

HPK1200296

Style: Farmhouse

Square Footage: 1,997

Bonus Space: 310 sq. ft.

Bedrooms: 2

Bathrooms: 2 ½

Width: 64' - 4"

Depth: 63' - 0"

Foundation: Crawlspace, Slab, Unfinished Basement

eplans.com

STONE PORCH SUPPORTS AND WIDE pillars lend a Craftsman look to this design. A truly elegant floor plan awaits within—an octagonal home office is just to the left of the entry, and a formal dining room sits to the right. The central living room offers a fireplace and a wall of windows that overlooks the deck; the nearby island kitchen includes a walk-in pantry and adjoins the breakfast bay. Access the greenhouse from the expansive side deck. Double doors open to the master bedroom, which provides a private bath with an angled soaking tub; two family bedrooms are found upstairs, where a balcony overlooks the two-story living room.

HOME PLAN

HPK1200263

Style: Transitional

First Floor: 1,530 sq. ft.

Second Floor: 469 sq. ft.

Total: 1,999 sq. ft.

Bedrooms: 3

Bathrooms: 2 ½

Width: 59' - 6"

Depth: 53' - 0"

Foundation: Unfinished Basement, Slab, Crawlspace

eplans.com

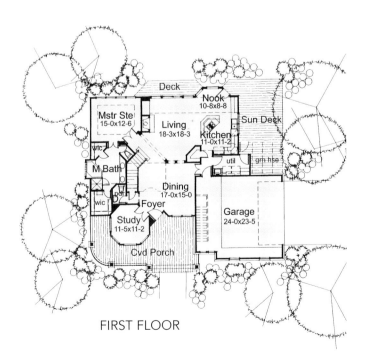

FIRST FLOOR

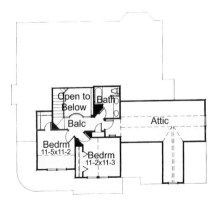

SECOND FLOOR

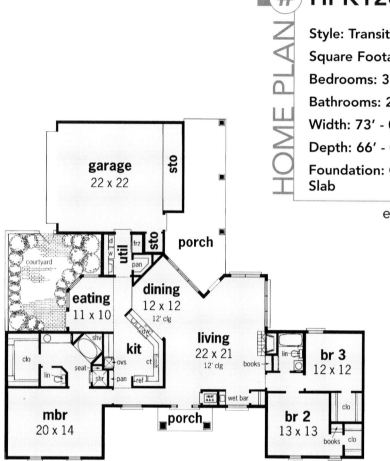

HPK1200254

Style: Transitional

Square Footage: 2,023

Bedrooms: 3

Bathrooms: 2

Width: 73' - 0"

Depth: 66' - 0"

Foundation: Crawlspace, Slab

eplans.com

CONTEMPORARY ELEGANCE IS YOURS for the taking in this charming ranch plan. The exterior is adorned with large brick quoins set against a stucco facade, keystone lintels, a prominent front-facing pediment and multiple rooflines. Special features include 12-foot ceilings in the kitchen and dining and living rooms. The kitchen/eating area accesses the courtyard, while the living room accesses the rear porch. The master suite is located on the left side of the plan, where it indulges in a walk-in closet and full bath with a garden tub and separate shower. Two additional bedrooms are on the right side and share a full bath.

HPK1200233

HOME PLAN #

Style: Country

First Floor: 1,219 sq. ft.

Second Floor: 809 sq. ft.

Total: 2,028 sq. ft.

Bonus Space: 342 sq. ft.

Bedrooms: 3

Bathrooms: 2 ½

Width: 58' - 0"

Depth: 55' - 0"

Foundation: Unfinished Basement

eplans.com

FIRST FLOOR

SECOND FLOOR

THIS UNUSUAL CONTEMPORARY DESIGN features a stunning facade enhanced by a two-story glass turret and a graceful curving staircase. Stairs lead up to a porch that accesses the main living area. The island snack-bar kitchen is open to the dining area, illuminated by the bayed sitting area. The combined living room and family area is warmed by a fireplace. Below, the first level is reserved for the family bedrooms. All three bedrooms feature double doors to the outdoors. The master suite features a private bath, while the two other bedrooms share a hall bath. A two-car garage with storage space completes the first floor.

HOME PLAN

HPK1200257

Style: Traditional

Square Footage: 2,053

Bedrooms: 3

Bathrooms: 2

Width: 67' - 8"

Depth: 58' - 0"

eplans.com

THE ALL-BRICK FRONT ELEVATION OF THIS HOME offers low maintenance to homeowners. A front porch opens to the living areas, all of which are universally designed to be wheelchair accessible. Counters designed in a U-shape define the kitchen. A pull-out shelf and snack bar offer convenience when entertaining and preparing meals. Bay windows provide a view in the breakfast area. An adjacent screened porch is accessible through patio doors and is an excellent place to dine or enjoy the outdoors. The master bedroom features bay windows that welcome a chair to read or take in the view. Bedroom 3 can be utilized as a den, features a window seat, and shares a skylit bath with Bedroom 2. A large utility room offers plenty of counter space to work. The two-car garage is extended to include a place for storage or a work area.

A TRULY ORIGINAL ANGLE at the entrance of this country home belies a much more traditionally designed floor plan. There are two sets of stairs in the foyer, one leading to the second level and the other to the basement. The island kitchen and dining room enjoy the glow of the living room fireplace. The master suite with walk-in closet and bathroom are on the main level and situated next to the two-car garage.

Up the short flight of stairs you'll find a convenient home office—or make it a sitting room to create a truly lavish second bedroom with a roomy closet and private bath. Finish the bonus space as a third bedroom if you wish.

HOME PLAN

(#) HPK1200281

Style: European Cottage

First Floor: 1,488 sq. ft.

Second Floor: 602 sq. ft.

Total: 2,090 sq. ft.

Bonus Space: 1,321 sq. ft.

Bedrooms: 2

Bathrooms: 2

Width: 60' - 0"

Depth: 44' - 0"

Foundation: Finished Basement

eplans.com

FIRST FLOOR

SECOND FLOOR

BASEMENT

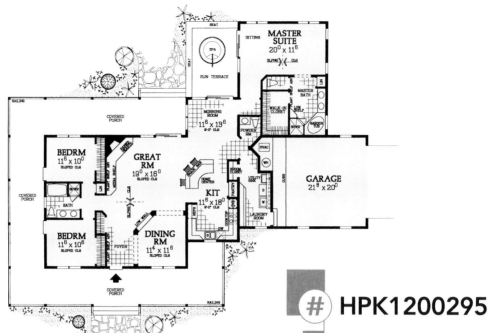

THIS CLASSIC FARMHOUSE ENJOYS

A WRAPAROUND porch that's perfect for enjoyment of the outdoors. To the rear of the plan, a sun terrace with a spa opens from the master suite and the morning room. A grand great room offers a sloped ceiling and a corner fireplace with a raised hearth. The formal dining room is defined by a low wall and graceful archways set off by decorative columns. The tiled kitchen has a centered island counter with a snack bar and adjoins a laundry area. Two family bedrooms reside to the side of the plan, and each enjoys private access to the covered porch. A secluded master suite nestles in its own wing and features a sitting area with access to the rear terrace and spa.

HOME PLAN

HPK1200295

Style: Farmhouse
Square Footage: 2,090
Bedrooms: 3
Bathrooms: 2 ½
Width: 84' - 6"
Depth: 64' - 0"
Foundation: Crawlspace

eplans.com

HOME PLAN

HPK1200276

Style: Country Cottage

First Floor: 1,060 sq. ft.

Second Floor: 1,039 sq. ft.

Total: 2,099 sq. ft.

Bedrooms: 4

Bathrooms: 2 ½

Width: 50' - 8"

Depth: 39' - 4"

Foundation: Unfinished Basement

eplans.com

THIS LOVELY COUNTRY DESIGN features a stunning wrapping porch and plenty of windows to provide the interior with natural light. The living room boasts a centered fireplace, which helps to define this spacious open area. A nine-foot ceiling on the first floor adds a sense of spaciousness and light. The casual living room leads outdoors to a rear porch. Upstairs, four bedrooms cluster around a central hall. The master suite sports a walk-in closet and a deluxe bath with an oval tub and a separate shower.

FIRST FLOOR

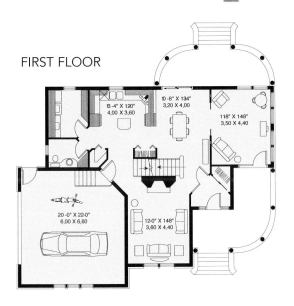

SECOND FLOOR

STEEP ROOFLINES AND COLUMNS make this home one to remember. Starburst windows align along the exterior and offer a nice touch of sophistication. Extra amenities run rampant through this one-story home. The sunroom can be enjoyed during every season. An eating nook right off the kitchen brightens the rear of the home. Utility and storage areas are also found at the rear of the home. A cozy study privately accesses the side porch. The master bedroom is complete with dual vanities and His and Hers closets. Two family bedrooms reside to the left of the plan.

HPK1200290

Style: Traditional

Square Footage: 2,160

Bedrooms: 3

Bathrooms: 2

Width: 68' - 0"

Depth: 64' - 0"

Foundation: Crawlspace, Slab

eplans.com

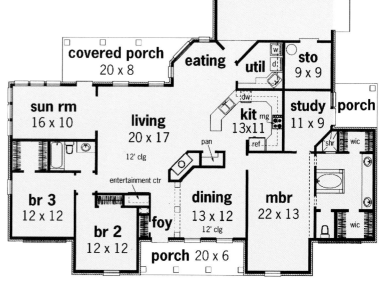

© 1991 Donald A. Gardner Architects, Inc.

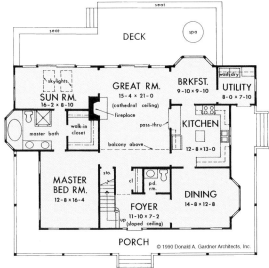

FIRST FLOOR

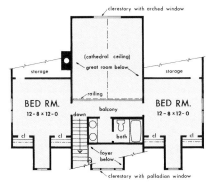

SECOND FLOOR

HOME PLAN

(#) HPK1200238

Style: Farmhouse

First Floor: 1,651 sq. ft.

Second Floor: 567 sq. ft.

Total: 2,218 sq. ft.

Bedrooms: 3

Bathrooms: 2 ½

Width: 55' - 0"

Depth: 42' - 4"

eplans.com

A WONDERFUL WRAPAROUND COVERED PORCH at the front and sides of this house and the open deck with a spa at the back provide plenty of outside living area. Inside, the spacious great room is appointed with a fireplace, cathedral ceiling, and clerestory with an arched window. The kitchen is centrally located for maximum flexibility in layout and features a food-preparation island for convenience. In addition to the master bedroom, with access to the sunroom, there are two second-level bedrooms that share a full bath.

(#) HPK1200371

Style: Transitional

Square Footage: 2,224

Bedrooms: 4

Bathrooms: 3

Width: 58' - 6"

Depth: 74' - 0"

Foundation: Slab

eplans.com

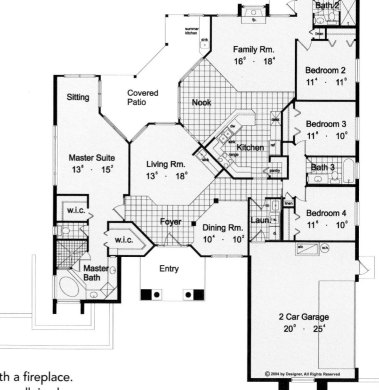

ARCHES CROWNED BY GENTLE, hipped rooflines provide an Italianate charm in this bright and spacious family-oriented plan. A covered entry leads to the foyer that presents the angular, vaulted living and dining rooms. A kitchen with a V-shaped counter includes a walk-in pantry and looks out over the breakfast nook and family room with a fireplace. The master suite features a sitting room, two walk-in closets, and a full bath with a garden tub. Two additional bedrooms share a full bath located between them. A fourth bedroom, with its own bath, opens off the family room, and works perfectly as a guest room

THIS RANCH-STYLE HOME HAS TONS OF CHARACTER and a functional floor plan for a design you're sure to love. Flower-box planters line the front of the home and welcome you into a formal entry. Living and dining rooms greet guests, as the casual family room invites relaxation ahead. Here, a beamed ceiling offers a rustic touch and the fireplace warms on chilly evenings. The kitchen is created to make your life simple and easily serves the eating bay and dining room. The master suite is situated for privacy and enjoys courtyard access and a soothing bath set off by turned-wood posts. Three additional bedrooms (or make one a study) are to the left and share a full bath.

HPK1200289

Style: Traditional

Square Footage: 2,240

Bedrooms: 4

Bathrooms: 2

Width: 74' - 6"

Depth: 50' - 0"

Foundation: Crawlspace, Slab

eplans.com

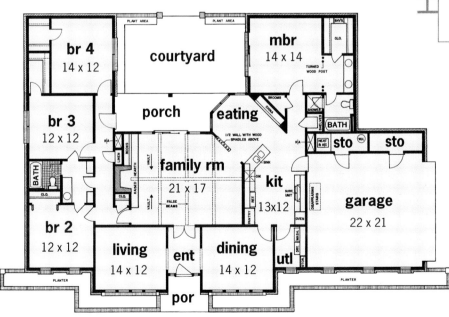

INTERESTING ROOFLINES, KEYSTONE ARCHES atop fanlight windows, and a dramatic covered entry precede the masterful plan within. The foyer opens to the dining room on the right and the living room that boasts a wonderful view to the rear porch and deck straight ahead. A sunny breakfast nook adjoins the angled kitchen on the right. The master suite on the left delights with a cozy corner fireplace, access to the deck, and a lavish bath. Two additional bedrooms share a full bath.

HOME PLAN # HPK1200259

Style: **Southern Colonial**

Square Footage: **2,240**

Bedrooms: **3**

Bathrooms: **2 ½**

Width: **71' - 10"**

Depth: **76' - 10"**

Foundation: **Pier**

eplans.com

Deck
31'x 10'

Porch
18'2"x 10'

Breakfast
11'10"x 11'

Ma. Bath

Master Bedroom
14'6"x 18'4"

Living
22'x 17'

Kitchen
11'10"x 12'

Walk-In Closet

Utility

Bath

WIC

Bedroom
11'8"x 12'6'

Foyer

Dining
13'8"x 12'

Pantry

1/2 Bath

Bedroom
11'4"x 13'

Porch

Three-Car Garage
21'2"x 34'8"

Courtyard

FINE FAMILY LIVING TAKES OFF in this grand two-story plan. The tiled foyer leads to a stately living room with sliding glass doors to the back terrace and columns separating it from the dining room. Additional accents include a corner curios niche and access to a covered porch. For casual living, look no further than the family room/breakfast room combination. On the second floor, the master bedroom offers a fireplace.

HOME PLAN # HPK1200241

Style: SW Contemporary

First Floor: 1,163 sq. ft.

Second Floor: 1,077 sq. ft.

Total: 2,240 sq. ft.

Bedrooms: 3

Bathrooms: 2 ½

Width: 36' - 0"

Depth: 63' - 0"

Foundation: Slab

eplans.com

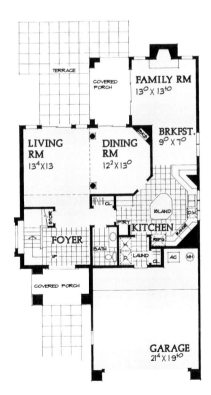

FIRST FLOOR

SECOND FLOOR

FIRST FLOOR

SECOND FLOOR

FROM THE WRAPAROUND COVERED PORCH, enter this attractive home to find the roomy master suite on the left and the formal dining room on the right. Leading through double doors from the dining area is a sunlit U-shaped kitchen with a breakfast island. This room then flows into a comfortable family room featuring a fireplace. Separate access to the garage and upstairs completes the first floor. The second floor is reserved for three family bedrooms that share a full bath.

HPK1200251

HOME PLAN

Style: Victorian

First Floor: 1,371 sq. ft.

Second Floor: 894 sq. ft.

Total: 2,265 sq. ft.

Bonus Space: 300 sq. ft.

Bedrooms: 4

Bathrooms: 3 ½

Width: 58' - 0"

Depth: 58' - 4"

Foundation: Unfinished Basement

eplans.com

HOME PLAN

HPK1200261

Style: Farmhouse

Square Footage: 2,293

Bonus Space: 536 sq. ft.

Bedrooms: 4

Bathrooms: 3

Width: 88' - 0"

Depth: 51' - 9"

Foundation: Slab, Unfinished Basement

eplans.com

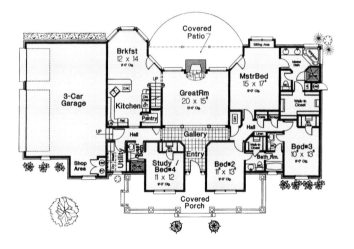

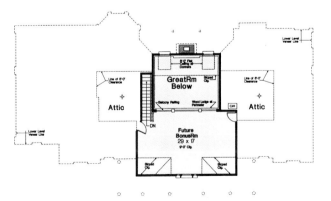

SPECIAL GATHERINGS AND EVENTS will take place in the heart of this splendid home. The great room, defined by columns, includes a hearth and views to the covered patio. The east wing is occupied by the sleeping quarters, with a master bedroom which features an exclusive master bath. Two family bedrooms both have walk-in closets and share a compartmented bath with twin vanities. The three-car garage opens to the hall where the utility room, the kitchen, and an additional bedroom/study can be accessed. A future bonus room is also available upstairs.

FIRST FLOOR

SECOND FLOOR

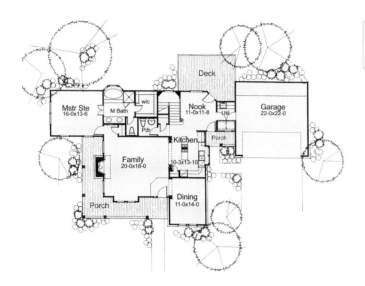

HPK1200299

Style: Farmhouse

First Floor: 1,468 sq. ft.

Second Floor: 830 sq. ft.

Total: 2,298 sq. ft.

Bonus Space: 235 sq. ft.

Bedrooms: 4

Bathrooms: 3 ½

Width: 79' - 10"

Depth: 44' - 2"

Foundation: Crawlspace, Slab, Unfinished Basement

eplans.com

THIS TWO-STORY FARMHOUSE DESIGN is happily enhanced by its family-friendly layout. The front wraparound porch directly accesses the family room warmed by a fireplace. The island kitchen is set between the formal dining room and breakfast nook. The first-floor master suite is located at the rear for privacy and features a private master bath and walk-in closet. A family garage completes this floor. Upstairs, three additional bedrooms share the second floor with two baths and attic space.

SOUTHERN COMFORT IS EXPRESSED with this house. Imagine all the entertaining that can be done with a full covered wrap-around porch! With dormers, French doors, and casement windows, this home is truly unique. The kitchen has an island with dual sinks and a four-stool snack bar. The dining and living areas share a fireplace. A master bedroom with its own French doors leading to the porch and a bathroom with both tub and shower are on the main floor. A spacious laundry room with shelving unit is also on the main floor. Upstairs, a lounge area, partly open to the main floor below, can provide extra space to study or read. Two bedrooms share a full-size bathroom. The dormer windows provide an added touch of charm.

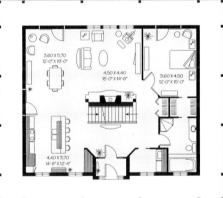

FIRST FLOOR

HOME PLAN

#HPK1200240

Style: Country Cottage

First Floor: 1,334 sq. ft.

Second Floor: 965 sq. ft.

Total: 2,299 sq. ft.

Bedrooms: 3

Bathrooms: 2

Width: 40' - 8"

Depth: 32' - 8"

Foundation: Unfinished Basement

eplans.com

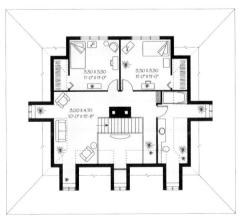

SECOND FLOOR

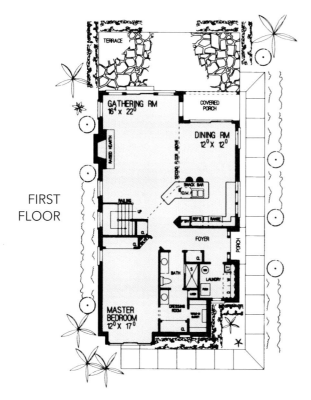

FIRST FLOOR

SECOND FLOOR

PERFECT FOR A NARROW LOT, THIS SHINGLE-AND-STONE
Nantucket Cape home caters to the casual lifestyle. The side entrance gives direct access to the wonderfully open living areas: gathering room with fireplace and an abundance of windows; island kitchen with angled, pass-through snack bar; and dining area with sliding glass doors to a covered eating area. Note also the large deck that further extends the living potential. Also on this floor is the large master suite with a compartmented bath, private dressing room, and walk-in closet. Upstairs, you'll find the three family bedrooms. Of the two bedrooms that share a bath, one features a private balcony.

HPK1200285

HOME PLAN

Style: Cape Cod
First Floor: 1,387 sq. ft.
Second Floor: 929 sq. ft.
Total: 2,316 sq. ft.
Bedrooms: 4
Bathrooms: 3
Width: 30' - 0"
Depth: 51' - 8"
Foundation: Crawlspace

eplans.com

© 1991 Donald A. Gardner Architects, Inc.

HOME PLAN

HPK1200270

Style: Farmhouse

First Floor: 1,756 sq. ft.

Second Floor: 565 sq. ft.

Total: 2,321 sq. ft.

Bedrooms: 4

Bathrooms: 3

Width: 56' - 8"

Depth: 42' - 4"

eplans.com

A WRAPAROUND COVERED PORCH at the front and sides of this house and an open deck at the back provide plenty of outside living area. The spacious great room features a fireplace, cathedral ceiling, and clerestory with an arched window. The island kitchen offers an attached skylit breakfast room complete with a bay window. The first-floor master bedroom contains a generous closet and a master bath with a garden tub, double-bowl vanity, and shower. The second floor sports two bedrooms and a full bath with a double-bowl vanity. An elegant balcony overlooks the great room.

FIRST FLOOR

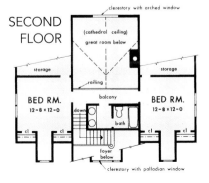

SECOND FLOOR

FIRST FLOOR

A VARIETY OF WINDOWS provides both sunshine and views for this attractive three-bedroom home. Just off the foyer, an office/study awaits. At the rear of the home, a spacious two-story living area features a warming fireplace and easy access to the dining area and kitchen. This room offers sliding glass doors to a private dining patio as well as to your own greenhouse! Secluded on the first floor, the master suite is complete with a walk-in closet, dual vanities, and separate tub and shower.

SECOND FLOOR

HOME PLAN

 # HPK1200292

Style: **Traditional**

First Floor: **1,606 sq. ft.**

Second Floor: **747 sq. ft.**

Total: **2,353 sq. ft.**

Bedrooms: **3**

Bathrooms: **2 ½**

Width: **56' - 0"**

Depth: **53' - 2"**

Foundation: **Unfinished Basement**

eplans.com

THIS VICTORIAN DESIGN is far more than just a pretty face. The turret houses a spacious den with built-in cabinetry on the first floor and provides a sunny bay window for the family bedroom upstairs. Just off the foyer, the formal living and dining rooms create an elegant open space for entertaining, while a focal-point fireplace with an extended hearth warms up the spacious family area. The cooktop-island kitchen and morning nook lead to a powder room and laundry area. Two second-floor bedrooms share a full bath, while the master suite offers a private bath with an oversized whirlpool tub, twin vanities, and a walk-in closet.

HOME PLAN

HPK1200268

Style: Victorian

First Floor: 1,337 sq. ft.

Second Floor: 1,025 sq. ft.

Total: 2,362 sq. ft.

Bedrooms: 3

Bathrooms: 2 ½

Width: 50' - 6"

Depth: 72' - 6"

Foundation: Crawlspace

eplans.com

FIRST FLOOR

SECOND FLOOR

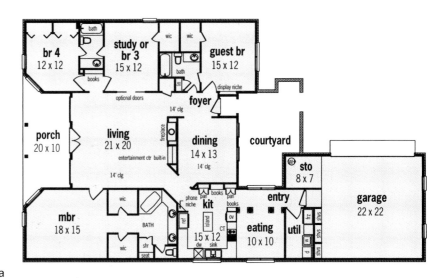

LOOKING A BIT LIKE A FRENCH COUNTRY manor, this alluring home maintains privacy with a stucco wall that encloses a splendid courtyard. Inside, 14-foot ceilings grace the family living areas. The foyer opens to the dining room on the left or to the brightly lit living room straight ahead. Thoughtful amenities in the living room include French doors to the rear porch, a fireplace, and a built-in entertainment center. The U-shaped kitchen is accentuated by an island and hosts bookshelves and a phone niche. Sleeping quarters begin with a guest room (with a semiprivate bath) and two secondary bedrooms, one of which also makes a perfect study. The master suite is separated for privacy, enhanced by a private bath with a garden tub and dual walk-in closets.

HPK1200272

HOME PLAN

Style: Traditional
Square Footage: 2,366
Bedrooms: 4
Bathrooms: 3
Width: 50' - 0"
Depth: 86' - 0"
Foundation: Slab

eplans.com

HOME PLAN

HPK1200372

Style: Country Cottage

Square Footage: 2,367

Bedrooms: 3

Bathrooms: 2 ½

Width: 72' - 0"

Depth: 62' - 0"

Foundation: Crawlspace

eplans.com

THIS GORGEOUS COUNTRY DREAM HOUSE brings down-home comfort to any neighborhood. A shaded, covered porch opens to a formal foyer with a niche, perfect for an entry table. On the left, a lovely dining room with a convenient butler's pantry overlooks the front yard. The great room is open and bright, enjoying a wall of windows, built-in media center, and cozy fireplace. The kitchen serves up delectable meals with ease. Bedrooms are situated on each side of the plan, featuring a lavish master suite with a magnificent bath. Two additional bedrooms and a den/study complete the home.

ONE-STORY LIVING TAKES A LOVELY TRADITIONAL turn in this brick home. The entry foyer opens to the formal dining room and the great room through graceful columned archways. The open gourmet kitchen, bayed breakfast nook, and keeping room with a fireplace will be a magnet for family activity. Sleeping quarters offer two family bedrooms, a hall bath, and a rambling master suite with a bayed sitting area and a sensuous bath.

(#) HPK1200278

Style: Traditional

Square Footage: 2,377

Bedrooms: 3

Bathrooms: 2

Width: 69' - 0"

Depth: 49' - 6"

Foundation: Finished Walkout Basement

eplans.com

HOME PLAN

HPK1200288

Style: Craftsman

Square Footage: 2,387

Bonus Space: 377 sq. ft.

Bedrooms: 3

Bathrooms: 2 ½

Width: 69' - 6"

Depth: 68' - 11"

Foundation: Slab, Crawlspace

eplans.com

THIS THREE-BEDROOM HOME brings the past to life with Tuscan columns, dormers, and fanlight windows. The entrance is flanked by the dining room and study. The great room boasts cathedral ceilings and a fireplace, with an open design that connects to the kitchen area. The spacious kitchen adjoins a breakfast nook and accesses the rear covered veranda. The master bedroom enjoys a sitting area, access to the covered veranda, and a spacious bathroom. This home is complete with two family bedrooms.

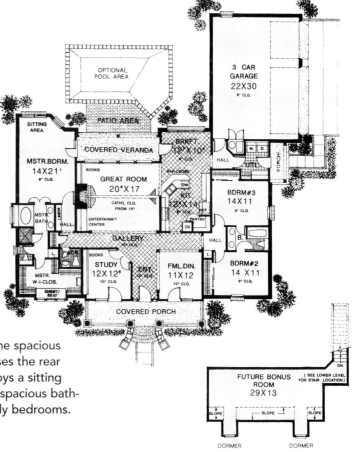

FIRST FLOOR

SECOND FLOOR

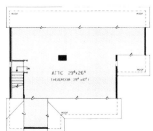

HOME PLAN

HPK1200294

Style: Farmhouse

First Floor: 1,375 sq. ft.

Second Floor: 1,016 sq. ft.

Total: 2,391 sq. ft.

Bedrooms: 3

Bathrooms: 2 ½

Width: 62' - 7"

Depth: 54' - 0"

Foundation: Unfinished Basement

eplans.com

COVERED PORCHES, FRONT AND BACK, are a fine preview to the livable nature of this Victorian home. Living areas are defined in a family room with a fireplace, formal living and dining rooms, and a kitchen with a breakfast room. An ample laundry room, a garage with a storage area, and a powder room round out the first floor. Three second-floor bedrooms are joined by a study and two full baths. The master suite on this floor has two closets, including an ample walk-in, as well as a relaxing bath with a tile-rimmed whirlpool tub and a separate shower with a seat.

HOME PLAN

HPK1200239

Style: Traditional

First Floor: 2,281 sq. ft.

Second Floor: 112 sq. ft.

Total: 2,393 sq. ft.

Bedrooms: 3

Bathrooms: 2 ½

Width: 60' - 0"

Depth: 71' - 0"

Foundation: Crawlspace, Slab

eplans.com

THE ASSORTMENT OF WINDOWS and double-columned stands that hold the front porch enhance the facade of this traditional home. The heart of the home is the spacious living room featuring a cozy fireplace and built-in entertainment center. An island kitchen gracefully serves the formal dining room—which displays a built-in china wall—through a pass-through. Sleeping quarters are found to the right of the home. Two family bedrooms share a full bath. The extravagant master suite gives you the option of relaxing in its sitting area or in the outside screened porch, which also leads to a large deck—great for outdoor barbecues!

FIRST FLOOR

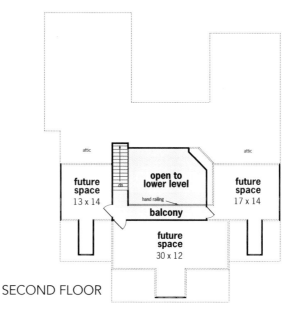

SECOND FLOOR

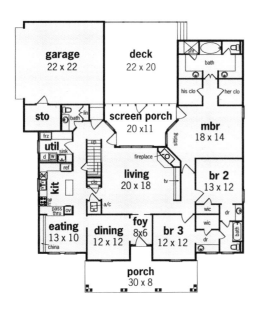

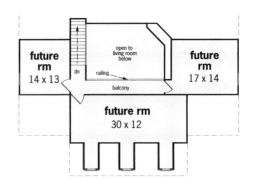

A CHEERFUL FACADE WRAPS AROUND a family-friendly plan in this home. The covered front porch opens to a foyer that leads to formal dining on the left and an all-purpose living area straight ahead. An entertainment center and corner fireplace grace the living room, which overlooks the screened porch and rear deck. An island kitchen and eating nook lie to the left side of the plan. The master suite and two family bedrooms are on the right. Upstairs is future space for additional bedrooms or a leisure room.

HOME PLAN

HPK1200245

Style: Traditional

First Floor: 2,281 sq. ft.

Second Floor: 112 sq. ft.

Total: 2,393 sq. ft.

Bonus Space: 866 sq. ft.

Bedrooms: 3

Bathrooms: 2 ½

Width: 60' - 0"

Depth: 71' - 0"

Foundation: Slab, Crawlspace

eplans.com

FIRST FLOOR

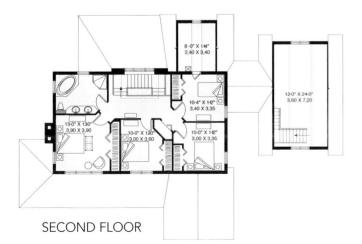

SECOND FLOOR

HOME PLAN

HPK1200273

Style: Contemporary

First Floor: 1,279 sq. ft.

Second Floor: 1,114 sq. ft.

Total: 2,393 sq. ft.

Bonus Space: 337 sq. ft.

Bedrooms: 4

Bathrooms: 2

Width: 68' - 0"

Depth: 36' - 0"

Foundation: Slab

eplans.com

COVERED PORCHES IN THE FRONT AND REAR of this contemporary design serve to facilitate a smooth indoor/outdoor relationship. First-floor living spaces are wide open—you'll never miss a word of conversation if you're cooking in the kitchen and serving friends and family in hearth-warmed family room or informal dining area nearby. Also on this level are the laundry room and a full bath. Venture upstairs to find four family bedrooms, each with a spacious closet, and another full bath. Dual sinks in this bathroom help ease the chaos of morning/bedtime rituals.

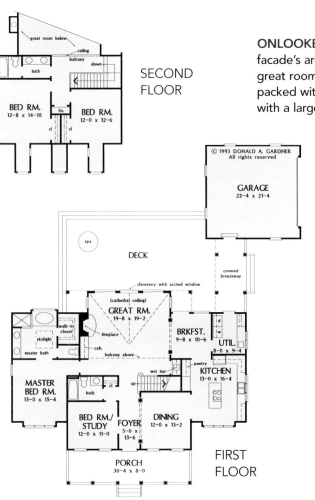

SECOND FLOOR

great room below.
railing
balcony
down
bath
BED RM.
12-8 x 14-10
BED RM.
12-0 x 12-6
lin.
cl cl

© 1993 DONALD A. GARDNER
All rights reserved

GARAGE
22-4 x 21-4

spa

DECK

covered breezeway

clerestory with arched window

(cathedral ceiling)
GREAT RM.
19-8 x 19-2

walk-in closet!
skylight
master bath
fireplace
cab.
balcony above

BRKFST.
9-8 x 10-6

d
w
UTIL.
8-0 x 9-4

MASTER BED RM.
13-0 x 15-4

bath
cl
wet bar
up

pantry
KITCHEN
13-0 x 16-4

BED RM./
STUDY
12-0 x 11-0

FOYER
5-0 x
13-6

DINING
12-0 x 13-2

PORCH
30-4 x 8-0

FIRST FLOOR

ONLOOKERS WILL DELIGHT in the symmetry of this facade's arched windows and dormers. The interior offers a great room with a cathedral ceiling. This open plan is also packed with the latest design features, including a kitchen with a large island, a wet bar in the great room, a bedroom/study combination on the first floor, and a gorgeous master suite with a spa-style bath. Upstairs, two family bedrooms share a compartmented hall bath. An expansive rear deck and generous covered front porch offer maximum outdoor livability.

HOME PLAN

HPK1200231

Style: Farmhouse
First Floor: 1,783 sq. ft.
Second Floor: 611 sq. ft.
Total: 2,394 sq. ft.
Bedrooms: 4
Bathrooms: 3
Width: 70' - 0"
Depth: 79' - 2"

eplans.com

HOME PLAN

HPK1200286

Style: French

First Floor: 1,566 sq. ft.

Second Floor: 837 sq. ft.

Total: 2,403 sq. ft.

Bedrooms: 5

Bathrooms: 4 ½

Width: 116' - 3"

Depth: 55' - 1"

Foundation: Unfinished Basement

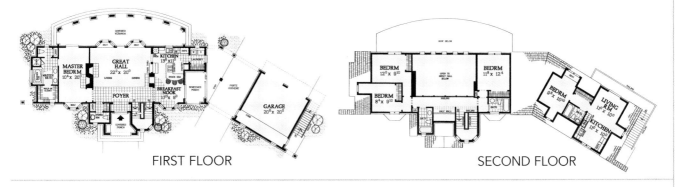

FIRST FLOOR

SECOND FLOOR

HOME PLAN

HPK1200287

Style: Traditional

Square Footage: 2,409

Bedrooms: 4

Bathrooms: 3

Width: 65' - 0"

Depth: 85' - 0"

Foundation: Slab

HOME PLAN

HPK1200269

Style: Farmhouse

First Floor: 1,250 sq. ft.

Second Floor: 1,166 sq. ft.

Total: 2,416 sq. ft.

Bedrooms: 4

Bathrooms: 2 ½

Width: 64' - 0"

Depth: 52' - 0"

Foundation: Unfinished Walkout Basement, Unfinished Basement

FIRST FLOOR

SECOND FLOOR

HOME PLAN

HPK1200298

Style: SW Contemporary

First Floor: 1,216 sq. ft.

Second Floor: 1,204 sq. ft.

Total: 2,420 sq. ft.

Bedrooms: 3

Bathrooms: 2 ½

Width: 52' - 4"

Depth: 34' - 8"

Foundation: Unfinished Basement

FIRST FLOOR

SECOND FLOOR

© 1985 Donald A. Gardner Architects, Inc.

HOME PLAN
HPK1200247

Style: Farmhouse

First Floor: 1,724 sq. ft.

Second Floor: 728 sq. ft.

Total: 2,452 sq. ft.

Bedrooms: 3

Bathrooms: 2 ½

Width: 61' - 4"

Depth: 46' - 6"

FIRST FLOOR

SECOND FLOOR

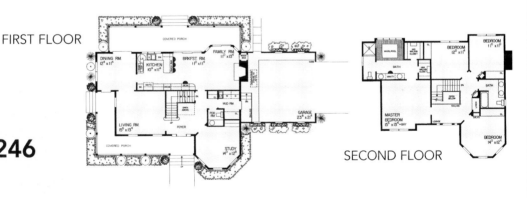

FIRST FLOOR

SECOND FLOOR

HOME PLAN
HPK1200246

Style: Victorian

First Floor: 1,269 sq. ft.

Second Floor: 1,227 sq. ft.

Total: 2,496 sq. ft.

Bedrooms: 4

Bathrooms: 2 ½

Width: 70' - 0"

Depth: 44' - 5"

Foundation: Unfinished Basement

Paradise Planned—Landscapes and Projects Complete the Picture

truly gratifying landscape design takes cues from the architecture of the home, your sense of style, and the natural properties of the land. You will also need to make a decision about the kind of landscape you desire. For instance, perennials and bulbs used throughout a design will establish a garden theme and provide cutting flowers for indoor bouquets. But remember that a garden will need a lot of care and constant attention. And a neglected garden will do nothing for a home's appeal. Similarly, edible gardens are very appropriate in a country-inspired design, but need to be protected from the elements. More shaded parts of the landscape call for sitting areas or outdoor structures, such as storage sheds or small barns.

The right landscaping design will effectively frame your home from the rest of the neighborhood. If your lot will not allow the placement of a tall fence or natural barrier between the home and the next-door neighbor, place "retreat" areas away from property lines. That is, resist the natural urge to place quiet areas in only the corners of the yard. With the right design, owners can create a relaxing getaway right in the middle of the plan.

The virtue of a predrawn landscape and project plan is that you can enjoy the benefits of a professional design without

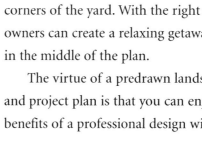

THE FULL BEAUTY of a landscape plan stems from how it can mature and grow naturally around the home. No two garden plans will be identical.

A GOOD LANDSCAPE DESIGN lets nature take its course. Only then will dwelling areas feel welcoming and special.

Karen Bussolini

paying for custom landscaping. Do-it-yourselfers can easily manage the tasks required to install a bed or build a gazebo. Your new landscape will improve your outdoor environment the day it's completed, and the initial investment will likely pay for itself by adding to the value of your home.

Ernest Braun

FIRST FLOOR

GARAGE
25/0 X 38/0 +

UP

SECOND FLOOR

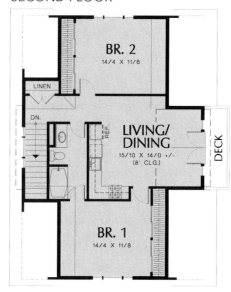

BR. 2
14/4 X 11/8

LINEN

DN.

REF.

LIVING/
DINING
15/10 X 14/0 +/-
(8' CLG.)

DECK

BR. 1
14/4 X 11/8

PERFECT FOR A VACATION COTTAGE or guest home, this contemporary design offers a cozy interior. The first-floor garage holds up to three cars—or use this additional space for storing seasonal vacation equipment such as skis or a family boat. Living space is found on the second floor. The kitchen is open to the combined living and dining area and is enhanced by 10-foot ceilings. This room opens through a set of double doors onto the petite front deck. Two family bedrooms feature ample closet space and share a full bath and linen storage.

HOME PLAN

HPK1200302

Style: Garage
First Floor: 1,079 sq. ft.
Second Floor: 908 sq. ft.
Total: 1,987 sq. ft.
Bedrooms: 2
Bathrooms: 1
Width: 41' - 0"
Depth: 43' - 6"
Foundation: Slab

eplans.com

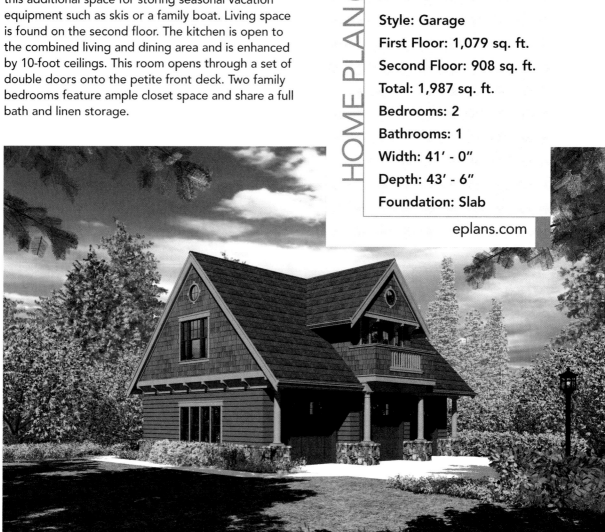

HPK1200303

Style: Contemporary

First Floor: 995 sq. ft.

Second Floor: 928 sq. ft.

Total: 1,923 sq. ft.

Bedrooms: 2

Bathrooms: 1 ½

Width: 32' - 0"

Depth: 32' - 0"

Foundation: Slab

eplans.com

AN ENDEARING COACH-HOUSE design gives modern practicality a touch of class. The garage holds room for two cars and provides a powder room. Upstairs, a two-bedroom apartment enjoys comfortable appointments such as an open great room featuring the dining and kitchen areas. A full bath is positioned between the bedrooms.

SECOND FLOOR

FIRST FLOOR

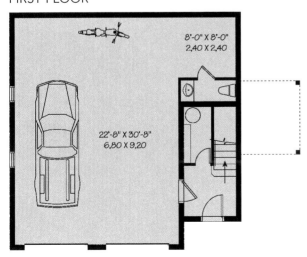

HOME PLAN

HPK1200304

Style: Contemporary

First Floor: 903 sq. ft.

Second Floor: 673 sq. ft.

Total: 1,576 sq. ft.

Width: 38' - 0"

Depth: 24' - 0"

Foundation: Slab

FIRST FLOOR

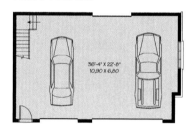

36'-4" X 22'-8"
10,90 X 6,80

SECOND FLOOR

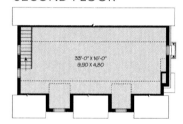

33'-0" X 16'-0"
9,90 X 4,80

FIRST FLOOR

two-car garage

SECOND FLOOR

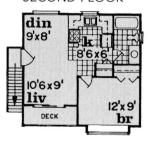

din
9'x8'

k
8'6x6'

10'6x9'
liv

DECK

12'x9'
br

HOME PLAN

HPK1200305

Style: Garage

First Floor: 528 sq. ft.

Second Floor: 484 sq. ft.

Total: 1,012 sq. ft.

Bedrooms: 1

Bathrooms: 1

Width: 27' - 6"

Depth: 22' - 0"

Foundation: Slab

HOME PLAN

HPK1200306

Style: Traditional

First Floor: 908 sq. ft.

Second Floor: 659 sq. ft.

Total: 1,567 sq. ft.

Bedrooms: 1

Bathrooms: 1

Width: 31' - 0"

Depth: 36' - 0"

Foundation: Slab

FIRST FLOOR

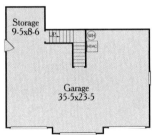

SECOND FLOOR

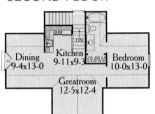

HOME PLAN

HPK1200307

Style: Garage

First Floor: 484 sq. ft.

Second Floor: 264 sq. ft.

Total: 748 sq. ft.

Width: 34' - 6"

Depth: 22' - 0"

Foundation: Slab

FIRST FLOOR

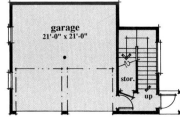

SECOND FLOOR

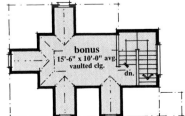

HOME PLAN #

HPK1200308

Style: Garage

Square Footage: 576

Width: 24' - 0"

Depth: 24' - 0"

Foundation: Slab

2 car garage

FIRST FLOOR

3-CAR GARAGE
33⁸ x 29⁴

SECOND FLOOR

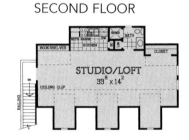

STUDIO/LOFT
33⁸ x 14²

HOME PLAN #

HPK1200309

Style: Garage

First Floor: 824 sq. ft.

Second Floor: 670 sq. ft.

Total: 1,494 sq. ft.

Bathrooms: 1

Width: 34' - 4"

Depth: 24' - 0"

Foundation: Slab

two car
garage
19'-4 x 21'-4

HOME PLAN #

HPK1200310

Style: Garage
Width: 20' - 0"
Depth: 22' - 0"
Foundation: Slab

HOME PLAN #

HPK1200311

Style: Garage
Square Footage: 264
Width: 12' - 0"
Depth: 22' - 0"
Foundation: Slab

garage
11'-4 x 21'-4

FLOWER
BOX

HOME PLAN #

HPK1200312

Style: Garage

Square Footage: 704

Width: 32' - 0"

Depth: 22' - 0"

Foundation: Slab

HOME PLAN #

HPK1200313

Style: Garage

Square Footage: 1,008

Width: 36' - 0"

Depth: 28' - 0"

Foundation: Slab

HOME PLAN
HPK1200314

Style: Garage
Square Footage: 484
Width: 22' - 0"
Depth: 22' - 0"
Foundation: Slab

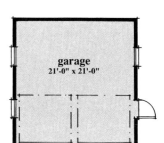

garage
21'-0" x 21'-0"

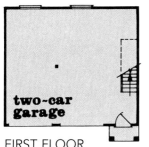

two-car garage

FIRST FLOOR

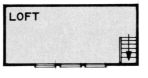

LOFT

SECOND FLOOR

HOME PLAN
HPK1200315

Style: Garage
First Floor: 672 sq. ft.
Second Floor: 320 sq. ft.
Total: 992 sq. ft.
Width: 28' - 0"
Depth: 27' - 0"
Foundation: Slab

LANDSCAPES & OUTDOOR PROJECTS

HOME PLAN

HPK1200316

Style: Traditional

First Floor: 672 sq. ft.

Second Floor: 588 sq. ft.

Total: 1,260 sq. ft.

Width: 28' - 0"

Depth: 24' - 0"

Foundation: Slab

FIRST FLOOR

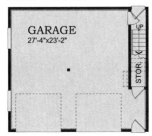

GARAGE
27'-4"x23'-2"

UP

STOR.

SECOND FLOOR

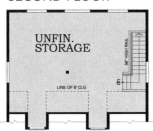

UNFIN.
STORAGE

30" HIGH RAIL

dn

LINE OF 8' CLG

HOME PLAN

HPK1200317

Style: Garage

First Floor: 816 sq. ft.

Second Floor: 618 sq. ft.

Total: 1,434 sq. ft.

Width: 32' - 0"

Depth: 26' - 0"

Foundation: Slab

FIRST FLOOR

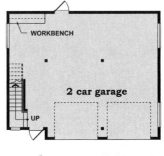

WORKBENCH

2 car garage

UP

SECOND FLOOR

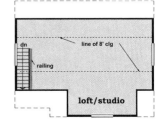

dn

line of 8' clg

railing

loft/studio

HOME PLAN #

HPK1200318

Style: Garage
Square Footage: 192
Width: 16' - 0"
Depth: 12' - 0"
Foundation: Slab

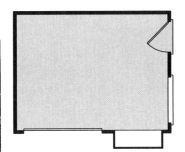

HOME PLAN #

HPK1200319

Style: Structure
Square Footage: 72
Width: 12' - 0"
Depth: 6' - 0"

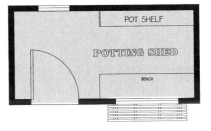

POT SHELF

POTTING SHED

BENCH

LANDSCAPES & OUTDOOR PROJECTS

HOME PLAN #

HPK1200320

Style: Structure

Square Footage: 288

Width: 20' - 0"

Depth: 16' - 0"

Foundation: Slab, Crawlspace

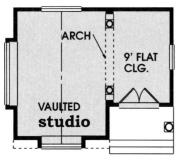

HOME PLAN #

HPK1200321

Style: Structure

Square Footage: 100

Width: 10' - 0"

Depth: 10' - 0"

Foundation: Slab

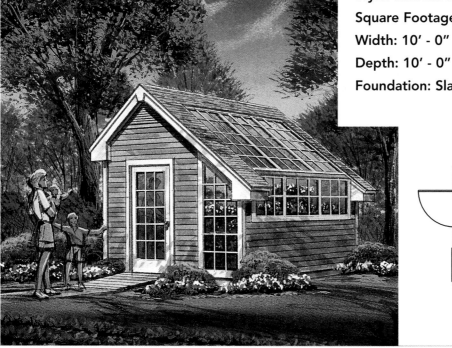

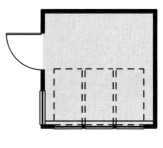

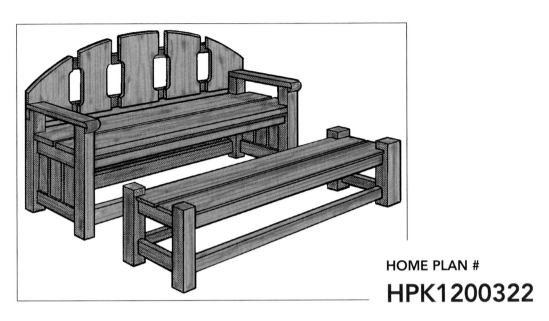

HOME PLAN #
HPK1200322

Style: Project

HOME PLAN #
HPK1200323

Style: Structure
Width: 8' - 0"
Depth: 8' - 0"

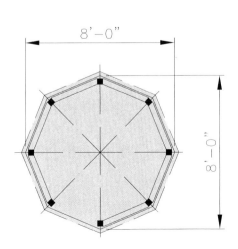

HOME PLAN #

HPK1200324

Style: Structure

Width: 20' - 0"

Depth: 30' - 0"

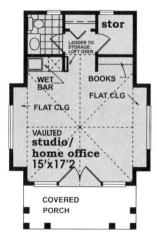

HOME PLAN #

HPK1200325

Style: Structure

Square Footage: 64

Width: 8' - 0"

Depth: 8' - 0"

Foundation: Pier (same as Piling), Block

HOME PLAN

HPK1200326

Style: Project

Square Footage: 64

Width: 8' - 0"

Depth: 8' - 0"

Foundation: Slab

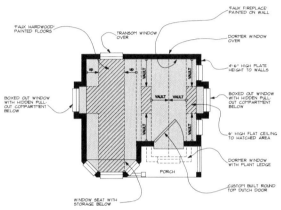

HOME PLAN

HPK1200327

Style: Structure

Square Footage: 160

Width: 16' - 0"

Depth: 12' - 0"

Foundation: Slab

PLAN

HPK1200328

Season: Summer

Design by: Maria Morrison

eplans.com

A ROMANTIC OLD-FASH-IONED ROSE BORDER is always in style. The voluptuous fragrance and heavy-petaled blossoms of roses bring charm to any sunny garden. Here, the designer chooses old garden roses, which offer scent as well as ease of care, unlike modern hybrid tea roses. Although many of these cherished plants bloom only once during the season, their other charms far outweigh the repeat-blossoms of their modern cousins. Many have excellent summer and fall foliage and a heavy crop of glossy rose hips in autumn. In this border design, these belles

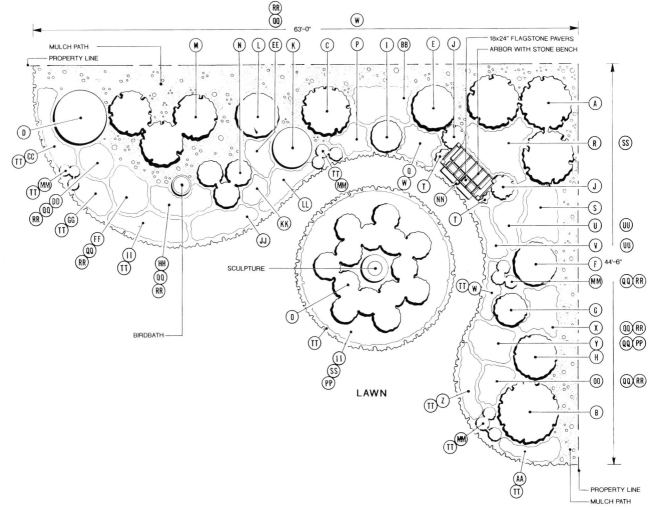

of the garden
are mixed with classic
perennial partners and bulbs to create
months of color and interest. A circular bed is tucked into this
pleasingly curved border and is separated by a ribbon-like strip
of lawn. A rose-covered pergola in the border frames a classical-
ly inspired sculpture in the bed's center, creating two balanced
focal points. A stone bench placed under the arbor provides a
lovely spot to contemplate the wonders of this flower-filled
haven. Mulched pathways at the back of the border allow easy
access for maintenance and for cutting flowers for the house.

**DESIGNED TO BEAUTIFY THE
CORNER** of a backyard, this
rose-filled border can be easily
turned into a freestanding
bed and placed in the center
of a lawn by rounding off the
straight sides into a more free-
flowing shape.

WHEN SMALL TREES, FLOWER-ING SHRUBS, PERENNIALS, and groundcovers are planted together, the result is a lovely mixed border that looks great throughout the year. The trees and shrubs—both evergreen and deciduous—provide structure and form in winter, while also offering dec-orative foliage and flowers in other seasons. Perennials and bulbs occupy large spaces between groups of woody plants and contribute leaf tex-ture and floral color to the scene.Even though this border contains a lot of

(#) HPK1200329

Season: Spring
Design by: Jim Morgan

PLAN

eplans.com

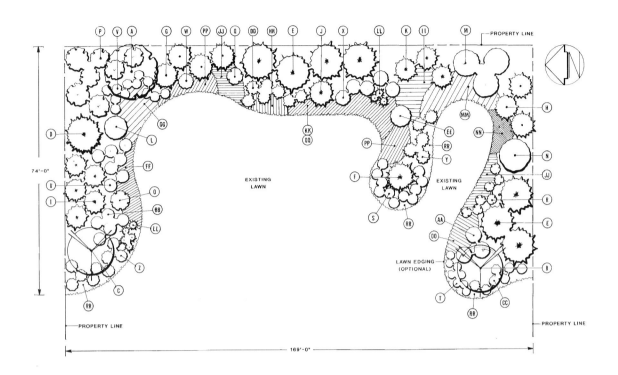

plants, it is easy to care for. That's part of the beauty of a mixed border—the woody plants are long-lived and need little pruning if allowed to grow naturally. By limiting the number of perennials and blanketing the ground with weed-smothering groundcovers, maintenance is kept to a minimum without sacrificing beauty.

You can install this mixed border in a sunny location almost anywhere on your property, though it's intended to run along the back of an average-sized lot. If your property is larger or smaller than the one in this plan, you can alter the design by either increasing or decreasing the number of plants in each grouping.

Evergreen and deciduous shrubs and small trees, mixed with drifts of bulbs and flowering perennials, create an ever-changing border that's gorgeous every month of the year.

A FLOWER-FILLED GARDEN CREATED IN THE ROMANTIC STYLE of an English border need not demand much care, as this lovely design illustrates. The designer carefully selects unfussy bulbs and perennials and a few flowering shrubs, all of which are disease- and insect-resistant and noninvasive, and don't need staking or other maintenance.

A balance of spring-, summer-, and fall-blooming plants keeps the border exciting throughout the growing season. Because English gardens are famous for their gorgeous roses, the designer includes several rosebushes, but chooses ones unharmed by bugs and mildew.

Hedges form a backdrop for most English flower gardens; the designer plants an informal one here to reduce pruning. A generous mulched path runs between the flowers and the hedge, so it's easy to tend them, and the edging keeps grass from invading and creating a nuisance.

Plant this border along any sunny side of your property. Imagine it along the back of the yard, where you can view it from a kitchen window or from a patio or deck, along one side of the front yard, or planted with the hedge bordering the front lawn and providing privacy from the street.

PLAN

HPK1200330

Season: Summer
Design by: Maria Morrison

eplans.com

BRIMMING WITH EASY-CARE FLOWERS from spring through fall, this low-maintenance flower border evokes the spirit of an English garden, but doesn't require a staff to take care of it.

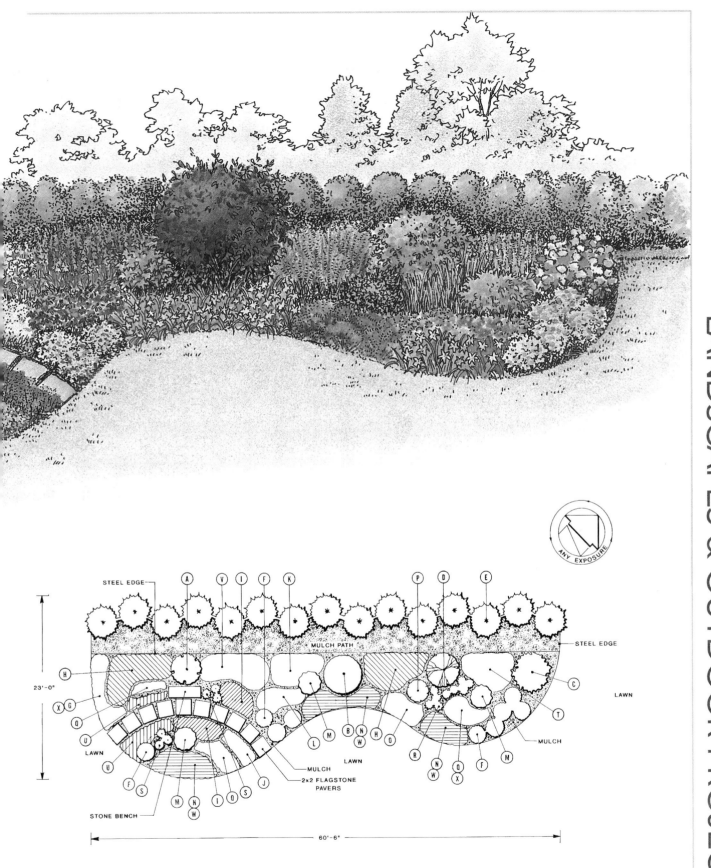

STEEL EDGE

MULCH PATH

STEEL EDGE

23'-0"

LAWN

LAWN

LAWN

MULCH

MULCH

2x2 FLAGSTONE
PAVERS

STONE BENCH

60'-6"

ANY EXPOSURE

IF YOU'D LIKE TO HAVE AN EASY-CARE GARDEN that offers more than a single burst of brilliant color, this season-spanning border packed with perennials is perfect for you. The designer selects a wide array of perennials that begin flowering in the spring, provide plenty of color throughout the summer and continue blooming into the fall. All you'll need to do is remove spent blossoms from time to time and divide plants every few years.

A deciduous hedge curves around the back of the border, providing a pleasant foil for the perennials throughout the growing season. Before dropping its leaves in autumn, the hedge puts on its own show of dazzling color just as the perennials are beginning to slow down. Once the perennials have finished blooming, you can leave the dried flower heads on the plants to add subtle beauty to the winter landscape.

The classic curved shape of this border will fit easily into a corner of your front- or back-yard. If you have a large yard, you may want to install this border on one side with its mirror image on the other and with a path set between them.

 # HPK1200331

PLAN

Season: Summer
Design by: Maria Morrison

eplans.com

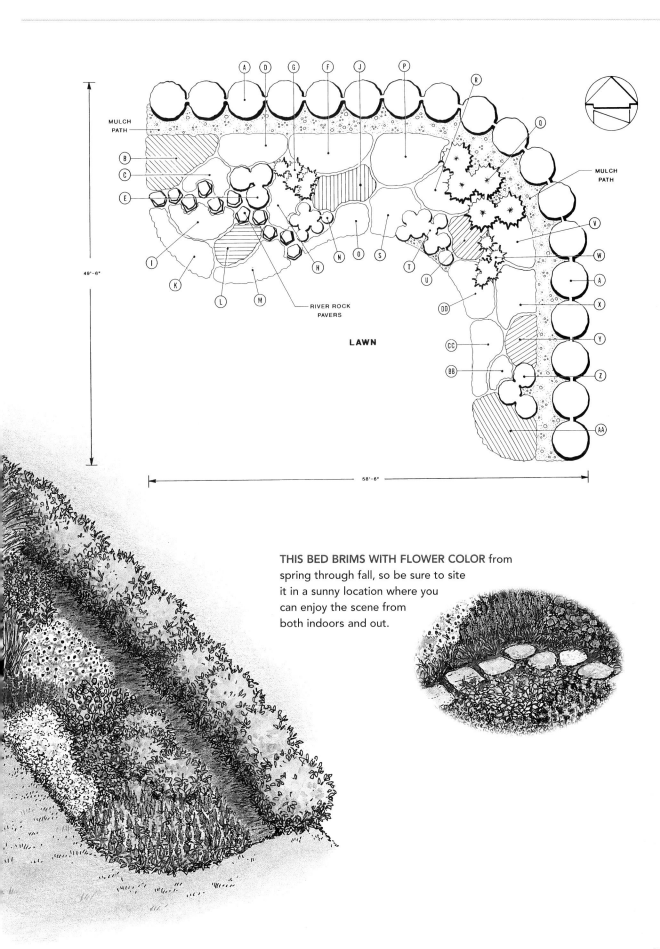

MULCH
PATH

MULCH
PATH

49'-6"

58'-6"

RIVER ROCK
PAVERS

LAWN

THIS BED BRIMS WITH FLOWER COLOR from
spring through fall, so be sure to site
it in a sunny location where you
can enjoy the scene from
both indoors and out.

PLAN

(#) HPK1200332

Season: Summer

Design by: Damon Scott

eplans.com

BLUE AND YELLOW FLOWERS PLANT-ED TOGETHER REWARD THE GAR-DENER with a naturally complementary color scheme that's as bright and pretty as any garden can be. It's hard to err when using these colors, because the pure blues and the lavender blues—whether dark or pastel—look just as pretty with the pale lemon yellows as with the bright sulfur yellows and the golden yellows. Each combination makes a different statement, some subtle and sweet as with the pastels, and others bold and demanding as with the deep vivid hues. But no combination fails to please.

The designer of this beautiful bed, which can be situated in any sunny spot, effectively orchestrated a sequence of blue-and-yellow-flowering perennials so the garden blooms from spring through fall. The designer not only combined the floral colors beautifully together, but also incorporated various flower shapes and textures so they make a happy opposition. Fluffy, rounded heads of blossoms set off elegant spires, and mounded shapes mask the lanky stems of taller plants. Large, funnel-shaped flowers stand out against masses of tiny, feathery flowers like jewels displayed against a silk dress.

Although the unmistakable color scheme for this garden is blue and yellow, the designer sprinkled in an occasional spot of orange to provide a lovely jolt of brightly contrasting color. A few masses of creamy white flowers frost the garden, easing the stronger colors into a compatible union.

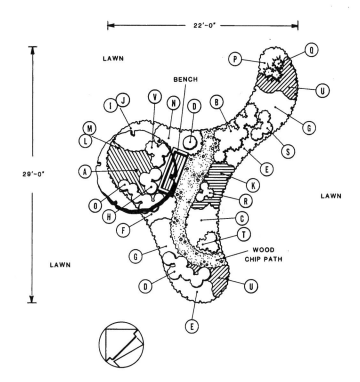

NATURAL COLOR COMPANIONS, BLUE AND YELLOW FLOWERS create a pleasing garden scene that looks great anywhere it's planted. This island bed works perfectly in an open sunny yard, but it could be modified to fit along the side of a house or to the back up against a fence or hedge along a property border.

THIS BORDER INCLUDES EVERYTHING BIRDS NEED— food, water, and nesting sites—and encourages them to become permanent residents of your yard. The design curves inward, creating a sense of enclosure and a sanctuary that appeals to even the shiest types of birds. The border's attractive design includes a pond, birdhouse, and birdbath, which act as focal points and make the garden irresistible to people as well. The large variety of pretty fruiting shrubs offers birds natural nourishment throughout much of the year, but you can supplement the food supply with store-bought bird food if you wish. Deciduous and evergreen trees provide shelter and nesting places, and the mulched

PLAN

 # **HPK1200333**

Season: Summer
Design by: Michael J. Opisso

eplans.com

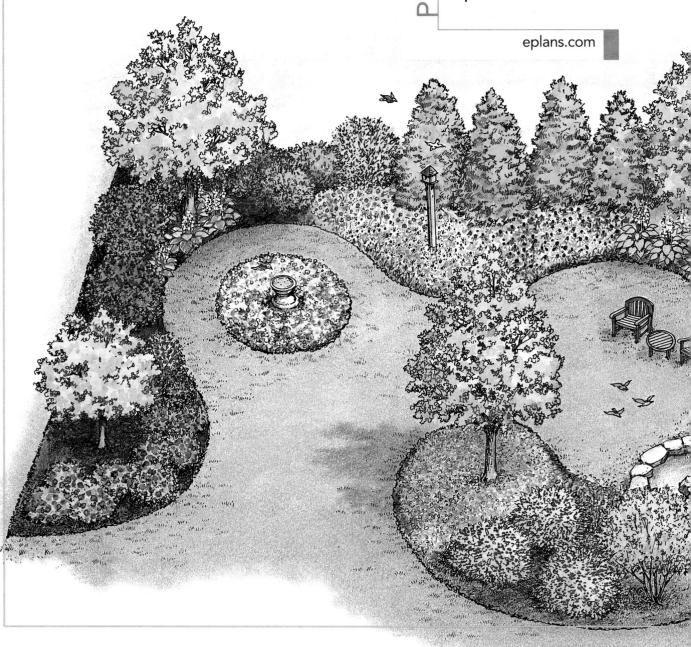

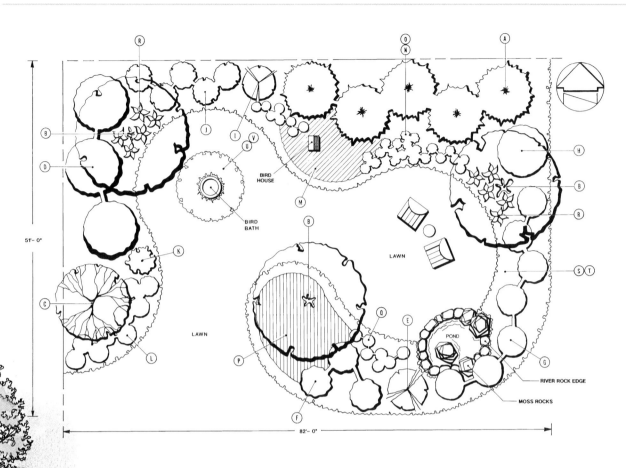

areas give birds a place to take dust baths and to poke around for insects and worms. Because water is so important to birds, the garden includes two water features: a small naturalistic pond, and a birdbath set in a circular bed. Both offer spots for perching, bathing, and drinking. In cold-weather climates, consider adding a special heater to the birdbath to keep the water from freezing; water attracts birds in winter even more than birdseed.

NOTE: The pond is not included in the landscape plans.

BIRDS FLOCK TO THIS BORDER, which provides them with ample supplies of food and water and locations for nesting and bathing. There's plenty of room for birdwatchers as well.

NATURE LOVERS WILL DELIGHT IN THE ABUNDANT NUMBER of birds that will flock to this beautiful garden. An attractive collection of berried plants and evergreens offers food and shelter for the wildlife, while creating a handsome, pastoral setting.

THERE IS NO BETTER WAY TO WAKE UP IN THE MORNING than to the sound of songbirds in the garden. Wherever you live, you will be surprised at the number and variety of birds you can attract by offering them a few basic necessities—water, shelter, nesting spots, and food. Birds need water for drinking and bathing. They need shrubs and trees, especially evergreens, for shelter and nesting. Edge spaces—open areas with trees nearby for quick protection—provide ground feeders with foraging places, and plants with berries and nuts offer other natural sources of food.

PLAN # **HPK1200334**

Season: Autumn

Design by: Michael J. Opisso

eplans.com

The garden presented here contains all the necessary elements to attract birds to the garden. The shrubs and trees are chosen especially to provide a mix of evergreen and deciduous species. All of these, together with the masses of flowering perennials, bear seeds, nuts, or

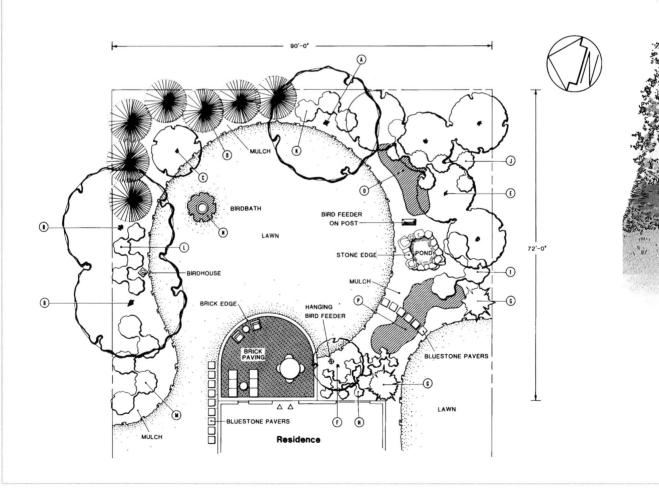

berries that are known to appeal to birds. The berry show looks quite pretty, too, until the birds gobble them up! Planted densely enough for necessary shelter, the bird-attracting plants create a lovely private backyard that's enjoyable throughout the seasons.

The birdbath is located in the lawn so it will be in the sun. A naturalistic pond provides water in a more protected setting. The birdhouses and feeders aren't really necessary—though they may be the icing on the cake when it comes to luring the largest number of birds—because the landscape provides abundant natural food and shelter. Outside one of the main windows of the house, a birdfeeder hangs from a small flowering tree, providing an up-close view of your feathered friends.

THIS NATURALISTIC GARDEN PLAN relies upon several different features to attract as many different species of birds as possible. A songbird's basic needs include food, water, and shelter, but this backyard plan offers luxury accommodations not found in every yard, and also provides the maximum opportunity for birds and bird-watchers to observe each other. Special features provide for specific birds; for example, the rotting log attracts woodpeckers and the dusting area will be used gratefully by birds to free themselves of parasites. In addition to plants that produce plentiful berries and seeds, the designer includes a ground feeder to lure mourning doves, cardinals, and other birds that prefer to eat off the ground. The birdhouse located in the shade of the

HPK1200335

Season: Summer
Design by: David Poplawski

eplans.com

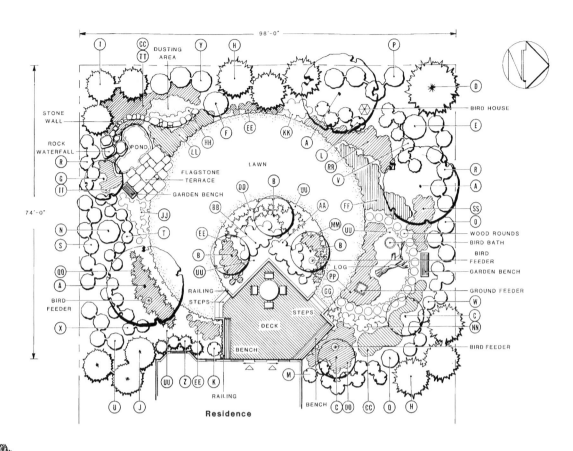

specimen tree to the rear of the garden suits a wide variety of songbirds.

The angular deck nestles attractively into the restful circular shapes of the garden. The designer encloses the deck amidst the bird-attracting plantings to maximize close-up observation opportunities and create an intimate setting. Two other sitting areas welcome birdwatchers into the garden. A bench positioned on a small patio under the shade of a graceful flowering tree provides a relaxing spot to sit and contemplate the small garden pool (not included in plan blueprints) and the melody of a low waterfall. Another bench—this one situated in the sun—may be reached by strolling along a path of wood-rounds on the opposite side of the yard. Both wildlife and people will find this backyard a very special retreat.

This large, naturalistic backyard design creates a wonderful environment for attracting a wide range of bird species, because it offers a plentiful supply of natural food, water, and shelter. The deck and garden benches invite people to observe and listen to the songbirds in comfort.

YOUR YARD WILL BE HOME TO JEWEL-TONED, quicksilver hummingbirds once you install this colorful bed. A rich display of bright annuals and perennials, specially selected to attract hummingbirds, creates a delightful setting. All birds need water, and hummingbirds are particularly attracted to flowing water, so the birdbath in this design features a small bubbler device. Informal flagstone pavers lead through the garden to a semicircular mulched area set with flagstones that surround the birdbath. The path to the wooden pergola (not included in plans), which creates a lovely sitting area, leads through the pretty flowers. Climbing vines and hanging planters attached to the pergola provide additional nectar and create a pleasant shady area where you can watch the hummers dart by. Hang the pots so you can watch the birds at eye level from the sitting area. Neutral-colored plastic pots look best and cut down on evaporation, minimizing watering chores.

HPK1200336

Season: Summer

Design by: Patrick J. Duffe

eplans.com

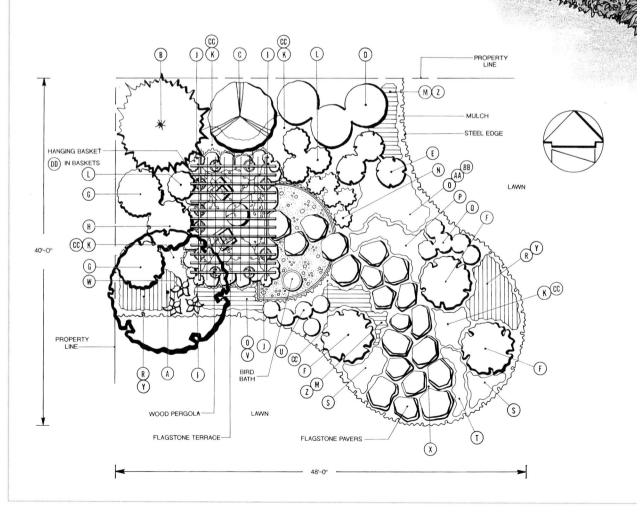

Site this
design in a sunny
location close to your
house so you can observe the birds from indoors as well. Or, if you
prefer, locate the bed in a quiet corner of your yard to
enhance the tranquil atmosphere.

Sit beneath the flower-draped pergola and enjoy
glimpses of hummingbirds as they pause in mid-
flight to drink nectar and splash in the birdbath.

THIS ATTRACTIVE BORDER DOES DOUBLE DUTY, because it serves both as a beautiful landscape planting as well as an effective wildlife sanctuary. Offering natural food sources, shelter, and water, the planting brings birds to your property throughout the year, and its informal but tidy design looks right at home in any suburban setting. Although they serve a practical purpose as well, the birdhouses, bird feeders, and birdbath add interesting architectural elements to the design. The shrubs and trees used in the border—and even many of the perennials and ornamental grasses—produce berries and seeds that attract birds. They are arranged informally and should be left

PLAN

(#) **HPK1200337**

Season: Autumn

Design by: Salvatore A. Masullo

eplans.com

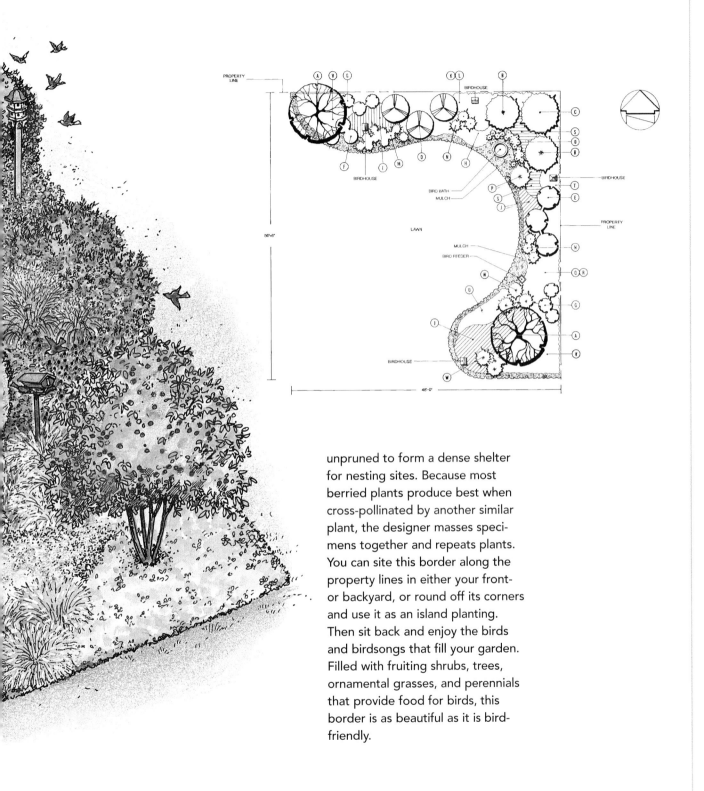

unpruned to form a dense shelter
for nesting sites. Because most
berried plants produce best when
cross-pollinated by another similar
plant, the designer masses speci-
mens together and repeats plants.
You can site this border along the
property lines in either your front-
or backyard, or round off its corners
and use it as an island planting.
Then sit back and enjoy the birds
and birdsongs that fill your garden.
Filled with fruiting shrubs, trees,
ornamental grasses, and perennials
that provide food for birds, this
border is as beautiful as it is bird-
friendly.

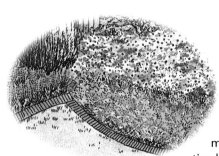

THIS DESIGN PROVES THAT "DROUGHT TOL-ERANT" and "low main-tenance" don't have to mean boring. This attrac-tive backyard looks lush, color-ful, and inviting but relies entirely on plants that flourish even if water is scarce. This means you won't spend any time tending to their watering needs once the plantings are established. Even the lawn is planted with a newly developed turf grass that tolerates long periods of drought.

The designer specifies buffalo grass, a native grass of the American West, for the lawn. The grass has fine-textured, grayish-green leaf blades, tolerates cold, and needs far less water to remain green and healthy than most lawns. It goes completely dormant during periods of extended drought, but greens up with rain or irriga-tion. To keep the lawn green throughout summer, all you need do is water occasionally if rainfall doesn't cooperate. And mowing is an occasional activity, too! This slow-growing grass needs mowing only a few times in summer to about one inch high. To keep the grass from spreading into the planting borders—and to

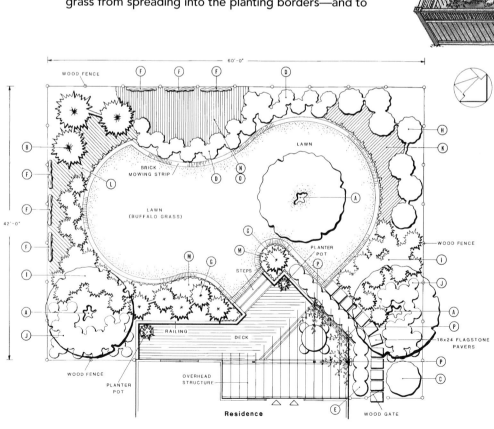

reduce weeding and edging chores—the designer calls for a decorative brick mowing strip surrounding the lawn.

Deciduous and evergreen trees and shrubs interplanted with long-blooming flowering perennials—all drought-tolerant—adorn the yard, bringing color every season. Against the fence grow espaliered shrubs, which offer flowers in spring and berries in winter. The vine-covered trellis shades the roomy, angular deck, where you can sit in cool seclusion and relax while your beautiful backyard takes care of itself.

This environmentally sound landscape plan won't strain the local water supply or burden you with gardening chores, because all the plants used here—from grass to flowers to trees—are easy-care, trouble-free kinds that flourish without frequent rain or irrigation.

PLAN

HPK1200338

Season: Summer
Design by: Damon Scott

eplans.com

WHEN A BUSY COUPLE WANTS A LANDSCAPE THAT IS DISTINCTIVE and requires little maintenance, the Japanese-style garden and backyard pictured here are a perfect solution. The essence of a Japanese garden lies in emulating nature through simple, clean lines that do not look contrived. The low, tight hedges underscore the plantings behind them, while providing a contrast in form. Looking straight out from the deck, the perimeter planting is a harmony of shades of green, with interest provided from contrasting textures. Paving stones border the deck because in the Japanese garden, every element has both an aesthetic and a functional purpose. The stones alleviate the wear that would result from stepping directly onto the lawn from the deck, and provide a visual transition between the man-made deck and the natural grass.

PLAN

HPK1200339

Season: Spring
Design by: Michael J. Opisso

eplans.com

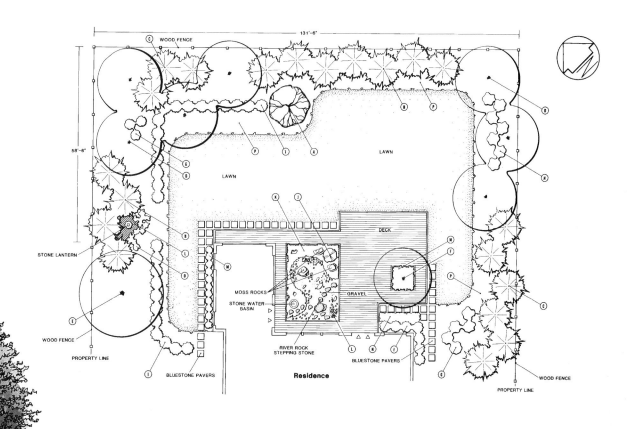

The pavers act as more than a path; they also provide a sight line to the stone lantern on the left side of the garden. The deck, like the rest of the landscape, has clean, simple lines, and provides the transition from the home's interior to the garden. It surrounds a viewing garden, one step down. In the Japanese tradition, this miniature landscape mimics a natural scene. The one large moss rock plays an important role—it is situated at the intersection of the stepping-stone paths that lead through the garden. Here a decision must be made as to which way to turn. The stone water basin, a symbolic part of the Japanese tea ceremony, is located near the door to the house, signaling the entrance to a very special place.

HPK1200340

Season: Summer
Design by: Salvatore A. Masullo

PLAN

eplans.com

A COLORFUL, EASY-CARE FLOWER BED LIKE THIS PAISLEY-SHAPED RAISED BED can be located almost anywhere on your property—it is perfectly suitable as an entry garden, or as a transition between different levels in a backyard. The bed's curving, organic shape echoes the sinuous stone wall that divides its upper and lower sections. Flagstone steps further divide the bed and lead visitors from the lower, more symmetrical area to the upper, more asymmetrical section of the garden. The designer incorporates lovely low-growing flowering perennials to spill over the wall, creating a curtain of flowers. Twin flowering shrubs flank the entry steps, and a sin-

gle specimen of the same type marks the exit. The rest of the bed is planted with a profusion of easy-care perennials, bulbs, ornamental grasses, and flowering shrubs. This garden bed requires only a little of your precious time for routine maintenance. You'll need to remove spent blossoms, do a bit of cleanup in spring and fall, and divide the perennials every few years. A curving stone retaining wall and small flowering tree give this flower garden dimension and form, which keep it attractive throughout the year.

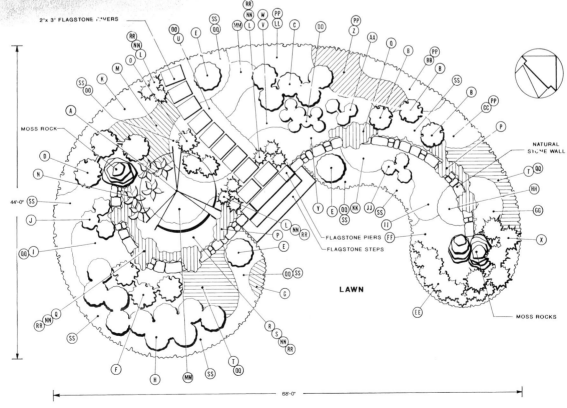

2'x 3' FLAGSTONE PAVERS

MOSS ROCK

44'-0"

NATURAL STONE WALL

FLAGSTONE PIERS

FLAGSTONE STEPS

LAWN

MOSS ROCKS

68'-0"

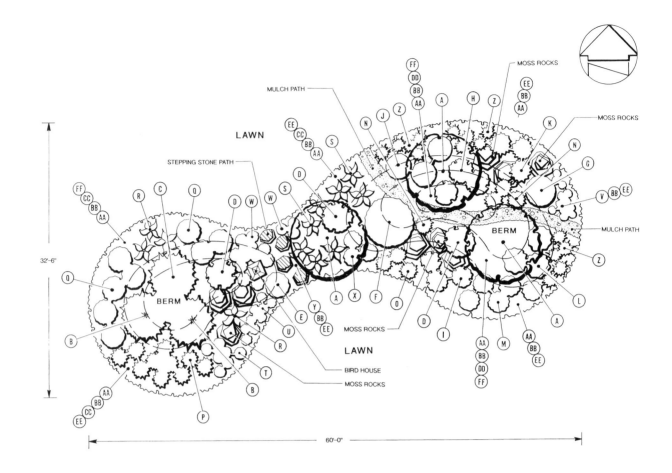

FF
DD
BB
AA

MOSS ROCKS

EE
BB
AA

MULCH PATH

N J Z A H Z

A

K

MOSS ROCKS

EE
CC
BB
AA

S

LAWN

STEPPING STONE PATH

D

S

D W W

BERM

N

G

V BB EE

MULCH PATH

FF
CC
BB
AA

R C Q

Z

Q

BERM

A X F O

D

L

A

Y
BB
EE

MOSS ROCKS

I

AA
M

AA
BB
EE

B

E

U

R

LAWN

D

AA
BB
DD
FF

32'-6"

AA

CC
BB
EE

T

B

BIRD HOUSE

MOSS ROCKS

P

60'-0"

ONE OF THE GREAT JOYS OF A LOVELY LOW-MAINTENANCE GARDEN is having the time to really enjoy it. If you'd like a garden bed that is eye-catching as well as easy-care, this design is for you. This bow-tie-shaped bed contains a delightful variety of low-maintenance perennials, evergreens, deciduous trees and shrubs, and spring bulbs. Such a diverse blend of easy-care plants guarantees you'll have both year-round color and the time to take pleasure in every season's display.

The berms at each end of the bed create a small valley that is traversed by a natural stone path. Trees screen the peak of the higher berm, adding a bit of mystery and encouraging visitors to explore. Two pathways—one of mulch, the other of stepping stones—make it easy to enjoy the plantings up close and to perform maintenance tasks, such as occasional deadheading and weeding. Moss rocks in three areas of the garden and a birdhouse near the stepping-stone path provide pleasing structure and interest.

Locate this easy-care bed in an open area of lawn in the front- or backyard to create a pretty view that can be enjoyed from indoors and out.

 HPK1200341

Season: Summer

Design by: Jeffery Diefenbach

eplans.com

PLAN

HPK1200342

Season: Spring

Design by: Maria Morrison

eplans.com

THE ROUGHLY C-SHAPED DESIGN OF THIS SHADY BED CREATES AN EYE-PLEASING CURVE. The garden's undulating interior edge forms all kinds of interesting nooks and crannies, which invite visitors to explore. Site this bed under the spread of high-canopied trees, which offer filtered shade—the kind that allows many types of shade-loving plants to flourish. Shade-loving shrubs dominate the bed, with drifts of spring-flowering bulbs, colonies of ferns and groups of perennials interspersed throughout to add more color. Bulbs dot the mulched areas between the shrubs in spring. Once the bulbs finish their display and go dormant, the mulch serves as pathways into the rest of the bed. Many of the shrubs have lovely

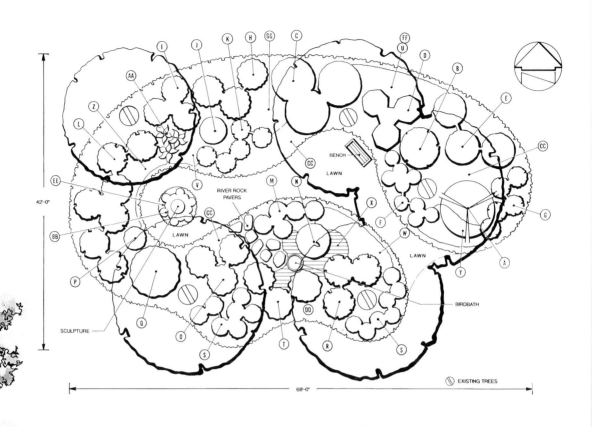

Labels on the plan: I, J, K, H, GG, C, FF/U, D, B, E, AA, Z, L, CC, BENCH, LAWN, EE, V, RIVER ROCK PAVERS, M, N, X, F, W, CC, G, BB, CC, LAWN, A, Y, P, Q, D, S, T, DD, R, S, SCULPTURE, BIRDBATH

42'-0"

68'-0"

⊘ EXISTING TREES

flowers during spring and summer, followed by showy berries that appear in fall and persist through winter. The designer adds a birdbath to accommodate the birds attracted by the berry-producing shrubs. Structural elements include a garden sculpture and a stepping-stone path that leads to a rustic bench, where visitors can sit and enjoy the naturalistic setting. A shady front- or backyard can be transformed into a lovely garden setting by planting this undulating border beneath the existing trees. Modify the plan to suit the locations of your existing trees and dig planting holes for shrubs only where you will not sever tree roots that are thicker than one inch in diameter.

LANDSCAPES & OUTDOOR PROJECTS

A SHADE GARDEN NEED NOT DEPEND ON FLOWERS—which usually need some sun to perform well—for color. You can enliven a shady area with a border that relies on a rainbow of foliage color to provide subtle, yet engaging beauty. An assortment of plants with variegated or unusually tinted foliage, such as burgundy, blue-green, golden yellow and chartreuse, thrives in shady conditions. This design contains an artful mix of foliage plants with colors and textures that range from understated to bold. In this gently curving border, the designer combines a variety of deciduous and evergreen shrubs and trees with perennials to provide year-round foliage color. Many of the plants also add floral accents to the design. The simple green of some of the evergreen plants acts as a foil for variegated and colored leaves in the border and helps to create a harmonious scene. A semicircular flagstone path leads to a bench, enticing visitors to sit in the cool shade and enjoy the splendor of the leafy display. Designed for a location where sunlight is insufficient to support most free-flowering plants, this showy border derives its color from an array of shade-loving shrubs and perennials featuring variegated, golden or purplish-red leaves.

HPK1200343

PLAN

Season: Summer

Design by: Michael J. Opisso and Anne Rode

eplans.com

PROPERTY
LINE

PROPERTY
LINE

LAWN

FLAGSTONE WALK

BENCH

EXISTING TREES

LANDSCAPES & OUTDOOR PROJECTS

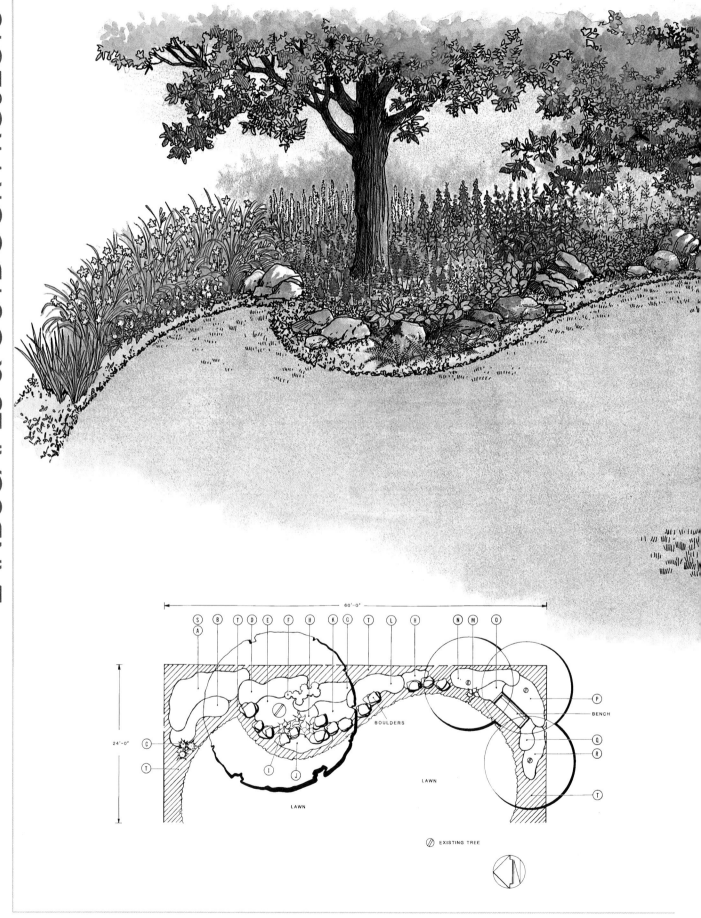

BOULDERS

BENCH

LAWN

LAWN

EXISTING TREE

60'-0"

24'-0"

IF YOU'RE CONSTANTLY COMPLAIN-ING THAT NOTHING WILL GROW in the shade of the trees in your backyard, consider planting this beautiful shady flower border. Lawn grass needs full sun and struggles to grow under trees, so why not plant something that flourishes in the shade and looks much prettier! This charming flower border features shade-loving perennials and ferns, fits under existing trees, and blooms from spring through fall. In this design, flowering perennials grow through a low evergreen groundcover, which keeps the garden pretty even in winter, when the perennials are dormant. Also providing year-round interest are rocks and boulders, as well as a bench that invites you to sit and enjoy the pretty scene. The designer shows this garden against a fence along the property border, but you could plant it in front of a hedge or other shrubbery and place it anywhere in your yard. If your property is smaller, you can easily eliminate the corner containing the bench and end the border with the group of three rocks to the left of the bench. This garden of shade-loving plants flourishes under trees where grass struggles to survive. Be sure to keep the plants healthy by providing plenty of water and fertilizer, especially if the garden plants compete for moisture and nutrients with thirsty tree roots.

HPK1200344

Season: Summer

Design by: Michael J. Opisso

eplans.com

PLAN

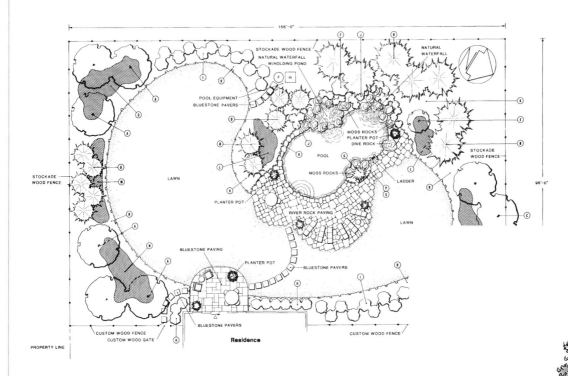

IF YOU LOOK AT THIS LANDSCAPE DESIGN and ask yourself, "Is that really a swimming pool?" then the designer is to be congratulated because he succeeded in his intention. Yes, it is a swimming pool, but the pool looks more like a natural pond and waterfall—one that you might discover in a clearing in the woods during a hike in the wilderness. Although the pool is not included in the blueprints for this design, the surrounding landscape lends itself to its placement. Leave the pool out for a pleasing rock garden, play area, or romantic gazebo hideaway. The designer achieves an aesthetically pleasing, natural look by employing several techniques. Large boulders form the waterfalls, one of which falls from a holding pond set among the boulders. If you do not choose to build a pool here, the boulders could empty into a pond or calming fountain. River-rock paving—the type of water-worn rocks that line the cool water of a natural spring or a rushing stream—adds a

HPK1200345

Season: Summer
Design by: Damon Scott

PLAN

eplans.com

touch of wilderness. The beautiful grassy areas of the landscape offer a serene setting with abundant floral and foliage interest throughout the year. For security reasons, a wooden stockade fence surrounds the entire backyard, yet the plantings camouflage it well. The irregular kidney shape of the lawn is pleasing to look at and beautifully integrates this naturalistic landscaping into its man-made setting. Abundant floral and foliage interest year-round, river-rock paving, and border plantings bring a wonderful, natural setting to your own backyard.

MANY CULTURES SEEM TO HAVE AN IDENTIFIABLE GARDEN STYLE—there are formal Italian fountain gardens, French parterres, English perennial borders, and Japanese contemplation gardens. For many years, we didn't have an American-style garden. Now, a new trend has arisen which the originators have dubbed the "New American Garden." This style of landscaping is naturalistic and relies on sweeps of ornamental grasses to create the feel of the prairies that once dominated much of the American landscape. The backyard garden presented here follows that

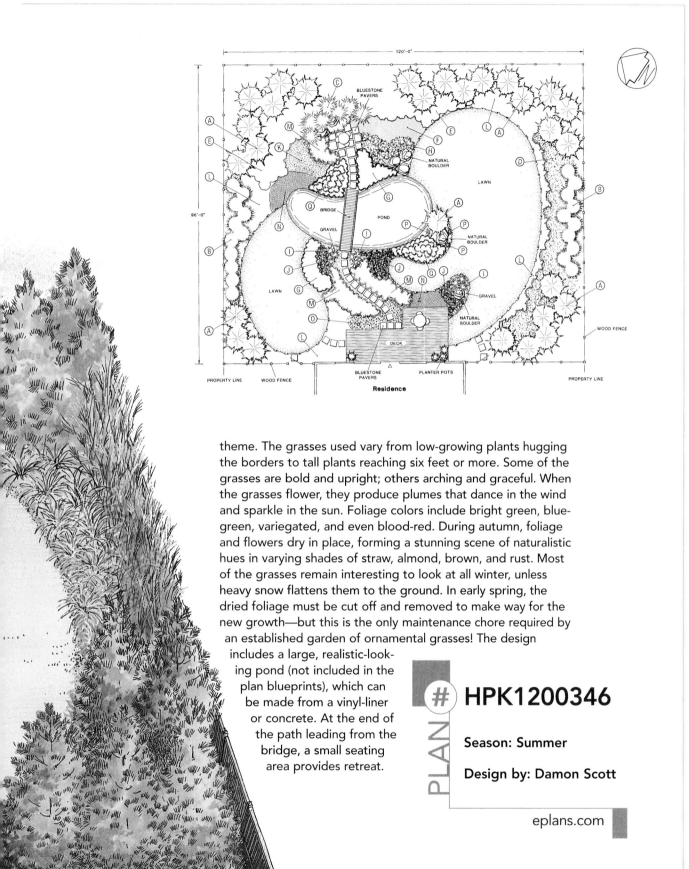

theme. The grasses used vary from low-growing plants hugging the borders to tall plants reaching six feet or more. Some of the grasses are bold and upright; others arching and graceful. When the grasses flower, they produce plumes that dance in the wind and sparkle in the sun. Foliage colors include bright green, blue-green, variegated, and even blood-red. During autumn, foliage and flowers dry in place, forming a stunning scene of naturalistic hues in varying shades of straw, almond, brown, and rust. Most of the grasses remain interesting to look at all winter, unless heavy snow flattens them to the ground. In early spring, the dried foliage must be cut off and removed to make way for the new growth—but this is the only maintenance chore required by an established garden of ornamental grasses! The design includes a large, realistic-looking pond (not included in the plan blueprints), which can be made from a vinyl-liner or concrete. At the end of the path leading from the bridge, a small seating area provides retreat.

PLAN

HPK1200346

Season: Summer

Design by: Damon Scott

eplans.com

DESIGNED TO BE AN OASIS IN THE SHADE, these garden beds surround a dramatic, yet naturalistic focal point—a small pond. The three lobes of the centrally located pond dictate the rhythm and design concept of the surrounding beds. Visitors enter via one of three entrances that divide the garden into three distinct beds: a large semicircular bed to the northwest, a roughly S-shaped bed to the southwest, and an island bed in the center, nearest the pond. Stepping-stones, set on a slightly sunken ridge, cut across the pond and allow visitors a panoramic view of the garden from the central stone. Midsize evergreens ring the entire garden, giving it a sense of privacy and seclusion. A diverse mix of shade-loving flowering shrubs

PLAN

HPK1200347

Season: Spring

Design by: Salvatore A. Masullo

eplans.com

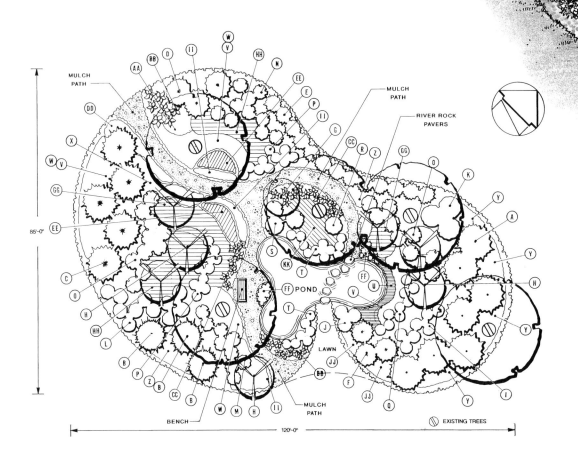

and trees, ferns, and perennials provide varying texture and color throughout the year. Site this garden under existing, high-canopied trees. To prevent fallen tree leaves from clogging the pond and fouling the water, cover the pond surface with bird netting in autumn. The black netting is almost invisible and allows you to easily catch and scoop out the leaves. Although the pond is not included in the blueprints for this design, the surrounding landscape lends itself to its placement.

HPK1200348

Season: Summer
Design by: Jeffery Dieffenbach

eplans.com

DESIGNED TO BE A BACKYARD OASIS, this mixed garden bed features a gently curving path that leads to a secluded patio and fountain. Deciduous trees and shrubs, evergreens, ornamental grasses, and perennials blend together to create a privacy screen around the seating area. The sense of enclosure is further enhanced with a low berm behind the wall sur-

rounding the fountain. In this intimate setting, you can sit and relax while listening to the music of the splashing fountain. The designer edged the semicircular fountain basin with stone that matches the patio and walkway to visually unite the design. The varied and dense plantings of this design are attractive to wildlife. As an added bonus, this heavily planted garden leaves little room for pesky weeds to take hold. And because this is a naturalistic garden, there's no need to keep a rigid maintenance schedule. Occasional deadheading and pruning to maintain plant health are the only gardening musts.

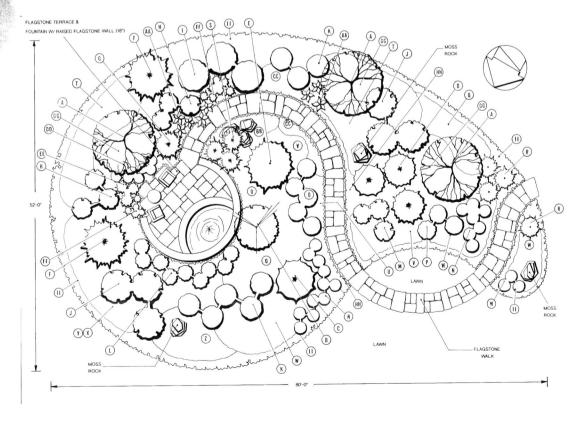

FLAGSTONE TERRACE & FOUNTAIN W/ RAISED FLAGSTONE WALL (18")

MOSS ROCK

52'-0"

MOSS ROCK

LAWN

LAWN

FLAGSTONE WALK

MOSS ROCK

80'-0"

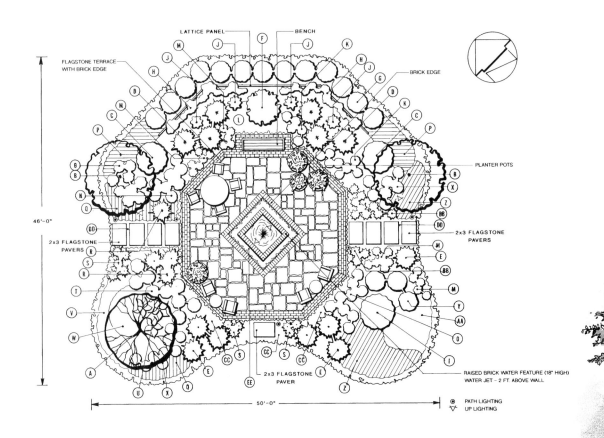

IMAGINE BEING ENGULFED IN DELICATELY SCENTED AIR as you relax on your patio. You can enjoy such sensory pleasures everyday by installing this intricate design filled with fragrant plants. Be sure to provide plenty of seating around the patio so you'll have places to sit and enjoy the perfumed air. This plan is as adaptable as it is beautiful. The designer includes a patio and combination fountain/planter, but you could plant the border around any existing patio. (NOTE: the fountain is not included in the landscape plans.) You might decide to add only a central planter or fountain, or both. You could locate the design right up against your house so that sliding glass or French doors open directly onto the patio—this allows you to enjoy the flowers'

HPK1200349

Season: Summer

Design by: Jeffery Diefenbach

PLAN

eplans.com

perfume from indoors as well. If you choose this option, site the planting so the lattice is directly opposite the wall of the house to capture and hold fragrance. The central planter and pots scattered about the patio are filled with fragrant annuals and tender perennials. During the cold winter months, try moving the pots to a sunny location inside the house, where they will continue to bloom and perfume the air.

THE PERFECT SETTING FOR AN OUT-DOOR PARTY—or for simply relaxing with family and friends—this backyard features an elegant wooden deck and brick patio that run the length of the house. The deck area on the right (not included in the plans) acts as an outdoor kitchen, featuring a built-in barbecue, serving cabinet and space enough for a dining table and chairs. For those who opt to mingle with the other guests rather than chat with the cook, a separate area has been provided at the other end.

Built at the same level as the house, and easily accessible from inside, the deck extends the interior living space to the outdoors. Three lovely flowering trees shade the deck

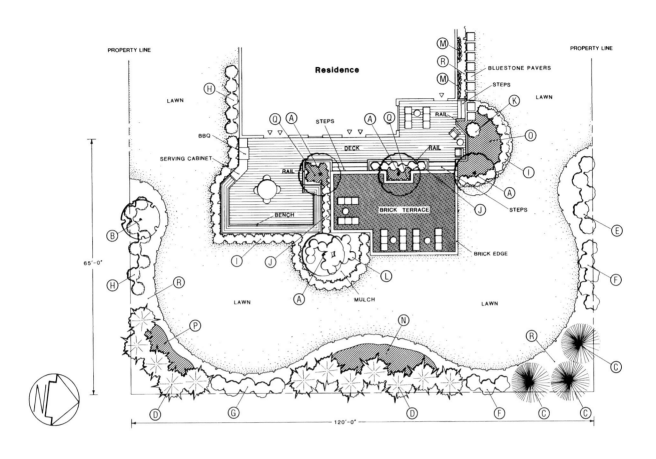

PLAN

HPK1200350

Season: Spring

Design by: Michael J. Opisso

eplans.com

and house, while creating a visual ceiling and walls to further reinforce the idea that these areas are outdoor rooms.

Down a few steps from the deck, the brick terrace makes a transition between the house (and deck) and the garden. Open on two sides to the lawn, this sunny terrace feels spacious and open, creating a great place in which people can mingle and talk during a cocktail party or sunbathe on a Saturday afternoon. From here, it's possible to enjoy the garden setting close at hand.

The plantings around the perimeter of the yard feature several kinds of tall evergreens to provide privacy. In front of the evergreens, large drifts of flowering perennials are perfectly displayed against the green background. Between the evergreens, masses of shrubbery provide a changing color show from early spring through fall.

Beauty .in **simplicity**

Break away from the conventional ideas of starter homes. HomePlanners titles prove that "budget" homes don't have to be boring homes. Elegant, yet affordable plans show how beautiful home design is available at every price range.

If you are looking to build an affordable starter home, look to HomePlanners first.

pick up a copy today!

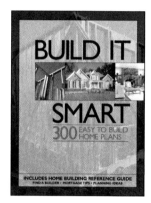

BUILD IT SMART
$9.95
ISBN 1-931131-30-9
(336 PAGES)

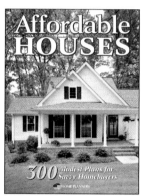

AFFORDABLE HOUSES
$9.95
ISBN 1-881955-93-1
(256 PAGES)

450 ONE-STORY HOMES
$9.95
ISBN 1-931131-07-4
(448 PAGES)

NEW!

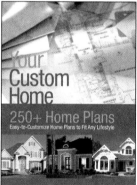

YOUR CUSTOM HOME
$11.95
ISBN 1-931131-38-4
(288 PAGES)

Toll-Free: **800.322.6797**
Online: **http://books.eplans.com**

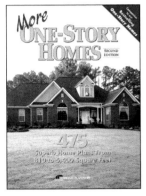

MORE ONE-STORY HOMES, 2ND ED.
$9.95
ISBN 1-881955-81-8
(448 PAGES)

200 BUDGET-SMART HOME PLANS
$8.95
ISBN 0-918894-97-2
(224 PAGES)

Finding the right
new home to fit

▶ Your style
▶ Your budget
▶ Your life

...has never
been easier.

NEW!

BIG BOOK OF HOME PLANS
$12.95
1-931131-36-8
(464 PAGES)

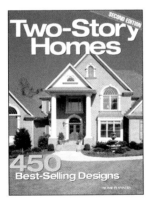

TWO-STORY HOMES, 2ND ED.
$9.95
ISBN 1-931131-15-5
(448 PAGES)

With more than 50 years of experience in the industry and millions of blueprints sold, Hanley Wood is a trusted source of high-quality, high-value pre-drawn home plans.

Using pre-drawn home plans is a **reliable, cost-effective way** to build your dream home, and our vast selection of plans is second-to-none. The nation's finest designers craft these plans that builders know they can trust. Meanwhile, our friendly, knowledgeable customer service representatives can help you every step of the way.

WHAT YOU'LL GET WITH YOUR ORDER

The contents of each designer's blueprint package is unique, but all contain detailed, high-quality working drawings. You can expect to find the following standard elements in most sets of plans:

1. FRONT PERSPECTIVE

This artist's sketch of the exterior of the house gives you an idea of how the house will look when built and landscaped.

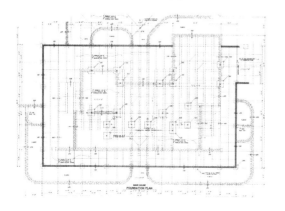

2. FOUNDATION AND BASEMENT PLANS

This sheet shows the foundation layout including concrete walls, footings, pads, posts, beams, bearing walls, and foundation notes. If the home features a basement, the first-floor framing details may also be included on this plan. If your plan features slab construction rather than a basement, the plan shows footings and details for a monolithic slab. This page, or another in the set, may include a sample plot plan for locating your house on a building site. Additional sheets focus on foundation cross-sections and other details.

3. DETAILED FLOOR PLANS

These plans show the layout of each floor of the house. Rooms and interior spaces are carefully dimensioned, doors and windows located, and keys are given for cross-section details provided elsewhere in the plans.

4. HOUSE AND DETAIL CROSS-SECTIONS

Large-scale views show sections or cutaways of the foundation, interior walls, exterior walls, floors, stairways, and roof details. Additional cross-sections may show important changes in floor, ceiling, or roof heights, or the relationship of one level to another. These sections show exactly how the various parts of the house fit together and are extremely valuable during construction. Additional sheets may include enlarged wall, floor, and roof construction details.

5. ROOF AND FLOOR STRUCTURAL SUPPORTS

The roof and floor framing plans provide detail for these crucial elements of your home. Each includes floor joist, ceiling joist, rafter and roof joist size, spacing, direction, span, and specifications. Beam and window headers, along with necessary details for framing connections, stairways, skylights, or dormers are also included.

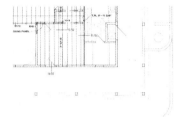

6. ELECTRICAL PLAN

The electrical plan offers a detailed outline of all wiring for your home, with notes for all lighting, outlets, switches, and circuits. A layout is provided for each level, as well as basements, garages, or other structures.

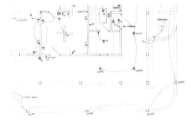

7. EXTERIOR ELEVATIONS

In addition to the front exterior, your blueprint set will include drawings of the rear and sides of your house as well. These drawings give notes on exterior materials and finishes. Particular attention is given to cornice detail, brick and stone accents, or other finish items that make your home unique.

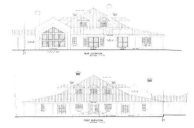

BEFORE YOU CALL

You are making a terrific decision to use a pre-drawn house plan it is one you can make with confidence, knowing that your blueprints are crafted by national-award-winning certified residential designers and architects, and trusted by builders.

Once you ve selected the plan you want or even if you have questions along the way our experienced customer service representatives are available 24 hours a day, seven days a week to help you navigate the home-building process. To help them provide you with even better service, please consider the following questions before you call:

■ Have you chosen or purchased your lot?

If so, please review the building setback requirements of your local building authority before you call. You don t need to have a lot before ordering plans, but if you own land already, please have the width and depth dimensions handy when you call.

■ Have you chosen a builder?

Involving your builder in the plan selection and evaluation process may be beneficial. Luckily, builders know they can have confidence with pre-drawn plans because they ve been designed for livability, functionality, and typically are builder-proven at successful home sites across the country.

■ Do you need a construction loan?

Construction loans are unique because they involve determining the value of something that is not yet constructed. Several lenders offer convenient contstruction-to-permanent loans. It is important to choose a good lending partner one who will help guide you through the application and appraisal process. Most will even help you evaluate your contractor to ensure reliability and credit worthiness. Our partnership with IndyMac Bank, a nationwide leader in construction loans, can help you save on your loan if needed.

■ How many sets of plans do you need?

Building a home can typically require a number of sets of blueprints one for yourself, two or three for the builder and subcontractors, two for the local building department, and one or more for your lender. For this reason, we offer 5- and 8-set plan packages, but your best value is the Reproducible Plan Package. Reproducible plans are accompanied by a license to make modifications and typically up to 12 duplicates of the plan so you have enough copies of the plan for everyone involved in the financing and construction of your home.

■ Do you want to make any changes to the plan?

We understand that it is difficult to find blueprints for a home that will meet all of your needs. That is why Hanley Wood is glad to offer plan Customization Services. We will work with you to design the modifications you d like to see and to adjust your blueprint plans accordingly anything from changing the foundation; adding square footage, redesigning baths, kitchens, or bedrooms; or most other modifications. This simple, cost-effective service saves you from hiring an outside architect to make alterations. Modifications may only be made to Reproducible Plan Packages that include the license to modify.

■ Do you have to make any changes to meet local building codes?

While all of our plans are drawn to meet national building codes at the time they were created, many areas required that plans be stamped by a local engineer to certify that they meet local building codes. Building codes are updated frequently and can vary by state, county, city, or municipality. Contact your local building inspection department, office of planning and zoning, or department of permits to determine how your local codes will affect your construction project. The best way to assure that you can make changes to your plan, if necessary, is to purchase a Reproducible Plan Package.

■ Has everyone—from family members to contractors—been involved in selecting the plan?

Building a new home is an exciting process, and using pre-drawn plans is a great way to realize your dreams. Make sure that everyone involved has had an opportunity to review the plan you ve selected. While Hanley Wood is the only plans provider with an exchange policy, it s best to be sure all parties agree on your selection before you buy.

CALL TOLL-FREE 1-800-521-6797

Source Key

HPK12

CUSTOMIZE YOUR PLAN – HANLEY WOOD CUSTOMIZATION SERVICES

Creating custom home plans has never been easier and more directly accessible. Using state-of-the-art technology and top-performing architectural expertise, Hanley Wood delivers on a long-standing customer commitment to provide world-class home-plans and customization services. Our valued customers—professional home builders and individual home owners—appreciate the convenience and accessibility of this interactive, consultative service.

With the Hanley Wood Customization Service you can:
■ Save valuable time by avoiding drawn-out and frequently repetitive face-to-face design meetings

■ Communicate design and home-plan changes faster and more efficiently
■ Speed-up project turn-around time
■ Build on a budget without sacrificing quality
■ Transform master home plans to suit your design needs and unique personal style

All of our design options and prices are impressively affordable. A detailed quote is available for a $50 consultation fee. Plan modification is an interactive service. Our skilled team of designers will guide you through the customization process from start to finish making recommendations, offering ideas, and determining the feasibility of your changes. This level of service is offered to ensure the final modified plan meets your expectations. If you use our service the $50 fee will be applied to the cost of the modifications.

You may purchase the customization consultation before or after purchasing a plan. In either case, it is necessary to purchase the Reproducible Plan Package and complete the accompanying license to modify the plan before we can begin customization.

Customization Consultation $50

TOOLS TO WORK WITH YOUR BUILDER

Two Reverse Options For Your Convenience – Mirror and Right-Reading Reverse (as available)

Mirror reverse plans simply flip the design 180 degrees keep in mind, the text will also be flipped. For a minimal fee you can have one or all of your plans shipped mirror reverse, although we recommend having at least one regular set handy. Right-reading reverse plans show the design flipped 180 degrees but the text reads normally. When you choose this option, we ship each set of purchased blueprints in this format.

Mirror Reverse Fee (indicate the number of sets when ordering). . . . $55
Right Reading Reverse Fee (all sets are reversed). $175

A Shopping List Exclusively for Your Home – Materials List

A customized Materials List helps you plan and estimate the cost of your new home, outlining the quantity, type, and size of materials needed to build your house (with the exception of mechanical system items). Included are framing lumber, windows and doors, kitchen and bath cabinetry, rough and finished hardware, and much more.

Materials List . . . .$75 each
Additional Materials Lists (at original time of purchase only). .$20 each

Plan Your Home- Building Process – Specification Outline

Work with your builder on this step-by-step chronicle of 166 stages or items crucial to the building process. It provides a comprehensive review of the construction process and helps you choose materials.
Specification Outline . . . .$10 each

Get Accurate Cost Estimates for Your Home – Quote One® Cost Reports

The Summary Cost Report, the first element in the Quote One® package, breaks down the cost of your home into various categories based on building materials, labor, and installation, and includes three grades of construction: Budget, Standard, and Custom. Make even more informed decisions about your project with the second element of our package, the Material Cost Report. The material and installation cost is shown for each of more than 1,000 line items provided in the standard-grade Materials List, which is included with this tool. Additional space is included for estimates from contractors and subcontractors, such as for mechanical materials, which are not included in our packages.

Quote One® Summary Cost Report $35
Quote One® Detailed Material Cost Report $140*
***Detailed material cost report includes the Materials List**

Learn the Basics of Building – Electrical, Plumbing, Mechanical, Construction Detail Sheets

If you want to know more about building techniques and deal more confidently with your subcontractors we offer four useful detail sheets. These sheets provide non-plan-specific general information, but are excellent tools that will add to your understanding of Plumbing Details, Electrical Details, Construction Details, and Mechanical Details.

Electrical Detail Sheet $14.95
Plumbing Detail Sheet $14.95
Mechanical Detail Sheet $14.95
Construction Detail Sheet $14.95
SUPER VALUE SETS:
Buy any 2: $26.95; Buy any 3: $34.95; Buy All 4: $39.95

Best Value

MAKE YOUR HOME TECH-READY – HOME AUTOMATION UPGRADE

Building a new home provides a unique opportunity to wire it with a plan for future needs. A Home Automation-Ready (HA-Ready) home contains the wiring substructure of tomorrow's connected home. It means that every room—from the front porch to the backyard, and from the attic to the basement—is wired for security, lighting, telecommunications, climate control, home computer networking, whole-house audio, home theater, shade control, video surveillance, entry access control, and yes, video gaming electronic solutions.

Along with the conveniences HA-Ready homes provide, they also have a higher resale value. The Consumer Electronics Association (CEA), in conjunction with the Custom Electronic Design and Installation Association (CEDIA), have developed a TechHome™ Rating system that quantifies the value of HA-Ready homes. The rating system is gaining widespread recognition in the real estate industry.

Developed by CEDIA-certified installers, our Home Automation Upgrade package includes everything you need to work with an installer during the construction of your home. It provides a short explanation of the various subsystems, a wiring floor plan for each level of your home, a detailed materials list with estimated costs, and a list of CEDIA-certified installers in your local area.
Home Automation Upgrade $250

GET YOUR HOME PLANS PAID FOR!

IndyMac Bank, in partnership with Hanley Wood, will reimburse you up to $600 toward the cost of your home plans simply by financing the construction of your new home with IndyMac Bank Home Construction Lending.

IndyMac's construction and permanent loan is a one-time close loan, meaning that one application—and one set of closing fees—provides all the financing you need.

Apply today at www.indymacbank.com, call toll free at 1-866-237-3478, or ask a Hanley Wood customer service representative for details.

DESIGN YOUR HOME – INTERIOR AND EXTERIOR FINISHING TOUCHES

Be Your Own Interior Designer! – Home Furniture Planner

Effectively plan the space in your home using our Hands-On Home Furniture Planner. It s fun and easy no more moving heavy pieces of furniture to see how the room will go together. The kit includes reusable peel-and-stick furniture templates that fit on a 12"x18" laminated layout board enough space to lay out every room in your house.
Home Furniture Planning Kit $15.95

Enjoy the Outdoors! – Deck Plans

Many of our homes have a corresponding deck plan, sold separately, which includes a Deck Plan Frontal Sheet, Deck Framing and Floor Plans, Deck Elevations, and a Deck Materials List. A Standard Deck Details Package, also available, provides all the how-to information necessary for building any deck. Get both the Deck Plan and the Standard Deck Details Package for one low price in our Complete Deck Building Package. See the price tier chart below and call for deck plan availability.
Deck Details (only) $14.95
Deck Building Package . . . . Plan price + $14.95

Create a Professionally Designed Landscape – Landscape Plans

Many of our homes have a front-yard Landscape Plan that is complementary in design to the house plan. These comprehensive Landscape Blueprint Packages include a Frontal Sheet, Plan View, Regionalized Plant & Materials List, a sheet on Planting and Maintaining Your Landscape, Zone Maps,  and a Plant Size and Description Guide. Each set of blueprints is a full 18" x 24" with clear, complete instructions in easy-to-read type. Our Landscape Plans are available with a Plant & Materials List adapted by horticultural experts to eight regions of the country. Please specify your region when ordering your plan see region map below. Call for more information about landscape plan availability and applicable regions.

LANDSCAPE & DECK PRICE SCHEDULE

PRICE TIERS	1-SET STUDY PACKAGE	5-SET BUILDING PACKAGE	8-SET BUILDING PACKAGE	1-SET REPRODUCIBLE*
P1	$25	$55	$95	$145
P2	$45	$75	$115	$165
P3	$75	$105	$145	$195
P4	$105	$135	$175	$225
P5	$145	$175	$215	$275
P6	$185	$215	$255	$315

PRICES SUBJECT TO CHANGE   * REQUIRES A FAX NUMBER

TERMS & CONDITIONS

OUR 90-DAY EXCHANGE POLICY

BUY WITH CONFIDENCE!

Hanley Wood is committed to ensuring your satisfaction with your blueprint order, which is why a we offer a 90-day exchange policy. With the exception of Reproducible Plan Package orders, we will exchange your entire first order for an equal or greater number of blueprints from our plan collection within 90 days of the original order. The entire content of your original order must be returned before an exchange will be processed. Please call our customer service department at 1-888-690-1116 for your return authorization number and shipping instructions. If the returned blueprints look used, redlined, or copied, we will not honor your exchange. Fees for exchanging your blueprints are as follows: 20% of the amount of the original order, plus the difference in cost if exchanging for a design in a higher price bracket or less the difference in cost if exchanging for a design in a lower price bracket. (Because they can be copied, Reproducible blueprints are not exchangeable or refundable.) Please call for current postage and handling prices. Shipping and handling charges are not refundable.

ARCHITECTURAL AND ENGINEERING SEALS

Some cities and states now require that a licensed architect or engineer review and "seal" a blueprint, or officially approve it, prior to construction. Prior to application for a building permit or the start of actual construction, we strongly advise that you consult your local building official who can tell you if such a review is required.

LOCAL BUILDING CODES AND ZONING REQUIREMENTS

Each plan was designed to meet or exceed the requirements of a nationally recognized model building code in effect at the time and place the plan was drawn. Typically plans designed after the year 2000 conform to the International Residential Building Code (IRC 2000 or 2003). The IRC is comprised of portions of the three major codes below. Plans drawn before 2000 conform to one of the three recognized building codes in effect at the time: Building Officials and Code Administrators (BOCA) International, Inc.;

CALL TOLL-FREE 1-866-473-4052 OR VISIT EPLANS.COM

the Southern Building Code Congress International, (SBCCI) Inc.; the International Conference of Building Officials (ICBO); or the Council of American Building Officials (CABO).

Because of the great differences in geography and climate throughout the United States and Canada, each state, county, and municipality has its own building codes, zone requirements, ordinances, and building regulations. Your plan may need to be modified to comply with local requirements. In addition, you may need to obtain permits or inspections from local governments before and in the course of construction. We authorize the use of the blueprints on the express condition that you consult a local licensed architect or engineer of your choice prior to beginning construction and strictly comply with all local building codes, zoning requirements, and other applicable laws, regulations, ordinances, and requirements. Notice: Plans for homes to be built in Nevada must be redrawn by a Nevada-registered professional. Consult your local building official for more information on this subject.

TERMS AND CONDITIONS

These designs are protected under the terms of United States Copyright Law and may not be copied or reproduced in any way, by

any means, unless you have purchased a Reproducible Plan Package and signed the accompanying license to modify and copy the plan, which clearly indicates your right to modify, copy, or reproduce. We authorize the use of your chosen design as an aid in the construction of ONE (1) single- or multifamily home only. You may not use this design to build a second dwelling or multiple dwellings without purchasing another blueprint or blueprints or paying additional design fees. Multi-use fees vary by designer—please call one of experienced sales representatives for a quote.

DISCLAIMER

The designers we work with have put substantial care and effort into the creation of their blueprints. However, because we cannot provide on-site consultation, supervision, and control over actual construction, and because of the great variance in local building requirements, building practices, and soil, seismic, weather, and other conditions, WE MAKE NO WARRANTY OF ANY KIND, EXPRESS OR IMPLIED, WITH RESPECT TO THE CONTENT OR USE OF THE BLUEPRINTS, INCLUDING BUT NOT LIMITED TO ANY WARRANTY OF MERCHANTABILITY OR OF FITNESS FOR A PARTICULAR PURPOSE. ITEMS, PRICES, TERMS, AND CONDITIONS ARE SUBJECT TO CHANGE WITHOUT NOTICE.

IMPORTANT COPYRIGHT NOTICE

From the Council of Publishing Home Designers

Blueprints for residential construction (or working drawings, as they are often called in the industry) are copyrighted intellectual property, protected under the terms of the United States Copyright Law and, therefore, cannot be copied legally for use in building. The following are some guidelines to help you get what you need to build your home, without violating copyright law:

1. HOME PLANS ARE COPY-RIGHTED

Just like books, movies, and songs, home plans receive protection under the federal copyright laws. The copyright laws prevent anyone, other than the copyright owner, from reproducing, modifying, or reusing the plans or design without permission of the copyright owner.

2. DO NOT COPY DESIGNS OR FLOOR PLANS FROM ANY PUBLICATION, ELECTRONIC MEDIA, OR EXISTING HOME

It is illegal to copy, change, or redraw home designs found in a plan book, CDROM or on the Internet. The right to modify plans is one of the exclusive rights of copyright. It is also illegal to copy or redraw a constructed home that is protected by copyright, even if you have never seen the plans for the home. If you find a plan or home that you like, you must purchase a set of plans from an authorized source. The plans may not be lent, given away, or sold by the purchaser.

3. DO NOT USE PLANS TO BUILD MORE THAN ONE HOUSE

The original purchaser of house plans is typically licensed to build a single home from the plans. Building more than one home from the plans without permission is an infringement of the home designer's copyright. The purchase of a multiple-set package of plans is for the construction of a single home only. The purchase of additional sets of plans does not grant the right to construct more than one home.

4. HOUSE PLANS IN THE FORM OF BLUEPRINTS OR BLACKLINES CANNOT BE COPIED OR REPRODUCED

Plans, blueprints, or blacklines, unless they are reproducibles, cannot be copied or reproduced without prior written consent of the copyright owner. Copy shops and blueprinters are prohibited from making copies of these plans without the copyright release letter you receive with reproducible plans.

5. HOUSE PLANS IN THE FORM OF BLUEPRINTS OR BLACKLINES CANNOT BE REDRAWN

Plans cannot be modified or redrawn without first obtaining the copyright owner's permission. With your purchase of plans, you are licensed to make non-structural changes by red-lining the purchased plans. If you need to make structural changes or need to redraw the plans for any reason, you must purchase a reproducible set of plans (see topic 6) which includes a license to modify the plans. Blueprints do not come with a license to make structural changes or to redraw the plans. You may not reuse or sell the modified design.

6. REPRODUCIBILE HOME PLANS

Reproducible plans (for example sepias, mylars, CAD files, electronic files, and vellums) come with a license to make modifications to the plans. Once modified, the plans can be taken to a local copy shop or blueprinter to make up to 10 or 12 copies of the plans to use in the construction of a single home. Only one home can be constructed from any single purchased set of reproducible plans either in original form or as modified. The license to modify and copy must be completed and returned before the plan will be shipped.

7. MODIFIED DESIGNS CANNOT BE REUSED

Even if you are licensed to make modifications to a copyrighted design, the modified design is not free from the original designer's copyright. The sale or reuse of the modified design is prohibited. Also, be aware that any modification to plans relieves the original designer from liability for design defects and voids all warranties expressed or implied.

8. WHO IS RESPONSIBLE FOR COPYRIGHT INFRINGEMENT?

Any party who participates in a copyright violation may be responsible including the purchaser, designers, architects, engineers, drafters, homeowners, builders, contractors, sub-contractors, copy shops, blueprinters, developers, and real estate agencies. It does not matter whether or not the individual knows that a violation is being committed. Ignorance of the law is not a valid defense.

9. PLEASE RESPECT HOME DESIGN COPYRIGHTS

In the event of any suspected violation of a copyright, or if there is any uncertainty about the plans purchased, the publisher, architect, designer, or the Council of Publishing Home Designers (www.cphd.org) should be contacted before proceeding. Awards are sometimes offered for information about home design copyright infringement.

10. PENALTIES FOR INFRINGEMENT

Penalties for violating a copyright may be severe. The responsible parties are required to pay actual damages caused by the infringement (which may be substantial), plus any profits made by the infringer commissions to include all profits from the sale of any home built from an infringing design. The copyright law also allows for the recovery of statutory damages, which may be as high as $150,000 for each infringement. Finally, the infringer may be required to pay legal fees which often exceed the damages.

BLUEPRINT PRICE SCHEDULE

PRICE TIERS	1-SET STUDY PACKAGE	5-SET BUILDING PACKAGE	8-SET BUILDING PACKAGE	1-SET REPRODUCIBLE*
A1	$450	$500	$555	$675
A2	$490	$545	$595	$735
A3	$540	$605	$665	$820
A4	$590	$660	$725	$895
C1	$640	$715	$775	$950
C2	$690	$760	$820	$1025
C3	$735	$810	$875	$1100
C4	$785	$860	$925	$1175
L1	$895	$990	$1075	$1335
L2	$970	$1065	$1150	$1455
L3	$1075	$1175	$1270	$1600
L4	$1185	$1295	$1385	$1775
SQ1				.40/SQ. FT.
SQ3				.55/SQ. FT.
SQ5				.80/SQ. FT.

PRICES SUBJECT TO CHANGE   * REQUIRES A FAX NUMBER

PLAN #	PRICE TIER	PAGE	MATERIALS LIST	QUOTE ONE®	DECK	DECK PRICE	LANDSCAPE	LANDSCAPE PRICE	REGIONS
HPK1200001	A2	24	Y						
HPK1200002	C2	68	Y						
HPK1200003	C1	79	Y						
HPK1200004	A4	22							
HPK1200005	C1	53	Y						
HPK1200006	A3	21	Y						
HPK1200007	A4	71							
HPK1200008	A3	31							
HPK1200009	A4	32							
HPK1200010	A4	52	Y	Y					
HPK1200011	C1	82	Y						
HPK1200012	C1	62	Y	Y					
HPK1200013	A4	73	Y			OLA004	P3	123568	
HPK1200014	C1	87							
HPK1200015	A4	70							
HPK1200016	A3	33	Y						
HPK1200017	C1	76	Y						
HPK1200018	A4	74	Y						
HPK1200019	A4	88							
HPK1200020	A3	63	Y						
HPK1200021	C1	41	Y						
HPK1200022	A4	67	Y						
HPK1200023	A2	20	Y						
HPK1200024	C1	56	Y	Y					
HPK1200025	A2	25							
HPK1200026	C1	46							
HPK1200027	A4	49	Y		ODA013	P2	OLA001	P3	123568
HPK1200028	A4	69							
HPK1200029	A2	23	Y						
HPK1200030	C1	42	Y						
HPK1200031	A3	37	Y						
HPK1200032	C3	91	Y						
HPK1200033	A4	65	Y						
HPK1200034	C1	48							
HPK1200035	A2	19	Y						
HPK1200036	A4	64							
HPK1200037	A3	40							
HPK1200038	A4	78	Y	Y					
HPK1200039	C3	77	Y						
HPK1200040	A4	66	Y						
HPK1200041	A3	34	Y						
HPK1200042	C1	57	Y						
HPK1200043	A4	17	Y	Y					
HPK1200044	A4	83							
HPK1200045	C1	55	Y						
HPK1200046	C1	44							
HPK1200047	A3	28	Y						
HPK1200048	C1	84	Y						
HPK1200049	A3	60							
HPK1200050	A3	59							
HPK1200051	A3	45	Y						
HPK1200052	A4	90	Y						
HPK1200053	A3	58	Y						
HPK1200054	C1	50	Y						
HPK1200055	C2	72	Y						
HPK1200056	A3	38							
HPK1200057	C1	35	Y						
HPK1200058	A4	75	Y						
HPK1200059	C2	81							
HPK1200060	A4	29	Y						
HPK1200061	A4	39							
HPK1200062	A4	18							
HPK1200063	A2	26	Y						
HPK1200064	A2	16							
HPK1200065	A3	36	Y						
HPK1200066	A3	30	Y						
HPK1200067	A2	23	Y						
HPK1200068	A3	43							
HPK1200069	A3	47							
HPK1200070	A4	86	Y						
HPK1200071	C1	88							
HPK1200072	C1	61							
HPK1200073	C1	67	Y	Y	ODA006	P2	OLA021	P3	123568
HPK1200074	C1	27	Y						

PLAN #	PRICE TIER	PAGE	MATERIALS LIST	QUOTE ONE®	DECK	DECK PRICE	LANDSCAPE	LANDSCAPE PRICE	REGIONS
HPK1200075	A4	85							
HPK1200076	C1	54	Y						
HPK1200077	A4	51	Y						
HPK1200078	C2	145							
HPK1200079	C1	159	Y						
HPK1200080	A3	101	Y						
HPK1200081	C1	142							
HPK1200082	A3	103	Y						
HPK1200083	A4	153	Y						
HPK1200084	C2	140	Y						
HPK1200085	A4	144	Y		ODA025	P3	OLA037	P4	347
HPK1200086	A3	96	Y	Y	ODA001	P2	OLA026	P3	1234568
HPK1200087	A4	120	Y	Y			OLA001	P3	123568
HPK1200088	A3	109	Y						
HPK1200089	C1	114							
HPK1200090	C1	117							
HPK1200091	A4	128	Y						
HPK1200092	C2	136	Y	Y					
HPK1200093	A3	94	Y	Y	ODA025	P3	OLA085	P3	12345678
HPK1200094	A3	122	Y						
HPK1200095	C2	157	Y						
HPK1200096	A3	95	Y						
HPK1200097	C2	133							
HPK1200098	C2	139	Y	Y					
HPK1200099	A3	105							
HPK1200100	A4	161	Y						
HPK1200101	C1	99							
HPK1200102	A3	112							
HPK1200103	A3	106	Y						
HPK1200104	A4	108	Y						
HPK1200105	C1	110	Y						
HPK1200106	C1	129	Y	Y			OLA037	P4	347
HPK1200107	C2	149							
HPK1200108	C1	156	Y	Y					
HPK1200109	C1	163	Y						
HPK1200110	A4	127	Y						
HPK1200111	C1	113	Y						
HPK1200112	C2	134	Y	Y					
HPK1200113	A4	135	Y	Y			OLA010	P3	1234568
HPK1200114	C2	155	Y						
HPK1200115	C2	126	Y						
HPK1200116	C2	160							
HPK1200117	A3	123							
HPK1200118	C1	143	Y						
HPK1200119	A3	107	Y				OLA001	P3	123568
HPK1200120	A4	131	Y						
HPK1200121	C1	163							
HPK1200122	A4	130	Y						
HPK1200123	A3	98	Y	Y			OLA006	P3	123568
HPK1200124	A2	97	Y	Y			OLA006	P3	123568
HPK1200125	C2	125							
HPK1200126	C2	137							
HPK1200127	C2	141	Y						
HPK1200128	C2	150	Y						
HPK1200129	A3	102	Y						
HPK1200130	A4	158	Y	Y			OLA088	P4	12345678
HPK1200131	C1	115							
HPK1200132	A3	118	Y						
HPK1200133	A4	124	Y						
HPK1200134	C1	162							
HPK1200135	C1	147	Y						
HPK1200136	C1	154	Y						
HPK1200137	A3	111	Y						
HPK1200138	A4	132	Y						
HPK1200139	A4	152							
HPK1200140	A3	116	Y		ODA013	P2			
HPK1200141	A4	119	Y	Y	ODA014	P2	OLA037	P4	347
HPK1200142	A4	239							
HPK1200143	C2	229	Y						

PLAN #	PRICE TIER	PAGE	MATERIALS LIST	QUOTE ONE®	DECK	DECK PRICE	LANDSCAPE	LANDSCAPE PRICE	REGIONS
HPK1200144	A3	202	Y						
HPK1200145	A2	168	Y						
HPK1200146	C2	225	Y						
HPK1200147	A3	193							
HPK1200148	A3	187	Y						
HPK1200150	C2	223							
HPK1200151	C1	217							
HPK1200152	A4	238							
HPK1200153	C1	210							
HPK1200154	A4	194	Y	Y	ODA012	P3	OLA083	P3	12345678
HPK1200155	SQ1	221	Y		ODA011	P2	OLA088	P4	12345678
HPK1200156	C1	185	Y						
HPK1200157	C2	239	Y						
HPK1200158	A4	177	Y	Y			OLA040	P4	123467
HPK1200159	C2	219							
HPK1200160	C2	237							
HPK1200161	C1	197							
HPK1200162	A4	232							
HPK1200163	C2	224							
HPK1200164	A2	178	Y						
HPK1200165	A3	191							
HPK1200166	A2	176	Y						
HPK1200167	A2	180	Y						
HPK1200168	A2	171							
HPK1200169	A4	211	Y						
HPK1200170	A2	170	Y						
HPK1200171	C2	233	Y	Y			OLA001	P3	123568
HPK1200172	A3	198							
HPK1200173	C1	192	Y						
HPK1200174	A3	200	Y						
HPK1200175	A3	195	Y						
HPK1200176	A3	172	Y						
HPK1200177	A2	175							
HPK1200178	A4	234							
HPK1200179	C2	213	Y						
HPK1200180	A3	186	Y						
HPK1200181	A1	188	Y						
HPK1200182	A3	174	Y						
HPK1200183	A3	183	Y	Y			OLA022	P3	123568
HPK1200184	C2	230							
HPK1200185	A4	238							
HPK1200186	C1	215	Y						
HPK1200187	C1	205							
HPK1200188	A4	179							
HPK1200189	C1	214							
HPK1200190	A4	196	Y	Y	ODA012	P3	OLA083	P3	12345678
HPK1200191	C1	201	Y						
HPK1200192	C3	227							
HPK1200193	C1	204	Y						
HPK1200194	C2	222	Y	Y					
HPK1200195	A3	184	Y						
HPK1200196	A4	208	Y		ODA011	P2	OLA083	P3	12345678
HPK1200197	A3	181	Y						
HPK1200198	A3	173	Y						
HPK1200199	A2	182	Y						
HPK1200200	C2	236	Y						
HPK1200201	A3	190	Y						
HPK1200202	C2	237	Y						
HPK1200203	C1	235	Y						
HPK1200204	A3	209							
HPK1200205	A4	212	Y						
HPK1200206	A3	207	Y						
HPK1200207	A4	220							
HPK1200208	A2	169	Y						
HPK1200209	A1	166	Y						
HPK1200210	A3	189	Y						
HPK1200231	C2	308	Y						
HPK1200232	A3	244	Y						
HPK1200233	A3	281	Y						

PLAN #	PRICE TIER	PAGE	MATERIALS LIST	QUOTE ONE®	DECK	DECK PRICE	LANDSCAPE	LANDSCAPE PRICE	REGIONS
HPK1200234	A4	250	Y	Y			OLA035	P3	1234567
HPK1200235	A3	254	Y						
HPK1200236	A3	258	Y	Y	ODA011	P2	OLA008	P4	1234568
HPK1200237	A3	268							
HPK1200238	C2	287	Y	Y					
HPK1200239	A4	305							
HPK1200240	A4	295	Y						
HPK1200241	A4	291	Y	Y			OLA039	P3	347
HPK1200242	A3	260	Y						
HPK1200244	A4	271	Y	Y			OLA088	P4	12345678
HPK1200245	A4	306							
HPK1200246	A4	311	Y	Y			OLA024	P4	123568
HPK1200247	C2	311	Y						
HPK1200248	C1	270	Y						
HPK1200250	A3	255	Y						
HPK1200251	C3	292	Y						
HPK1200252	A4	245	Y						
HPK1200253	A4	261	Y	Y	ODA018	P3			
HPK1200254	A4	280	Y						
HPK1200255	A3	273	Y						
HPK1200256	C1	259	Y						
HPK1200257	C1	282	Y						
HPK1200258	C1	262	Y						
HPK1200259	A4	290							
HPK1200260	C1	274	Y						
HPK1200261	C1	293							
HPK1200262	C1	257	Y	Y					
HPK1200263	A3	279	Y						
HPK1200264	A3	277	Y	Y	ODA001	P2	OLA008	P4	1234568
HPK1200265	C1	256					OLA024	P4	123568
HPK1200266	C1	272	Y						
HPK1200267	A3	269	Y						
HPK1200268	SQ1	299	Y						
HPK1200269	C1	310	Y						
HPK1200270	C2	297	Y						
HPK1200271	A3	266	Y						
HPK1200272	A4	300							
HPK1200273	C2	307	Y						
HPK1200274	A4	247							
HPK1200275	A4	252	Y	Y			OLA025	P3	123568
HPK1200276	C1	285	Y						
HPK1200277	A4	264	Y	Y					
HPK1200278	C2	302	Y	Y					
HPK1200279	A3	275							
HPK1200280	A3	253	Y						
HPK1200281	C2	283	Y						
HPK1200282	A2	242	Y						
HPK1200283	C1	267	Y						
HPK1200284	A2	243	Y	Y			OLA006	P3	123568
HPK1200285	A4	296	Y						
HPK1200286	C1	309	Y	Y			OLA025	P3	123568
HPK1200287	A4	309	Y						
HPK1200288	A4	303							
HPK1200289	A4	289	Y						
HPK1200290	A4	286	Y						
HPK1200291	A3	263	Y						
HPK1200292	A3	298	Y						
HPK1200293	A3	265							
HPK1200294	SQ1	304	Y	Y			OLA010	P3	1234568
HPK1200295	C1	284	Y		ODA012	P3	OLA010	P3	1234568
HPK1200296	C1	278	Y						
HPK1200297	A3	246	Y						
HPK1200298	A3	310	Y	Y	ODA016	P2	OLA034	P3	347
HPK1200299	A4	294							
HPK1200300	A3	276	Y						
HPK1200301	A3	251	Y						
HPK1200302	P6	314							
HPK1200303	A2	315							
HPK1200304	P6	316							

PLAN #	PRICE TIER	PAGE	MATERIALS LIST	QUOTE ONE®	DECK	DECK PRICE	LANDSCAPE	LANDSCAPE PRICE	REGIONS
HPK1200305	P6	316	Y						
HPK1200306	P5	317							
HPK1200307	P5	317							
HPK1200308	P4	318							
HPK1200309	P6	318							
HPK1200310	P4	319							
HPK1200311	P4	319							
HPK1200312	P4	320							
HPK1200313	P4	320	Y						
HPK1200314	P4	321							
HPK1200315	P5	321	Y						
HPK1200316	P6	322							
HPK1200317	P5	322	Y						
HPK1200318	P2	323							
HPK1200319	P1	323							
HPK1200320	P4	324							
HPK1200321	P2	324							
HPK1200322	P1	325							
HPK1200323	P2	325							
HPK1200324	P4	326							
HPK1200325	P1	326							
HPK1200326	P4	327	Y						
HPK1200327	P1	327							
HPK1200328	P3	328					OLA120	P3	1235678
HPK1200329	P3	330					OLA108	P3	12345678
HPK1200330	P2	332					OLA107	P2	12345678
HPK1200331	P2	334					OLA122	P2	1235678
HPK1200332	P2	336					OLA079	P2	12345678
HPK1200333	P3	338					OLA131	P3	1234678
HPK1200334	P3	340					OLA046	P3	12345678
HPK1200335	P4	342					OLA076	P4	12345678
HPK1200336	P3	344					OLA132	P3	1234678
HPK1200337	P3	346					OLA129	P3	12345678
HPK1200338	P3	348					OLA067	P3	12345678
HPK1200339	P3	350					OLA042	P3	12345678
HPK1200340	P3	352					OLA121	P3	1235678
HPK1200341	P3	354					OLA124	P3	12345678
HPK1200342	P3	356					OLA126	P3	123568
HPK1200343	P3	358					OLA125	P3	12345678
HPK1200344	P2	360					OLA078	P2	12345678
HPK1200345	P4	362					OLA049	P4	12345678
HPK1200346	P4	364					OLA047	P4	12345678
HPK1200347	P3	366					OLA128	P3	123568
HPK1200348	P3	368					OLA134	P3	1234678
HPK1200349	P3	370					OLA139	P3	1235678
HPK1200350	P3	372					OLA041	P3	12345678
HPK1200351	C1	80							
HPK1200352	A4	89							
HPK1200353	A3	100							
HPK1200354	A3	104							
HPK1200355	A4	121							
HPK1200356	A4	138							
HPK1200357	A4	146							
HPK1200358	C1	148	Y						
HPK1200359	A4	151							
HPK1200360	C2	162							
HPK1200361	A2	167							
HPK1200362	A4	199							
HPK1200363	A4	206							
HPK1200364	A4	216							
HPK1200365	A4	218							
HPK1200366	C1	226							
HPK1200367	C1	228							
HPK1200368	C1	231							
HPK1200369	A4	248							
HPK1200370	A3	249							
HPK1200371	C1	288	Y						
HPK1200372	A4	301	Y						
HPK1200373	C1	203	Y						